TROUBLESOME GROUND

TROUBLESOME GROUND

*Farming Trees & Green Policy
in Rural Ireland*

JODIE ASSELIN

UNIVERSITY PRESS OF COLORADO
Denver

© 2025 by University Press of Colorado

Published by University Press of Colorado
1580 North Logan Street, Suite 660
PMB 39883
Denver, Colorado 80203-1942

All rights reserved

 The University Press of Colorado is a proud member of Association of University Presses.

The University Press of Colorado is a cooperative publishing enterprise supported, in part, by Adams State University, Colorado School of Mines, Colorado State University, Fort Lewis College, Metropolitan State University of Denver, University of Alaska Fairbanks, University of Colorado, University of Denver, University of Northern Colorado, University of Wyoming, Utah State University, and Western Colorado University.

ISBN: 978-1-64642-773-4 (hardcover)
ISBN: 978-1-64642-774-1 (paperback)
ISBN: 978-1-64642-775-8 (ebook)
https://doi.org/10.5876/9781646427758

Library of Congress Cataloging-in-Publication Data

Names: Asselin, Jodie, 1980– author.
Title: Troublesome ground : farming trees and green policy in rural Ireland / Jodie Asselin.
Description: Denver : University Press of Colorado, [2025] | Includes bibliographical references and index.
Identifiers: LCCN 2025016649 (print) | LCCN 2025016650 (ebook) | ISBN 9781646427734 (hardcover) | ISBN 9781646427741 (paperback) | ISBN 9781646427758 (ebook)
Subjects: LCSH: Rural development—Ireland—Cork (County) | Rural development—Ireland—Duhallow (Barony) | Agriculture—Ireland—Duhallow (Barony) | Agriculture—Ireland—Cork (County) | Land use, Rural—Ireland—Duhallow (Barony) | Land use, Rural—Ireland—Cork (County) | Ethnology—Ireland—Cork (County) | Ethnology—Ireland—Duhallow (Barony) | Duhallow (Ireland : Barony)—Rural conditions. | Cork (Ireland : County)—Rural conditions.
Classification: LCC HN400.3.A8 A77 2025 (print) | LCC HN400.3.A8 (ebook)
LC record available at https://lccn.loc.gov/2025016649
LC ebook record available at https://lccn.loc.gov/2025016650

This book will be made open access within three years of publication thanks to Path to Open, a program developed in partnership between JSTOR, the American Council of Learned Societies (ACLS), University of Michigan Press, and The University of North Carolina Press to bring about equitable access and impact for the entire scholarly community, including authors, researchers, libraries, and university presses around the world. Learn more at https://about.jstor.org/path-to-open/.

This work is licensed under CC BY-NC-ND 4.0.

Cover photograph by Jodie Asselin

To small farmers, wherever they might be, whose efforts and
stories shape our world and its many residents

Contents

	Acknowledgments	ix
1.	Introduction	3
	Elusive Characters	29
2.	The Nature of Marginal Land: A Brief History of Upland Farming in Duhallow	33
	Abundant Travelers	55
3.	The Family Farm	59
	Itinerant Residents	82
4.	Containing the Unruly: Life as Told Through Incentives, Regulations, and Calendars	85
	Permanent Residents	109
5.	What Is a Forest, and Who Gets to Decide?	112
	Farm Fields as Multi-Species Entanglements	139
6.	The Salvage Value of Rural Livelihood: Flexible Economies on the Margin	143
7.	Conclusion	164
	References	169
	Index	189
	About the Author	193

Acknowledgments

This book has been at least six years in the making and has been made possible through the support and labour of a small army of individuals. The privilege of my career is not one I take lightly, and neither is the challenge to continue to learn and grow. Any mistakes within these coming pages are entirely my own. Please know that I will build from them and strive to improve.

Funding for this research was provided through the University of Lethbridge and the Social Sciences and Humanities Research Council of Canada. Such funding is one of the primary mechanisms by which Canadians can engage in research, and I am forever grateful for a system that prioritizes the telling of important stories.

I want to acknowledge the residents of Duhallow who shared their stories with me, in particular, the character known as Maeve and the team of IRD Duhallow whose support meant I might have a chance to tell a small part of this tale. Your work and ingenuity are the stuff worlds are made of. Thank you to the residents of this beautiful corner of the world who opened their homes to me and shared their stories. I hope you see yourselves in these pages and that I have treated your words with the respect they deserve.

I would also like to thank the anonymous reviewers of this book, whose detailed critiques were much appreciated, as well as those colleagues who took the time to read selected chapters and provide feedback. The peer review process is one I take to heart, and it was a delight to receive and grow from your feedback.

Finally, I would like to acknowledge the support of my family, who have traveled, often literally, on this journey with me. Gabriel, I am forever grateful for your critical feedback and support. Your integrity is a benchmark I strive to meet daily.

TROUBLESOME GROUND

I

Introduction

LOOKING FOR HEN HARRIERS

My first proper encounter with the uplands of northwest County Cork came by way of an invitation a week after I arrived: Would I like to accompany a monitoring team for an afternoon as they searched for an endangered bird, the hen harrier? My arrival at the small farming community had been eased by the friendliness of a local community development organization, and it seemed it had also coincided with the arrival of a distinguished UK visitor who was there to tour the organization's environmental projects. Knowing nothing of the hen harrier or the area we were to visit, I counted myself lucky and gladly tagged along, notebook in hand.

Our field day started with a dawn chorus walk through one of the last remaining deciduous forests in the area. The lush green forest was a popular walking destination for birders, and we had a good-sized group of local enthusiasts with us. Afterward, our small group—consisting of an Irish scientist leading a hen harrier habitat mitigation project, the UK representative with similar project goals, and me, a Canadian anthropologist who wanted to understand upland livelihood—climbed into a car and headed out of town.

The rest of the day found us with gazes drawn to the sky, searching for the rare shapes of hen harriers. I learned that members of the local European Union (EU)–funded project were trying to determine how many active nests were in the area, and a food pass between male and female birds was a good indication. In three-hour shifts, we spent our time at two sites. The first saw us in a forest cut block, sitting among the debris of cleared trees, looking outward across the heavily forested valley that sloped downhill toward a small stream at the bottom. We sat between ditches dug into the earth, allowing the boggy upland to drain enough for non-native conifer trees to grow. Twice, we saw the silver silhouette of what was apparently a male hen harrier in the distance but failed to see a female. After pushing our vehicle out of a particularly mucky road edge, we moved to our second site, an upland blanket bog with the road at times cut eight feet below the surface. Our chosen watching post rested along a high hill, with the deep green of forests on the opposite hillside and wind turbines visible on its crest. As we walked from our car to the hilltop, I could see the small, tidy squares of farm fields at the valley's distant edge, their margins clearly outlined by thick hedges. Spreading out from our watching spot were the soft white fluff of bog cotton in bloom and the tidy stacks of turf laid out and drying, each brick in piles of three or four, resting upright. Partway into our surveillance, I watched an elderly couple slowly make their way up the hill to our right and begin turning over bricks of turf. Without taking her eyes from the sky, the Irish scientist told me this was their parcel of turf: "They're turning it to better dry out before taking it home to heat their house" (figure 1).

In the following hours, I learned that this region was part of a Special Protected Area (SPA), declared so by the Irish government to appease European regulations that protected endangered birds (Council Directive 2009/147/EC). The designation meant that low-intensity land use was favoured and that new activities needed to go through a review process. Controversially, this included changes in farm field use, such as draining and improving fallow fields or planting fields with trees. My eyes told me that while it was an SPA, the area was also an energy extraction site—in local turf and the wind turbines that dotted the hill across from us. I learned that locals and outsiders alike debate both types of extraction, framing their merits and faults in terms of environmental, economic, and cultural impact. I initially thought the forests on this hillside across from us were unremarkable; however, I was surprised to hear my companions discuss them the most. At one point they referred to the forest as a "green desert," unable to support local biodiversity and largely devoid of upland life. "Yes, it's worrying," the UK representative suggested, "but surely they are also good for carbon sequestration?" This comment was a point of discussion for part of our day: whether planting trees on upland bog had environmental benefits.

At the core of all of this was the farm pasture visible at the end of the valley that kept drawing my eye. Both of my companions felt that farmers in Ireland and the UK needed to be better informed and educated about their land and its ecological potential. Unbeknownst to me at the time, I was sitting at the centre

Figure 1. Community members turn turf to dry on Mount Eagle; bog cotton in the foreground, conifer plantations and wind turbines in the background. Picture taken while surveying for hen harrier. The bog and plantations are part of a Special Protected Area. Author photo.

of the dominant narratives that would shape my time in the region: farms, forests, environmental protection, rural development, and the people who feel they should have a say in the area's future.

THIS BOOK

This book is an ethnographic account of the relationship between land and Irish upland farmers in north County Cork, Ireland. It takes place amid the colliding influences of agricultural professionalization, a global environmental crisis, and the subsequent implementation and rotation of various politically motivated projects meant to spur economic growth and simultaneously better the environment. As such, it is a story about the challenges farmers in one region face in the conflicting worlds of program payments, shifting policy initiatives, and the joint cultural and economic requirements of farming. Consequently, in addition to expected topics like family farms, crops, and livestock, this book spends considerable time on forestry and EU subsidy programs, each an integral component of what it means to farm in Ireland today. In telling this tale, I have two distinct yet interconnected goals. Foremost, I aim to provide an ethnographic account of what it means to live in these uplands and, in doing so, contribute to an anthropology of rural Ireland. Second, I want to contribute to an understanding of how the ephemeral worlds of green discourse and development plans manifest in rural areas, making a case that ethnographic description can help illuminate and acknowledge the realities of conflicting development and conservation strategies—indeed, that it is imperative that we do so.

Ethnography demands that the messiness and contradictions of life be acknowledged, and this contribution is particularly significant today because, like many so-called marginal regions, the uplands of north County Cork often hold the position of a catch-all geography for others' dreams of nation-building and economic development. I argue in the coming pages that the landscape is conceptually stretched and oversaturated, containing any number of possible futures and the contradictions inherent within those futures. In recent decades, the pressure to address climate change and declining biodiversity has, in many cases, further saturated such areas with even more potential. Many family farms now persist in what Charles J. Godfray and colleagues (2010) have termed the "perfect storm"—that is, the intersection of rising demand for food, an increasing role for farms in energy production, greater demand for water, and a need for the agricultural sector to adapt to and mitigate climate change. Much of this demand has been formalized through the language of multifunctional agriculture, which, as a policy focus, supports and recognises the diverse contributions of farms while simultaneously increasing the expectation of such diversity (Heatherington 2011; O'Rourke et al. 2016). As farmers navigate these competing pressures, their core roles in the nation shift, with farms functioning less and less as purely production-centred spaces and begin filling leisure, recreation, and living space demands for urban areas (McDonagh et al. 2010). In this, the role of farmers has shifted. For example, Jeremy MacClancy (2015) argues that within the EU, once seen as an exploiter of agricultural potential, farmers are now just as often understood as stewards or guardians of the land. I would amend this observation slightly, however, to say that many of today's small European farmers are both agricultural exploiters *and* stewards of the collective environment, and it is increasingly their role to navigate any resultant contradictions.

In Duhallow, where I spent most of my time, I argue that oversaturation or expectation is primarily due to a failure to address the contradictions inherent within and among environmental policy, economic development goals, and land-use regulations that are collectively meant to outline the road to sustainable rural development. While the story provided here is a regional case study and cannot be taken as a stand-in for Ireland as a whole, the experiences many Duhallow farmers face are not unique. Andrea Rissing and Bradley M. Jones (2022, 195) note in their exploration of landscape value through an anthropological lens that "processes of inscribing landscapes with market value always exist in tension with the diverse values simultaneously ascribed to the same landscapes—in the past, present, and future." Such colliding values exist in the economic sense—a monetary exchange on the market, for example—and certainly in the sense of a broader sphere of human meaning, including a cultural sense of place, belonging, and obligation. However, more recently, the murky spaces in how species and landscape conservation is valued and by whom have increasingly been entwined with tenuous economic ties to green economic growth, where market value asserts itself in new ways. For instance, many of the opportunities and challenges facing Duhallow farms today result from a broader neoliberal strategy to address climate change and declining biodiversity through mechanisms that can, in theory, also support local economic development. Firmly linking conservation and development is part of a more global emphasis on neoliberal conservation, described by Robert Fletcher (2023, 75) as "an ambitious effort to render the capitalist system as a whole sustainable in the face of increasing skepticism concerning this possibility as well as mounting obstacles to continued accumulation posed by global natural resource depletion and associated pollution buildup including climate change producing greenhouse gas emissions." Among the concrete contradictions that will be encountered in this book—to plant and not to plant, for instance—is a deeper thread that is the unaddressed tension between growth and sustainable practices and the subsequent misalignment in what economic value means to the orbit of the many individuals who have a stake in small farms.

Together, the entwined subjects of rural livelihood and green development and discourse provide a rich case study in staying with the trouble (Haraway 2016) of unpacking the lived consequences of today's competing demands on rural regions. I understand this attention as significant on at least four fronts. First, it is important in itself to refuse to explain away, overlook, or ignore the incompatibility of many rural narratives. The material and discursive over-allocation of what this region can provide and what it symbolizes results in cumulative exhaustion from living in an overstretched and imagined landscape that cannot be all things at once. The tensions that emerge from competing visualizations of place and development are not theoretical quandaries; they manifest *somewhere*. Much as colonial imaginings manifest(ed) in landscapes deemed or cultivated as empty, the merger of economic growth and environmental interventions moves into these same areas—places that are unlikely to meet the shifting visions and requirements of what others hope them to be but where people and their non-human companions exist, persist, and on occasion thrive in unpredictable ways. Failure to critically examine the tension between the dual pulls of growth and de-growth, green spaces and development, and human spaces and spaces for non-human companions results in people failing to see what is occurring around them and losing track of the everyday facts of life in exchange for high-level data. This potentially undermines programs meant to better our collective futures.

Second, I hope the book's focus contributes to a critical examination of how the proliferation of green language, especially as symbolic rhetoric, can perpetuate unequal power relations and mask exploitative patterns for humans, landscapes, and companion species. This is particularly the case in so-call marginal areas where narratives that position rural regions as empty and comparatively lacking in value justify and even oblige political and economic intervention. Duhallow residents and landscapes are less easily incorporated into scalable enterprises, proving simultaneously vexing for frustrated planners and bureaucrats and providing imaginative fodder for future plans. The land is wet; bogs slide; rain falls in overabundance or not at all; uninvited species spread; and the temporal rhythms of trees, peat, and migratory animals do not always coincide well with human calendars. Local farmers are aware of this precarity, of being vulnerable to others and living without the promise of stability (Tsing 2015), and they respond with flexible economies that have sustained upland regions over centuries. It is this flexibility that is at risk in many of Ireland's green development plans. In particular, among the myriad overlapping influences in this region, forest plantations succeed in rationalizing rural landscapes and people where other ventures have failed. In one swoop, forest plantations have the potential to render land and people compliant (though not completely) by reshaping the farmer-farm relationship while only superficially meeting the designation of forest as a land type. This shift in land meaning has received inadequate attention, mainly because forest discourse, although not its materiality, can strategically meet competing demands in this oversaturated place—economic, environmental, and cultural.

Third, a focus on how conservation and development programs and policies manifest in the space between farmer and land offers an opportunity to see *how* change does or does not occur while prioritizing the position of local actors who might otherwise be seen as isolated case studies, too subjective or poorly informed to be taken seriously. Rather than resting on the often uncritically cited narratives of rural decline and a lack of modernization, a focus on lived realities can position local livelihood as an integral landscape component rather than an isolated economic feature. This book reminds its readers that the ever-shifting theoretical and discursive tension apparent in political strategy manifests in real-world ways, and it is those who are least in control of such rhetoric who must find ways to live with its consequences. Many upland residents I met felt frustrated, powerless, and angry about living in a complex bureaucratic system where they often could not recognise their land when it was described. Ethnographic detail can help portray the context in which such feelings emerge and support more meaningful discussions about our collective futures.

Finally, such an approach reorients a focus on contested spaces to allow for the less obvious ways place and landscape are redefined. Adrian Peace (2005, 509), in his ethnographic examination of contested landscapes in western Ireland, makes the important point that anthropologists must focus on the processual character of contested space, as irrevocable social change is the most likely substantive outcome. However, while necessary, prioritizing obviously contested areas and clear public disputes can sometimes overshadow the more insidious ways rural areas are reimagined and the everyday and mundane ways people resist and bear the burden of resistance. As such, this book contributes to the chronicling of Irish culture and land, recording and attempting to honour people's ongoing struggles and triumphs in a region that otherwise might go unnoticed by many.

In the remainder of this chapter, I briefly introduce the region; outline the context that shaped this research, including my methods; and situate this work in relation to research in the domains of anthropology, political ecology, and landscape.

WELCOME TO DUHALLOW

Upland Duhallow is a rural region of northwest County Cork in southern Ireland that encompasses 1,800 square kilometres. Off the main track, it seldom sees tourists, although the roads that lead to popular tourist destinations like Killarney National Park and Blarney Castle are not far off. Well-established motorways skirt the region, so most travelers are likely to stick to those main roads unless they are local enough to know the winding routes that might reduce travel time. Less visually arresting than some coastal regions or more northern upland areas, Duhallow's elevation gain is gradual; as a result, its peaks (in the Mullaghareirk Mountains, at a maximum of 451 meters at Knockfeha) are less evident than those in some celebrated upland regions like Wild Nephin National Park to the northwest. To the outsider, the inland area is a typical Irish mix of narrow winding roads bordered by thick hedges, stone walls, small towns scattered 10 to 15 kilometres apart, deep green fields, and small farms that focus on either dairy cattle (lowland areas) or beef (suckler) cattle in the higher elevations. When driving, the primary indication that one is moving upland is the fact that fields become less uniformly green, and the uneven brownish-green of rushes fills in some fields' edges or their entirety. The soft rush (*Juncus effusus*) appears as a cluster of pointy stems, usually over a foot tall, and can look like stiff grass to the outsider. Indicative of wet, acidic soils, rushes reduce grazing ground for cattle and are often taken as a visual indicator of poor land or a farmer failing to care for their fields. In Duhallow and many other rural Irish areas, the rough and patchy look of bog or rushes, once familiar, has now often given way to the deep green of conifer plantation forests, which are often planted on poor farmland. Overall, the area is often seen as somewhat unremarkable, a place most people except those who live there move through to get somewhere else.

Duhallow is not a name locals use extensively. In fact, much like Carles Salazar's (1996) "Three Districts" in his ethnographic account of farm economies in rural County Galway, Duhallow as a precise location does not really exist. The term refers to the original barony, one known for its wet mountainous land to the north, and it was of little historical interest to the various waves of English development, except insofar as it offered safety to Irish rebels. Largely rural, the broader barony consists of thirty-six small villages and four larger market towns. The region's southern reaches tend to be wealthier, having more lowland fertile ground, with the northern edges that border County Limerick and County Kerry having smaller, less prosperous farms. Locally, the term *Duhallow* differentiates this region from the broader and more prosperous County Cork, and it claims a unique regional landscape and heritage. The northwest part of Duhallow, especially the Mullaghareirk Mountains and surrounding regions straddling the Cork-Kerry-Limerick border where I spent most of my time, is the heartland of Slieve Luachra—a cultural region associated with rich musical, dancing, storytelling, and poetic traditions. These mountains and their surrounding towns and farms are the primary setting of this research, and my choice of this name mimics local organizations that likewise employ it. This regional or landscape-scale approach is an intuitive way to explore the intersection of local ecology, economic exchanges, and cultural and social identities that are not always bound to a single community, and it well suits contemporary anthropologists in Ireland who query political and economic processes beyond the village scale by theorizing the nature of space, place, and territory (Wilson 2013, 24).

Aside from the shifting nature of farming and land consolidation, the most significant land-use change in Duhallow over the last fifty years has been afforestation, planting trees where none have been before, at least in recent history. Some estimates suggest that as much as 45 percent of the region's SPA (called the Stack's to Mullaghareirk SPA) is afforested (National Parks and Wildlife Service Ireland 2015), although the forest officials I spoke to disagreed. Wind turbines have also proliferated in the area over the last ten years. In 2015, there were twelve working wind farms with 152 turbines in the SPA and an additional eleven turbines on wind farms that were only partly inside the SPA. By the end of 2017, there were 317 turbines inside the SPA, including those within 500 metres of its boundary. Aside from the inherent uniqueness of the place and the people themselves—it is a beautiful countryside with kind and welcoming residents—what is distinctive about this region is the constellation of factors that overlap in these not-quite uplands. An intersection of low-intensity farming, afforestation, wind turbines, and conservation through Ireland's second-largest SPA has led to considerable local debate about what land means, how it should be used, and who should decide.

Economically, the area struggles compared to its southern County Cork neighbours, and it is still grappling with the booms and busts of recent decades. In particular, remnants of the Celtic Tiger economy are scattered across the landscape in the shape of abandoned houses built on speculative development schemes. The Celtic Tiger economy, a time of economic growth in Ireland from the mid-1990s to 2007, saw a dramatic transformation of social and economic life, followed by a massive downturn after the global financial crises of 2008 and the collapse of Ireland's property bubble. In the 1990s—embracing neoliberal policies—Ireland moved toward deregulation, the privatization of public goods, and support of free-market principles, which, among other things, focused on economic integration between states. The Celtic Tiger is understood by many as a period of economic and cultural reinvention wherein a poor and peripheral state rapidly shifted its economy, saw high population growth, reduced the number of long-term unemployed and socially excluded people, and went from having one of the lowest gross domestic products (GDPs) in Western Europe to one of the highest (Clinch et al. 2002; O'Connell et al. 2007; Smith 2005).

This economic and social shift is detailed in David Stead's (2011) account of economic changes in south County Cork from the 1960s onward. He paints a stark picture in which West Cork was an area of extensive economic decline and chronic population reductions for over a century, with more than three-fifths of workers involved in forestry, agriculture, and fishing—with agriculture the dominant practice and a low degree of integration into the market economy. Stead outlines how this region's economy, social structure, and population shifted throughout the Celtic Tiger era. This shift included moving away from the resource sector—which by 2006 accounted for only 14.6 percent of total employment—toward tourism, retail, services, and information and communication technology, transforming the region's economy and social structure.[1] However, the subsequent collapse of the property and banking sectors led to a contraction in the wider economy, with the drying up of credit, markets, and tax receipts. This resulted in a huge hole in the public purse, an extensive bank bailout,[2] bank recapitalization, massive state

---

[1] During this period, workers also received a smaller share of total profits as the gap between the wealthy, middle, and lower classes widened (Allen 2000).

[2] Including the establishment of the National Assets Management Agency (NAMA), which has acquired €74 billion of property debt from Irish banks.

borrowing, rising unemployment, and plummeting house prices (Kitchin et al. 2012)—all of which led to an €85 billion International Monetary Fund (IMF)–EU bailout in 2010 and a precarious Irish economy that is still working its way out of a massive downturn.

This moment was in the not-too-distant past when I began fieldwork, and its economic and ideological ramifications are still present. I was particularly interested in how all this had shaped both the idea of development and the right kind of Irish citizen. For instance, Peadar Kirby and colleagues (2002), writing during the Celtic Tiger era, criticized the way Irish culture was commodified and restrained during the economic boom years. The authors argue that in framing Ireland's past as a form of undeveloped dark ages, recent history is often read as a bogeyman story that directs people toward open market development: "Either you accept the deregulated ruthlessness of the market, or you will be cast back into the eternal night of emigration and high unemployment" (7). The authors observe that through this rhetoric, those who oppose the politics of development are framed as naive, ungrateful, retrograde, or irresponsible, making it very difficult to speak out against neoliberal improvements. Readers will notice this thread throughout the coming pages, in the ways marginal Irish farmers and their sometimes inconsistent attitudes toward development projects are framed.

AN ANTHROPOLOGICAL METHOD OF INQUIRY

I came to know Duhallow as the result of a happy juncture of events. My work as an anthropologist had been limited mainly to North America, focusing on rural livelihood, the pulls of place, and how multiple land-use issues manifest in rural residents' lives—especially in forestry, farming, and hunting. Having grown up in a farming and forestry family in rural western Canada, I was drawn to the ways people shape and apply meaning to the non-human world and how the politics of place and rural-ness are expressed in daily life. A short stay in Oulu, Finland, as a visiting scholar and a collaboration with a Polish colleague had introduced me to European forest dynamics and policies (Asselin and Konczal 2014), but I had ventured no further in that direction.

After securing a position at the University of Lethbridge in western Canada as an environmental anthropologist, I had the rare opportunity to rethink my research goals. In doing so, I attended a Canadian conference on rural revitalization that focused on community voices. One of the speakers was a community member from Duhallow who had been working tirelessly to support her region economically and socially. She commented on the uselessness of much rural development advice— "Lord help me if one other person suggests the ladies sell jam" (a nod toward entrepreneurial crafting as a rural fix-all)—and I was drawn to both her humour and the parallels between our observations on rural development. After the event, we kept in correspondence, and I secured a small grant to spend six weeks in the Duhallow region, collecting preliminary information and establishing the groundwork for a project that might have a small community benefit. A year later, I resided in the area with my family from June through November, and the following year I was able to visit again in the fall to present our co-written land-use report and continue fieldwork. The Covid pandemic enveloped the world that winter and a subsequent field visit was canceled the following year, although I kept up correspondence. This book is a result of these experiences.

Although this project was independent, the community-based organization IRD Duhallow (IRD stands for Integrated Rural Development) offered desk space, and the staff answered my endless questions and regularly let me tag along on various environmental field programs so I could better understand the region. This collaboration eventually resulted in the publication of a local land-use report based in part on a two-year survey with farmers who had SPA land, which I helped conduct and analyze in its second year (Asselin and Mee 2019).

This work also resulted in some community-based conference presentations; partly because of this, preserving the anonymity of the research area—a common tradition in anthropology—is not possible. I am also not sure it would be to Duhallow's benefit to do so. In a reflection on her ethnographic work in Ireland, Nancy Scheper-Hughes (2000) has suggested that anonymity protects the researcher more than it does the community members, shading us from the consequences of our own words, and I am inclined to agree. However, I also recognise that ongoing land-use tensions result in considerable frustration among land users, neighbours, and community members. It is not my intention to place anyone in the spotlight, particularly as the activities spoken of in these pages are not always in the spirit of a law or payment scheme requirements. For this reason, most names in this book are pseudonyms, although a few that could not be reasonably anonymized are kept in full. To support this intent, clear identity markers such as some professions, place names, and—where doing so did not change the meaning—family structure (number of siblings, for instance) and farm size were altered to protect speakers' identity. Duhallow is a large area, and I refer only loosely to communities within it. Drafts of the central chapters were shared with key community members, and, where possible, sections pertaining to particular individuals were shared with them in advance for comment and adjustment. These stories are meant to represent the tight weave of humans, non-human species, and the landscape itself. While each thread is significant and unique, the threads cumulatively reveal patterns of import that reach beyond these green fields and cool cement homes.

At its heart, the ethnographic method is simple enough: Engage as fully as possible in community life, wherever that might be, for as long as feasible while asking questions that ideally emerge from locals themselves and reflect their priorities, concerns, and experiences. This process fixed my research focus on the lived yet highly political experience of landscape in all its variations. While my original idea had been to explore the relationship between farmers and water, the dominance of concerns over the intensely bureaucratic nature of the land and the expansion of upland forestry quickly reshaped my queries. My first visit in 2017 resulted in collecting, summarizing, and analyzing relevant land-use policies as the environmental team within IRD Duhallow sought clarification on apparent contradictions community members had cited (Asselin 2022; Asselin et al. 2022). I also monitored hen harriers and volunteered my labour with local farmers in Ireland's rural development scheme. During this time, I began to conduct open-ended interviews with community members, primarily focusing on the experiences of local farming, forestry, and land-use policy.

In 2018, ethnographic fieldwork resulted in thirty-five interviews with farmers, forest and agriculture officials, farm advisers, park wardens, and others, in addition to countless informal conversations with residents that were equally, if not more, important. Interviews often occurred in people's homes or while walking in farm fields, driving through the region, or moving through forests. While I interviewed most professionals in their offices, conducting interviews while on the land whenever possible was a deliberate strategy because the meaning and feel of what land meant were easier to share and experience. My interview questions were loosely outlined, asking people about their farm and field history and their thoughts on land-use trends in the area—most often forestry, the SPA, and the schemes or programs they were involved in. However, for the most part, once we began to talk, I followed the farmers' leads. Living in the community allowed me to follow up with interviewees later if I still had questions or to go out on the land with them again, helping out if I could. I did not deliberately seek out information on political or religious leanings, which is perhaps a failing of this book. However, the land itself was the focus, and I chose to follow those topics farmers most often raised; overwhelmingly, the topics involved family, what it meant to farm, and the specific choices and policy tensions that shaped their days. While the specifics of local politics seldom came up, where farmers stood in relation to national and EU-level decisions as they related to land policy was a common topic of discussion.

Landscape invariably stretches outward, and I therefore often found myself in larger centres—Dublin, Cork, and elsewhere—talking to people about the various policies, laws, and material flows that extend inward and outward from this region. But most of my time was spent in Duhallow, where I helped build fences, walked fields with farmers and inspectors, monitored hen harriers with local biologists, pulled and sprayed invasive species as part of an EU-funded community development program, helped move and transport cattle among fields, farms, and markets, attended livestock auctions, and, as much as possible, fully engaged with the daily life and community events on which this book is grounded. That engagement also meant I had the pleasure of attending music sessions at the local pub, attending a Slieve Luachra culture night, and participating in céilí dance (pronounced kay-lee); in addition, my children, who had accompanied me for a portion of this work, could take advantage of local sports teams and events. In all of this, I had the pleasure of the friendship and support of Maeve, a tireless local advocate and rural dweller I met in my first days in Duhallow who was kind enough to take me and eventually my family under her wing. The openness of this community toward myself and my family touched us all, and I am grateful for the kindness we were shown. Above all, I hope its residents can see themselves in these pages.

AN ANTHROPOLOGY OF IRELAND

Rural and community-based research has deep roots in Ireland, as it lays claim to one of the first European ethnographies with the seminal study of a western Irish community by Conrad M. Arensberg and Solon T. Kimball in the 1930s (1968). The structural-functionalist examination of poor farmers was remarkably detailed in presenting a community-based, kinship-centric account of rural life. While influential in shaping the decades of social research in Ireland that followed, the waves of subsequent critique of that literature have been equally significant, so much so that Keith M. Egan and Fiona E. Murphy (2015) have argued that rehashing, responding to, and addressing these roots have stymied attempts to reimagine national anthropologies. Despite the warning, I briefly present this research arc below to better position my argument that a more fulsome return to the rural in Irish anthropology is necessary to address and acknowledge the significant role of green discourse and programs in shaping rural livelihood, property systems, and the reach of environmental policy more generally.

Many early Irish anthropologists built off Arensberg and Kimball's work, taking their case study as representative of a wider Ireland; in doing so, they emphasized crumbling tradition and decline set against the apparent stability of earlier years. Although some argue that this was a misinterpretation of the Arensberg and Kimball study (see Wilson 1984; Wilson and Donnan 2006), this research cumulatively produces what Thomas M. Wilson and Hastings Donnan call the prevalent theme of the dying peasant community in southern Irish research. For example, Hugh Brody's (1973) study of a rural parish in western Ireland focused on what he saw as rural demoralization, as locals lost belief in the social advantages and moral worth of their society when faced with drastic economic change. Robin Fox (1978), in his ethnographic account of island life off the coast of Donegal, detailed romantic and exotic people clinging to the rubble of change surrounding that area. Scheper-Hughes (1979), in her study of mental illness in a small western Irish community, painted a picture of crumbling familialism and social decline in the face of economic change. In such works, modernity and the quick pace of change were understood to have undermined peasant culture, resulting in a socially unhealthy rural populace. While focusing less on decline, others built on the Arensberg and Kimball legacy that examined kinship and stability at the core of community life. For example, Rosemary Harris's (1972) examination of farming and faith in the small market town of Ballybeg in Northern Ireland emphasized the endurance of long-standing tradition. In another Northern Ireland example, Elliott Leyton (1975) traced kinship and labor patters in a small coastal village of fishing trawlers and small farms, again emphasizing the stability of village life. Yet, by the last third of the twentieth century, this tendency to focus on stability and decline was already being critiqued.

Examples of such critics include Peter Gibbon (1973), who directly critiqued the Arensberg and Kimball study and those since for a tendency to measure decline from a prior point of stability that never existed in the first place, arguing that what many saw as stability was a single moment within centuries of change. Similarly, anthropologist Adrian Peace (1989) has been a strong critic of the primitivism and romanticism common in much twentieth-century Irish writing, particularly the ever-elusive vanishing Gael (citing, among others, Fox [1962, 1975]), or what he referred to as "thatched cottage primitivism" (Peace 2001, 137). Peace (1989, 104) argues that many of the negative assessments of rural Irishness are set against the apparently healthy economy and society of urban centres, particularly the modern and urban West. Anthropologist Mark T. Shutes (1991), who has worked extensively in western Ireland on the topics of farm culture and economy since Ireland's first incorporation into the European Community, has offered a similar critique of early to mid-twentieth-century ethnographies and their tendency to focus on isolated and unchanging village life. Both Shutes's and Peace's works were part of a swelling criticism in Ireland of the failure to examine the power structures that shape the dominant discourse around rural or so-called marginal areas, a critique expanded on and extended through Egan and Murphy's (2015) more recent review of the anthropology of Ireland. The authors trace this representation, arguing that the Irish played the role of the "savage slot" for Europe in which they were discursively othered through reliance on a series of tropes, including representations as an edge people; a stable, homogeneous national community; a society marked by repressed sexuality; and a pathological nation. The authors note that "what makes this early anthropology of Ireland truly spectral are the forms of Irish identity it produced for so long" (137). Despite these criticisms, twentieth-century Irish ethnography did produce extensive and detailed case studies of people and communities that would have otherwise often been overlooked, particularly, as others have pointed out (Wilson 1984; Wilson and Donnan 2006), because anthropologists tend to ask different questions and speak to different people than do those in many other disciplines.

By the late 1970s and early 1980s, these criticisms and broader disciplinary shifts opened ethnography to new subject areas. Those still focusing on rural areas began to take on a different tone, particularly as they dealt with political structures rather than kinship systems. For example, both Paul Martin Sacks (1976) and Mart Bax (1976) addressed the formation of machine-style politics in Ireland. Each provided detailed accounts of constituency-level politics and found a particular political culture stemming from a rural/peasant heritage that allowed machine-style politics to take hold. Other rural ethnography, such as Peace's (1986) manuscript on an Irish village through three cultural domains (village, farm, and sea), emphasized resilient and diverse research subjects in contrast to the Irish homogeneity found in earlier ethnography. All three of these sources exemplify how this ethnographic shift opened an inquiry into rural Irish culture beyond the narrow village model that had dominated prior research.

Increasingly, however, anthropological inquiry has focused on urban areas and underrepresented communities, opening ethnographic research to largely unexplored areas, including gender and unemployment (McLaughlin 1989), religion (Taylor 1989, 1995), political violence (Vincent 1989), nationalism (Shanks 1994), immigration and racism (Maguire and Murphy 2012), and the arts (Wulff 2017). In much of this research, the increasing influence of globalization also became a growing topic of interest, with a focus on flows of people, goods, capital, and ideas—flows that had intensified when Ireland joined the European Community in 1973, further strengthened in the economic boom of the Celtic Tiger era, and continued well after its decline.

While less dominant than urban-focused research, rural ethnography continued to make significant contributions to our understanding of Irish society and culture during the late twentieth and early twenty-first centuries, particularly at the intersection of the rural and the global. For example, Salazar's (1996) study of rural economic systems traced the connection between farming communities and the external world through commodity exchanges. Wilson (2013) built on his 1970s County Meath research to trace the impacts of European Economic Community (EEC) membership on the political workings of a large farming community. Peace

(2001) continued his work to emphasize community heterogeneity and relations between community and state. Adam R. Kaul (2009) worked in the west coast village of Doolin to provide an account of the intersection of tourism, traditional Irish music, and the rapid social change resulting from constant intercultural interactions. Irene Ketonen (2019) worked among farmers in Northern Ireland, exploring Brexit through the lens of faith and cultural value.

Despite the ongoing contribution of such works, the decline in rural ethnography in Ireland and throughout Europe eventually became a noted concern. Jeremy MacClancy (2015), whose own work examines the role of newcomers, or blow-ins, in a rural west Ireland village, has been particularly critical on this point and notes that the shift toward the urban and the apparently modern has left a concerning gap. Marion Demossier (2011) points to a shift away from the rural in anthropology as a European-wide phenomenon that should be rectified, especially given the increasingly broad role agriculture is supposed to fulfill in multifunctional rhetoric. As evidence of this shift, MacClancy notes, among others, turn-of-the-century texts such as Irène Bellier and Wilson's (2000) *Anthropology of the EU*, John Borneman and Nick Fowler's (1997) review, and Jaro Stacul and colleagues' (2006) review of population movement in the EU—all of which failed to account for rural areas altogether. MacClancy's work argues for a return to the rural and, among others (Gray 2000; Heatherington 2011), highlights the dynamic and changing nature of the countryside as important points of focus.

I see the present book as contributing to an ethnographic discussion of rural Ireland, where rurality is not the emptying home of tired traditionalism (MacClancy 2015) but a site of important processes, including those of Europeanization and globalization, and—important for this manuscript—a space where the broader processes of neoliberal conservation, green development, and green policy manifest. While MacClancy's observations show that rural ethnographies are perhaps less abundant than our time demands, many are still doing this critical work and increasingly do so in the context of environmental change, political change, or both. To this end, Shutes's (2015a) observations of how ecology and economy can jointly produce flexible social relationships on farms will be a thread picked up in upcoming chapters. Likewise, Kirby's (2013) exploration of the nature of capitalism in rural Ireland; Paul Collinson's (2015) research at the intersection of environmental attitudes and local politics; Tony Varley's critical account of agricultural modernization (Moser and Varley 2013), rural populism (Varley and Curtin 2002), and rural partnerships (Varley and Curtin 2006); and Wilson's past and ongoing work on the implications of Europeanization in Ireland and across Europe (Bellier and Wilson 2000; Ilieva and Wilson 2011; Wilson 2013) are central to my understanding of contemporary politics and ecology in rural Ireland.

Building on lessons learned in prior research, I approach community members as resilient, active participants in life, where process rather than a typology of community is my focus and landscape rather than village is the scale. Yet, it is also important to remember that the lure of rural romanticism and crumbling communities in the face of modernity is not a trend bound to mid-twentieth-century anthropology. While critical examination by academics has resulted in fuller portraits of Irish lives, such ideas have remarkable staying power in mainstream and political discourse. The core of such "myths that defined Ireland" (Egan and Murphy 2015, 137) is more insidious and more broadly applicable than can be contained within the bounds of a single discipline and place. Marginality, decline, bounded culture, and backwardness are colonial tools, and they are as common in neoliberal (and green) agendas today as they have been in decades past; subsequently, they demand attention in the coming pages.

Yet, as Wilson and Donnan (2006) point out, it is not because of a recognition that communities are perhaps less stable and identifiable than previously discussed and its inhabitants less uniform that place should not be a focus. In contrast, they remind us that the politics of identity are also the politics of community, and both are about the politics of place (115). In a similar line of thought, MacClancy (2015, 7) writes that "political discourses of rurality are not stable, and it is the job of anthropologists to track and analyze their continuing evolution." The importance of place is now clearer than ever, particularly in contributing to and informing contemporary policy and understanding how the contradictions inherent in the political are experienced by those living on the land.

THE POLITICS OF ENVIRONMENT

Beyond anthropology, the domain I draw from most for this book is the kaleidoscope of material often understood as political ecology, which, at its broadest, refers to an analytical approach that recognises power and institutions' role in shaping human-environment relations. The history of political ecology is often traced through two dominant trajectories, the earliest focusing on the material realities of the natural world and the distribution of resources. In this domain, an often-cited definition of political ecology comes from Michael Watts (2000, 257), wherein a political ecology approach aims to understand the complex relationship between humans and their environment by paying particular attention to forms of access and control over resources and their implications for livelihood and environmental health. A second thread of political ecology emerged in the 1990s, emphasizing the capacity for discourse to shape human-environment experiences and increasingly recognizing the contingency of nature as a concept (see Tetreault 2017 for a rich discussion of these two approaches). Scholars who take this approach pay particular attention to meaning, value, and the epistemological and ontological assumptions inherent in the very idea of nature or resource. The latter approach is what I draw from most, as I am interested in how landscape is discursively constructed and nature more broadly imagined. More generally, while diverse approaches to political ecology are abundant, I'm inclined to agree with Paul Robbins (2019), who argues that a common thread in all political ecology is the rejection of apolitical ecology—that is, the argument that environmental problems can be understood through such lenses as resource scarcity, population pressure, or want of modernization without considering the influence of political structures.

Moreso, these approaches need not be exclusive of each other. Instead, I see an emphasis on the materialities of resource access, control, and risk or on discourse and meaning to be threads in the broader attempt to understand how systems of power shape the non-human environment and people's relation to it. As Arturo Escobar (1999) outlines succinctly, the crisis of nature is also the crisis of nature's identity, a truth that does not dispute nature's biophysical reality but emphasizes that what we perceive as natural is also cultural and social. The power of this recognition is seen in the examples offered by scholars working to dissect contemporary understandings of landscape and insist on the fundamental importance of diachronic readings of land and people, regardless of their placement as political ecology or not. For example, James Fairhead and Melissa Leach's (1995) groundbreaking study of forest dynamics in sub-Saharan Africa, Raymond Williams's (1975) examination of the countryside in Britain, and Roderick Frazier Nash's (2001 [1967]) exploration of wilderness in the United States critically examine what is natural or material; from that, they build in-depth detail of the cultural priorities and anxieties of their chosen communities over time. My inclusion of the historical perspective of power and environment in parallel with the more contemporary-oriented political ecology is deliberate. In Ireland, there is no escaping history; furthermore, neither the material truths of resource distribution and state power nor the interpretive and cultural value of land should be sidestepped or neatly disentangled from each other. Still, we are left with the simple truth, as Robbins (2019) aptly points out, that there is no ecology without politics and no politics without ecology.

A valuable tool in understanding this entanglement is recognizing that individuals live with the ongoing process of statecraft and, increasingly, modern environmental statehood. Statecraft is the making of the modern state, a recognition that nations do not exist as isolated, unchanging entities but are continuously made through processes, one of which, as James C. Scott (1998) argues, is the administrative simplification of nature and space. Statecraft, as Scott outlines, is devoted to rationalizing and standardizing what was a social hieroglyph into a legible and administrability more convenient format. The term *legibility* is central to my study—that is, paying particular attention to how the state creates space, nature, and people as legible items to be tracked, ordered, profited from, and managed. Scott's work has been important for many scholars who work with the debris of social and environmental simplification, a process that never fully represents reality and tends to leave a host of problems in its wake. Throughout this account of upland farming, I draw from Scott, exploring how simplified narratives of nature (or resources) ease the state's conflicting goals for development and conservation. This political exploration is done less with a focus on specific political actors or parties and more through attention to policies, schemes, and regulations that turn agriculture into a bureaucratic exercise.

As environmental problems increasingly demand organized interventions, however, the ongoing work of statecraft also involves environmental statehood, that is, the combination of discursive, ideological, and material efforts by the state to deal with socioecological problems (Ioris 2014). Antonio Ioris argues that the search for sound environmental management by many states constitutes a strategy to preserve existing economic activities, often those that depend on appropriating and exploiting common resources (4). While many states increasingly address a wide range of environmental problems through policy, laws, and programs, the state plays the role of mediator of socioecological conflict and a driver of additional environmental change. Ioris's work lays out the long process of bringing the commons into mainstream socioeconomic activities, including how the language of environmental governance and its associated concepts of green economy, ecological modernization, and sustainable development (98) fit well within the neoliberal model—which emphasizes the importance of private property, rational management, individualistic values, and short-term economic priorities. Ioris (100) lays out the contradictions inherent in the neoliberalization of socio-nature as follows: "On the one hand, the neoliberal state has had to react to pressing demands to resolve environmental degradation and related conflicts, which has required some level of state independence from the groups involved in disputes. On the other hand, the advance of neoliberalism by the state has been an integral driving-force behind the reinvigoration of capitalist social relations, which makes it permeable to hegemonic political interests and undermines its ability to contain the environmental degradation caused by capital accumulation pressures."

An Irish example of this process is provided by Mark Boyle (2002), who explores this tendency of statehood through the political application of scale in Ireland around waste management, arguing that by scaling ecological problems or potential fixes in a certain way—that is, central or local—the Irish state can ensure the legitimacy of its own regime of accumulation while promoting certain kinds of interventions and foreclosing others. Boyle argues that the Irish state appears to be more concerned about organizing consent around acceptable pollution levels rather than radically attacking the root of the problem in the first place, suggesting that waste itself is a threat to the Irish state—a material manifestation of the cracks in its own logic. In a different example, Ireland's commitment to the importance of private property and rational management is laid out in Patricia Wood's (2017) work with Irish Travellers. Wood argues that the policing of Travellers, particularly those who keep horses, is part of a landscape transformation led by the Irish state that aims to modernize rural landscapes toward intensive dairy and beef production. Wood argues that through this process, land came to have new and lucrative potential for development, and state actors had an increased aversion toward "disorderly" land that did not fully benefit the state. Much like my own argument, both Boyle and Wood illuminate how state-led visions and narratives of what land and people should be have material consequences for local human-environment relations.

Of course, environmental statehood tends to extend beyond the borders of a single nation. Extensive anthropological work has taken place in the domain of European integration, the process of bringing member states together in an "ever closer union," and Europeanization, the complex processes of making people, ideas, practices, and institutions more cohesively European (Ilieva and Wilson 2011). These twin processes materially shape people's lives across Europe, but they are also transformative for society as a whole. Wilson in particular has been building an anthropology of Europeanization for some time (Bellier and Wilson 2000; Ilieva and Wilson 2011; Wilson 1993, 2013) and has emphasized the relevance of anthropological models in understanding what the EU may mean in citizens' everyday lives (1993, 3). Most anthropologists today would be hard-pressed not to incorporate European influences into even the most site-specific work. Shutes's (2015b) examination of decision-making and control in an Irish farming community, for example, is grounded in a query of how individual farmers respond to the programs and incentives available to them through EU priorities. Europeanization, as "spirit, vision, and process" (Borneman and Fowler 1997, 510), is part of people's lives at almost every scale, shaping political systems, economic opportunities, education, identities, and so on. As Cris Shore's (2000) ethnography of the work of Europeanization shows, it is also a deliberate strategy that aims to shape European identity, cultural heritage, symbols, and ideas of citizenship through practices and discourses that weave their way into the lives of Europeans in multiple ways. In such a way and in the Irish context more broadly, concern with statecraft and environmental statehood must inherently also consider the influence of EU policies and priorities.

Of particular relevance for this project are the ways Europeanization through environmental policy has led to significant changes within the state, moving environmental concerns to the foreground of state development and supporting a constellation of shifting programs that subsidize small upland farms. Many of these programs require farmers to adjust their farm activities to receive payment. Despite the impact of such programs on farm viability, many have argued that such changes have not led to a paradigm shift in Irish planning. For example, Bernadette Connaughton (2010) argues that Ireland is generally slow to change, with drawn-out implementation processes and reprimands from Europe needed before concrete action is taken. Likewise, others have suggested that EU environmental plans are met with delays, politicking, and general mismanagement in Ireland. For example, Brendan Flynn (2009) traces the implementation of the Birds Directive (a piece of legislation that directly led to the SPA in upland Duhallow), suggesting that its application was half-hearted and minimalist and that it gave in to the demands of "lobby groups." Flynn goes so far as to suggest that farmers who want compensation for lost value because of designation (many of the farmers I was working with) were "rent-seeking" lobby groups who needed to be "bought off." While Duhallow and most marginal Irish regions more generally are seldom the direct focus of such broad-level discussion, they are nevertheless often the subjects of its articulation, the material manifestation of such discursive and legislative volleying.

My intent in this brief summary is to emphasize that the processes and tensions that are part of statecraft and environmental statehood are woven into upland livelihood. The physical making and unmaking of places, together with the discursive construction of resources, political initiatives, and history, are part of residents' everyday lives. Anthropology's focus on the everyday, mundane aspects of life and its commitment to engaged methods that prioritize local values have a critical role in telling this story. In particular, contemporary anthropologists can articulate the context within which people live their lives, not through romanticizing and narrowing such features into unchanging constructs of place and community but through leaning into the tension inherent within them.

TURNING TO LANDSCAPE

I stated earlier that this book is an ethnographic account of the relationship between land and Irish upland farmers. Through this relationship, I see most clearly the conflicting aspirations of various powerful others downloaded onto the shoulders of people who must navigate resulting tensions through everyday decisions. As Anu Lounela and colleagues (2019, 9) point out, in the context of the massive environmental challenges facing us all, what is increasingly at issue "are landscapes as meaningful social and material entanglements and relations"—relations among institutions, neighbours, and nations but also extending to spirits, ancestors, winds, daylight, and so on. This approach is also apparent in Ethel Crowley's (2006) *Land Matters*, a sociological examination of how the Irish countryside is subject to several competing constructions that discursively zone land for production or ecological purposes. For Crowley, like me, landscape is the intersection of intimate and specific lived realities with broader, often global, processes. Landscape is both physical description (topography) and emotional experience, both of which incorporate the collective presence of people and the non-human world, the past and the present, physical attributes and associative values (McGrath 2013).

Duhallow as landscape and landscape as social and material entanglement determine the parameters of this inquiry. I understand environments as the consequence of continuous human and non-human entanglements, and the idea of socio-nature is a recognition of this entanglement—of the political, ecological, social, and natural, which co-produce any given place. In this way, I ground this work in the engagement of farmers who dwell in this region, at once sensed, lived, and imagined—not as something separate from themselves but, drawing from Tim Ingold (2000) and others who have followed his suit, as organisms in their environment co-creating the world in which they live.

However, while this is my starting point, many of the following pages describe conversations that occurred not in fields but in offices. In the last few decades, it has become apparent that humans want increasingly more from their environments. Subsequently, greener energy production and consumable products often add to human demands rather than replace or lessen them (Hughes 2021). Likewise, as my early discussion of environmental statehood indicates, conservation efforts increasingly add onto, rather than genuinely shift, the kinds of engagements people have with the other-than-human. As a local example, chapter 4 introduces a bureaucrat who tells me that "we [various government departments] are all chasing the same marginal land." He said this while discussing the unrealistic land-use goals set before him and his colleagues and how each of them desires something different from the same scarce resource. In this context, I discuss the curation of landscapes—that is, how places can be discursively cultivated through emphasizing, rationalizing, or simplifying landscape features and inhabitants in language, *combined* with policy and regulation that materially shape livelihoods.

Landscape as a concept foregrounds places, scales, processes, and the links between them. Increasingly freed from tight geographic boundaries, it helps visualize international flows that are a part of people's lives. For example, while most of the residents I spoke to framed the European Union as somewhere "over there" rather than "right here," all were in agreement that European policy, especially such things as the Common Agricultural Policy (CAP), is a central component of upland farming and livelihood. The European Union is a major agent of social change within its member states. Indeed, Collinson (2005), in his work in County Donegal, has argued that the influence of the EU—particularly through various funding schemes that are built off of such central concepts as subsidiarity, partnership, participation, social exclusion, and community—can go so far as to reshape local power relations. But what exactly is the EU? As Bellier and Wilson (2000) pointed out twenty-five years ago, the EU is many things at once—a formal institutional integration of economic and political structures based on international treaties, to be sure, but also the institutions within those treaties, as well as the wider evolving social systems of its member states within which nearly everything is impacted. More so perhaps, the EU is an arena of cultural relations set in almost continuous redefinition. However you define it, the EU is undoubtedly a part of Duhallow, although residents might not always feel the inverse is true. A phenomenological approach to landscape does not need to exclude such political aspects; instead, it is in full bodily engagement with all around us, including people, animals, and soil, where politics manifest.

WHAT LIES AHEAD

Between each pair of main chapters of this book, readers will find short stories that invite an examination of the various relationships that co-occur with those described in this book. These stories explore the world-making activities of non-human companions alongside the logic and impact of decision-making processes that alternatively welcome or discourage particular types of residents, both human and otherwise. I have borrowed this presentation of a brief rush of stories from Anna Tsing (2015), who deftly urges us all to lean into messy multi-species entanglements. In presenting such stories, I mean to counter the ontological flattening present within the legislative meanderings that dominate these chapters. By ontological flattening, I mean the ways the heterogeneity of life-worlds is translated into one-dimensional categories of market exchange (Fitz-Henry 2017), wherein the natural world is fragmented and flattened into exchangeable units dominant in the green economy and where non-human natures become legible as natural capital (Sullivan 2014)—farms and farmers as firms, forests as carbon and raw material production centres, fields measured in outputs.

In contrast, these stories are about landscape as gatherings in the making: gatherings of humans, non-humans, animate and inanimate features, at once engaging in collaborative and precarious survival, resulting in heterogeneous patches of activity and weedy configurations (Tsing 2019). Existing within different timelines, scales, and entangled relations, such features are collectively the essence of the Duhallow landscape, and they disrupt, or perhaps even contradict, the book's primary chapters. These stories introduce several of the simultaneous gatherings I became aware of during fieldwork and are perhaps more likely to confuse than clarify. It is not my intent to clean them up and produce legibility but instead to hint at the cacophony of relations, processes, and beings that are part of upland livelihood.

Chapter 2 examines the marginal land narrative over time. The idea that this area is "poor land," "marginal," "wet," and "shit" in comparison to the green fields of the lowlands is established by sharing local stories from both farmers and officials. The chapter then moves on to a concise genealogy of marginal land in Ireland, which undoes this accepted truth by locating the concept within ever-shifting national goals of development and progress. Recent praise of high nature value farming for its ecological benefits—which, at its core, is an acknowledgment of non-intensive and less productive land use—completes this discussion as farmers and bureaucrats struggle to see such land through a new lens. In taking this trajectory, this chapter establishes the connection between shifting definitions of marginal and changing national development priorities. Rather than a material descriptor of land type, the idea of marginal lands and communities is grounded in the failure of locals (human and non-human) to cooperate with attempts to produce scalable and homogeneous outputs.

In the following chapter I explore the connection among inheritance, work, land, and gender. The family farm model is an important part of Irish farm structure and decision-making. In acknowledging that the rural demise narrative—a straightforward and simplified approach to rural history—fails to account for why rural communities continue to exist, this chapter casts a wide net to examine the work of community building in part by extending farm labour to the community more generally.

Chapter 4 is grounded in farmers' experiences with regulation changes and "farming to scheme" (conducting the minimum amount of work necessary to benefit from payment schemes). This chapter explores how bureaucracy is materially, discursively, and conceptually woven throughout farming and lived as a series of specific rules attached to various payment schemes and land designations. The sense and absurdity of intersecting regulations is told through local experiences. For instance, small fields are painstakingly cut in strips to cultivate biodiverse habitats set within a sea of dense monoculture forests. Much of this chapter also focuses on interviews with various government workers and their perception of interdepartmental uncertainty regarding jurisdiction, regulatory confusion, and access points for land users. The chapter concludes by arguing that Duhallow, as told through government mechanisms such as policy, and the fields and hills themselves cultivate two separate places—one as told on paper and one as lived by farmers.

Both detested and celebrated, at the centre of Duhallow landscape and discourse are conifer plantations, and chapter 5 focuses on this forest model. In parts of Duhallow, plantations cover a significant portion of the landscape, a number that would be higher if the Special Protected Area had not placed a temporary moratorium on planting. Dense, linear, and dark, these near-monocultures have come to dominate most hillsides. This chapter explores the intense debate currently unfolding in Ireland about the core nature of such forests. I argue that far from economic machines that support biodiversity, they are more akin to green illusions whose economic and environmental impact discourages people from remaining in the countryside. The discursive techniques of borrowing from the broad cultural capital of forests as fundamentally beneficial are traced through regional, national, and European Union–level policies, which shift the meaning of plantations on paper while the material form remains unchanged. This story is then further confused by introducing upland farmers who dislike forests and see them as "community killers" but who work to regain their right to plant trees within their Special Protected farming areas. This contradiction is unpacked by outlining the entwined nature of land prices, farming, wind turbines, and forest plantations with flexible upland livelihoods. The facts that forest must remain so in perpetuity and that farmers themselves are responsible for the costs of replanting and maintenance after the first harvest and state-funded fifteen-year annual payments emphasize the degree to which national priorities materially and symbolically shape local landscapes. The labour of keeping up such narratives falls on the shoulders of local residents who navigate the tensions between creating the desired landscapes and benefiting from the brief economic opportunities that are possible on poor land. This chapter concludes that the widespread upland afforestation has made advances in making land productively cooperative while simultaneously severing the ties between farmer and farm.

Chapter 6 outlines Duhallow residents' creative engagements with the local and global economies. Rather than development-oriented policies wiping out the small farm as predicted, farms and farming families have changed their shape, output, and structure while firmly remaining tied to the idea of inherited farms. When you encounter a resident in Duhallow, you are likely speaking to a farmer even if the person is foremost the local doctor, plumber, office worker, or schoolteacher. Each person, or their children or siblings, is likely to live on a small family farm. If married, each also probably has a spouse with similar connections. In addition to farming to scheme, most farmers have several income-generating methods, including renting out farm equipment, transporting local cattle, or receiving monies from children or siblings abroad or in the city. Peri-capitalism is an acknowledgment of those income-making activities that occur outside of the regularly sanctioned work and wage system and that may fall more within the domestic economy. Rather than failed projects, peri-capitalist activities are central to the functioning of an economic system that can never entirely provide for the needs of all actors. This chapter points to the reality that flexible, adaptive economies are central to upland livelihoods and have always been important to the cultural and economic systems of marginal rural areas more generally. Moreover, this flexibility is part of the core thread that connects farm and farmer in areas where the land itself can be seen as a burden even to those who work tirelessly to keep it. I argue that an unanticipated consequence of the Special Protected Area in Duhallow is how it has limited such flexible opportunities, including wind energy and afforestation.

The concluding chapter places the book's central arguments within a discussion of upland futures more generally. Collectively, these arguments act as a material reminder that the enticing futures brought into view through the shallow rhetoric of green development are not innocent. Real landscapes and residents are forced to navigate their consequences while often simultaneously labouring to produce them. However, the flexible nature of rural livelihood likewise incorporates or obfuscates the cyclical opportunities and limits that come with shifting bureaucratic landscape management. What farming, rural living, and land ownership mean has historically been adaptable and continues to be so. For the moment, EU efforts to support the link between small farmers and farms through basic farm payments are, at least in some cases, having the desired effect. Yet until the ideas of productivity and marginality themselves are challenged as core assumptions of what it means to have good land and to be a good farmer, efforts to reshape the human-environment relationship will remain conceptual rather than material, adding yet another layer of symbolic meaning onto an already overburdened region.

Elusive Characters

Non-human species and processes are important parts of world making. In recognition of this simple truth, many people are directly concerned with the minutiae of non-human agency. For example, land-use planners, conservation biologists, or farmers might work to cultivate certain species and processes, track small bodies as they move across the fields and sky, plant trees with roots that will, it is hoped, hold soil still, or attempt through other means to hold soil still when given to the embrace of water. As much as these moments represent the attempted containment of environmental processes, they likewise emphasize how much is unknown and how things like movement—of water, dirt, animals, and time—remain outside human control. While most of my time in Duhallow was human-centric, I still found myself engaged in counting (birds and plucking posts), containing (plants and germs), moving (cows and plants), shaping (forests, fields, and rivers), and talking about these activities and the various creatures that fill human lives.

For instance, one day I had the opportunity to spend an afternoon with a local scientist and summer student who were working to assess the types and numbers of predators of ground-nesting birds. The site we visited was at the source of the Blackwater River, Ireland's second-largest river. This area would have been indistinguishable from others I had been exploring with farmers if not for the presence of a bench and a few signs indicating the water source (figure 2). The Blackwater River begins in a boggy upland area with a trickling of water too small to call a stream

Figure 2. A sign leading to a short walkway into bog indicates the source of the Blackwater River. Author photo.

seeping out from dense grasses. The water gathers at the base of a shallow valley and eventually heads downhill to welcome similar flows into its body until it is recognizable as a river.

We were there to move mammal traps and spent roughly one-and-a-half hours walking bog to pick up cages baited with raw chicken. Each cage had a

Figure 3. Four predator traps freshly baited and waiting to be placed. Author photo.

motion-activated camera that would take an image if an animal tried to steal the bait, and the camera cards needed to be downloaded or swapped out at regular intervals. The team was tracking mammals that were in the area of potential hen harrier nests. The summer student, who had spent months moving traps and reviewing the data, told me they primarily saw fox and other bird species in the photos, although marten and mink made a rare appearance. With each trap, we picked up the stinky cage, brought it back to the truck, downloaded the images, re-baited, and then walked to a different area and set it up again. Each transect had five cages, 100 metres apart. They would stay with a transect for two weeks and then move to another (figure 3).

Small mammals are tricky to track in Ireland, particularly the fox—an animal I heard about in casual conversations with farmers and scientists. It was often on the edge of our discussions although seldom a focus, much as in real life. The red fox (*Vulpes vulpes*) is common in rural and urban areas throughout Ireland. Elusive and nocturnal, foxes tend to stay where cover is abundant, particularly along forest edges. For this reason, many farmers feel that tree plantations increase fox predation of chickens, farmed mink, and pets. Fox predation of hen harrier nests is a concern of conservationists (McMillan 2014); however, tracking exact instances is tricky. On two occasions, I learned of predated hen harrier nests from scientists monitoring the bird; the monitoring team thought it was likely a fox, and I could tell they felt the setback strongly. Because foxes are opportunistic champions, their numbers are high throughout the country, and many farmers target the species when seen on their property.

I later learned that the red fox is of interest for other reasons beyond its problematic appetite. It is also an easy host for a wide variety of other organisms that make worlds within the fox and, as a vector, other species. For example, *Angiostrongylus vasorum* is a nematode (an insect with a smooth, unsegmented body, sometimes referred to as roundworm) that can infect dogs and lead to life-threatening illness. A recent study of samples across Ireland found a 39.9 percent positivity rate for *Angiostrongylus vasorum* among foxes, the second-highest rate in Europe (McCarthy et al. 2016). Other studies have also explored the fox as host for *Alaria alata*, an intestinal parasite (Murphy et al. 2012), and hookworm (*U stenocephala*), among others (Wolfe et al. 2001). In the local survey I helped conduct concerning hen harriers, numerous farmers stated that they felt the fox was a problematic species, although none expanded on their concerns of predation to include the fox as a host.

All of the above research, including the project I briefly engaged in, acknowledged non-human species' capacity to shape or create a landscape. If there are landscapes on a leaf and a continent (Tsing 2019), surely there are landscapes within a fox. Yet the details of these entanglements are murky; for scientists and farmers alike, the fox is an elusive, ever-present companion, and I (unsurprisingly) did not come across a fox myself—although perhaps one encountered me.

2

The Nature of Marginal Land

A Brief History of Upland Farming in Duhallow

The marginal land problem was described succinctly in an interview with a National Parks and Wildlife Service employee who told me: "We need to decide as a nation what to do with unproductive land. Is the land ever going to be profitable? Do we want to keep people on the land?" The reality that Duhallow land and residents fall short of a national standard is pervasive in regional descriptors, including local accounts. At times, this failure is a point of pride for locals whose history is firmly rooted in rebellion and survival; more often, it is a mark of frustration for those "who have the bad luck" to be born with such land. Yet the ease of such statements underscores the degree to which outsiders, even relatively low-level government employees, feel entitled to give input on the future of so-called marginal regions and their inhabitants. Positioning marginal land as both an obvious problem and a national question highlights the view that small-scale farms and farmers hinder Ireland's effort to be productive and developed, something I heard often.

I approach marginality in this chapter much as John Gray does the notion of the rural. Building from Keith H. Halfacree (1993), Gray's (2009) analysis of the impacts of Europe's Common Agricultural Policy distinguishes between the rural as a locality and a social representation. As a locality, a specific spatial dimension can be analyzed, mapped, and observed. The same can be said of marginality when built into funding schemes, for example, that support farms on challenging terrain with specific requirements for eligibility. However, using Halfacree's initial observation, rurality as social representation is a morally charged discourse about a de-spatialized cultural concept more than a reference to a particular geography. Gray adds that in this frame, "the rural is something expressed rather than observed, interpreted rather than explained" (16). I argue in this chapter that the marginal label is more often a moral judgment of an area's (or a farmer's) failure to enfold itself in scalable economic enterprises more fully than just as a meaningful material reference.

While the marginal land narrative was common among farm professionals I interacted with—that is, the broad sphere of individuals whose work intersects with farm life—I also found that the history of individual farms, the Duhallow region, and Irish independence was a common point of discussion with farmers who positioned their current situation within a longer time line. In taking their stories seriously, this chapter weaves together historical and contemporary contexts for Duhallow livelihoods, entwining farmers' experiences with historical sources to interrogate the notion of marginality. I provide three approaches to this subject: considerations of marginal land as a long-standing historical discourse, a strategic decision, and a lived reality. Placing statements like this in historical context illuminates how claims of marginality are often another way of saying that places and people refuse to be subsumed entirely into broader economic or production systems. Moreso, I mean to draw attention to how the inherent vagueness of the term allows so-called marginal places, ever those in perceived need of help, to meet the shifting political and economic realities of any particular period.

THE MAKING OF MARGINAL LAND: A SHORT PIECE OF A LONG STORY

To say that the English fight for "possession of the soil," as James Godkin (1870) refers to it, has been a central theme in Irish history is an understatement. However, the relatively more recent history of Duhallow, as described to me by locals and detailed below, emerges from this longer story of land confiscations and settlement beginning at least with the twelfth-century initial Norman conquests, although more often traced to the mid-sixteenth- to seventeenth-century initiation of English plantations. During this time, the English Crown carried out its organized policy of land colonization to control the local populace and secure access to natural resources. Such campaigns involved confiscating lands and converting local practices and belief systems while introducing settlers who would reorder the physical landscape and its management by creating towns, roads, and new settlement and ownership practices. The Crown used plantations to quell rebellions, such as the Munster Plantation of 1580 in response to the Desmond rebellion and the Plantation of Ulster, Ireland's largest and most comprehensive exclusion of existing landholders (Canny 2001). The formalization of land confiscations continued to evolve after the 1641 rebellion, when various acts again resulted in the seizure of Irish lands—including the Adventurers Acts of 1642, under which Irish lands forfeited as a result of uprisings were offered for sale to British subjects, and during the Cromwellian period the 1652 Act for the Settling of Ireland and the 1653 Act of Satisfaction, which "set out the final blueprint for plantation and transplantation" (Cunningham 2010, 922). Waves of settlement continued in the eighteenth century, wherein the Irish continued to be banned from speaking their language, wearing Irish clothing, owning many forms of land, and freely practicing their faith.

It is in this context that Europe was also embracing the agricultural revolution, which began to take place in the second half of the eighteenth century and during which states began to realize the "possibility of transforming agriculture into an increasingly dynamic sector capable of continuous growth" (Moser and Varley 2013, 15). In Duhallow, many residents trace their farm history to the early nineteenth century, when centuries of land struggles intersected with an increased state desire to formalize and modernize agricultural production. Duhallow residents often positioned their comments on land use, land type, and current policy within this historical context, often referencing the relatively late establishment of the region's infrastructure, the origin of contemporary farm divisions, and the prideful role in regional rebellion that pushed the land issue leading up to independence. This regional history is essential in understanding how locals see their role in the landscape, their families, and the region's position within the Irish state. It is also a valuable tool in defamiliarizing the notion of marginal by opening our inquiry to include the ways colonial and, later, state power relations employed the term to justify development goals, subsequently jointly constructing rural and marginal subjects.

Prior to the nineteenth century, poor soils and rugged, wet terrain delayed extensive English settlement and control of the Barony of Duhallow (Clifford 1986). Upland Duhallow's isolation relative to main coastal ports, navigable rivers, and existing roads meant that extensive development and farm intensification occurred later than in low-lying areas. During the Munster Plantation of the 1600s, for example, where Irish-owned land was confiscated and given to British settlers, few English wanted to settle the boggy interior, leaving much of the region as undeveloped Crown land on which locals continued to subsist with somewhat less interference than occurred in lowland and coastal areas.

Early accounts of Duhallow describe the area as lagging behind more profitable regions: marked by small farms, limited profit, and what outsiders saw as a lack of improvement. While this is hardly unique to rough rural areas under the control of colonial powers, it is part of an established narrative that predictably reflects development priorities as much as local character. For example, between 1776 and 1778, Englishman Arthur Young toured Ireland, including the Barony of Duhallow. He later published his travel observations in which he described Duhallow as dominated by poor land and economic circumstances, writing that "Duhallow has much mountains and unimproved lands; vast tracts of it is heath" (Young 1780, 55) and going on to state that locals were likely to exhaust the land as rapidly as possible. The Reverend Horatio Townsend, a native of County Cork writing on behalf of the Dublin Society in 1810 (401), shared a similar assessment: "The western part of this Barony consists of high moorland and mountain, all of which, except, perhaps, the more lofty parts of the latter, seems very capable of improvement . . . One of the greatest obstructions to its improvement at present is the want of good roads for the carriage of limestone, and occasionally fuel." Speaking of what today we know as upland Duhallow, Townsend wrote that the moorlands west of Kanturk remained largely unimproved and "still in much want of cultivators" (420), adding that regions that were only used for coarse summer pasture could be converted into productive land. As James S. Donnelly described (1975), smaller acreages were still dominant in the uplands even though farms of more than fifty acres were increasingly common in areas with better soil.

Duhallow residents were likewise characterized as problematic during this time. Local landlords up to the nineteenth century were uninterested in estate improvements in such a politically and geographically insignificant area. Consequently, landlords did not establish necessary infrastructure, such as roads passable by carriages, until after 1822 (Cullory 1986). By that time, locals had gained a reputation for lawlessness, a characteristic blamed mainly on Irish rebels' ability to hide in the boggy and mountainous landscape. Richard Aldworth, whose family remained established at Newmarket court until the early 1900s (IRD Duhallow's current office location), wrote to the Lord Lieutenant concerning his estate and the surrounding lands, stating: "Newmarket in the County of Cork is a village in the centre of a most lawless and uncivilized part of the country. This district has therefore ever been as the Highlands of Scotland formerly were, a hiding place for plunderers, from the surrounding country, a refuge for delinquents and consequently a stronghold and nursery for Rebellion" (quoted in Cullory 1986, 68). The connection between roads and lawlessness is confirmed in the *Dublin Penny Journal* in which the region is distinguished by "a more than ordinary indolence, discontentedness, and turbulence, in its inhabitants; and their abodes being inaccessible for want of roads, crime frequently escaped unpunished. During the disturbances of the winter of 1821 and the spring of 1822, this district was the asylum for Whiteboys, smugglers, and midnight marauders. Stolen cattle were constantly driven into it, from the surrounding flat and fertile country, as to a safe and impenetrable retreat" (Folds et al. 1832, 166).

As the article suggests, building roads in the region became a priority during the Whiteboy campaign of 1822 and later. Whiteboys was a secret agrarian organization wherein bands of local men protested evictions, extortion, land enclosure, and landlordism's injustices by working to disrupt English rule, often destroying local infrastructure such as fences. To deter lawlessness and establish English dominance in the region, the relative isolation of the Mullaghareirk Mountains was penetrated in the following decades by roads built from Newcastle by Abbeyfeale to Castleisland, Listowel, and Newmarket and from Newmarket to Charleville. These changes were further entrenched in the 1830s with the establishment of the model village of Kingwilliamstown, today known as Ballydesmond, an important town in Duhallow.

The establishment of Kingwilliamstown, which today sits near the Cork-Kerry border, is where many contemporary farmers began their historical accounts of regional history during interviews, as the layout of many of today's roads and farm boundaries dates back to this period. The fact that the ancestry of upland farm families was grounded in resistance to English rule and that their ancestors could persist on land others thought too difficult was a matter of pride for many I spoke to, although it was often also coloured with resignation.

Early Development in Duhallow

From the early nineteenth century onward, if not earlier, efforts have been under way to fold upland Duhallow into more extensive plans for a developed and productive Irish countryside. Some of the early plans for the development of northwest County Cork are accessible today through a series of communication papers among civil engineer Richard Griffith, his partner James Weale, and the Commissioner of the Woods (Griffith and Weale 1834). Griffith was charged with establishing formal infrastructure in the region and is a well-known historical character. In the letters we can see the shape of Duhallow farms beginning to form, including infrastructural changes that were swiftly implemented once approved. For instance, on March 2, 1832, the Commissioner of the Woods wrote in support of proposed improvements, including the site and road construction for Kingwilliamstown. Less than a year later, all of the roads discussed were complete except one (Knocknaboul to Castleisland, ten miles). In 1834, Griffiths also recommended establishing "farms in sizes of 60, 80, 160 and 200 acres with the smaller farms at the southern extremity where the climate was better, and the larger at the northern end where the elevation was greater and soil inferior" (44). As lime was essential to this scheme, two limestone quarries were also secured. Many of today's farmers date the establishment of their farms back to this decision.

Griffith's work was one of the first efforts to jointly improve the region and its inhabitants. During this time, efforts were also made to educate Duhallow residents in modern farming methods, directly reshaping locals' knowledge and practices to achieve desired development goals. For instance, Weale initiated a scheme whereby nine young men, sons of tenant farms, were "placed in situations in other parts of the country where as farm labourers they might gain farm knowledge and skills needed for the regional development of farming" (Griffith and Weale 1834, 66). This effort would be the first among many in the following 180 years to educate farmers in "modern" agricultural techniques and shape their land-use practices.

With reliable roads, resources such as lime (needed as fertilizer and to reduce soil acidity) became more easily accessible and contributed to the region's accelerated development. Landlords began paying more attention to their estates' well-being, and agriculture outputs increased while the population began to rise. In response to increased demand for land and labour, many farmers began to sublet portions of their holdings to smaller farmers. This cottier, or laborer, system was viewed as problematic by landlords who worked to limit the number of individuals farming their lands. Nevertheless, subletting land persisted until high local mortality and emigration resulting from the potato famine lessened the population.

As in much of Ireland, the famine of 1845–1849 and its subsequent effects were devastating in Duhallow. The potato crop failure killed between 1 million and 1.5 million people nationally, and in the six years from 1847 to 1852, perhaps as many more Irish emigrated (Turner 1996). In her account of emigration from Duhallow to Oregon in the United States, Marie Keller (1985, 72) cites a population decline of over 26,000 people in Duhallow between 1841 and 1851, adding that in 1846, 40 percent of the population in the Kanturk Union (a large section of which is upland Duhallow) were landless, with another 17 percent having holdings valued at or less than four pounds. Michael Turner's (1996) detailed account of the agricultural sector post-famine argues that the Irish population decline had two significant consequences for farming: a decrease in total consumption and a labour supply crisis in what was traditionally a labour-intensive sector. Certainly, the famine was a turning point in Duhallow agricultural history. The labourer system had been perceived as a "formidable barrier to investment in estate improvements" (Donnelly 1975, 163–164), and the famine's devastation along with stricter rules virtually eliminated the practice while increasing local land tension.

Post-famine years, characterized by some as the final shift of the agricultural economy toward pastoral farming (Donnelly 1976), were tumultuous for agriculture, particularly with the agricultural depression of 1859–1864. The second half of the nineteenth century witnessed both increasing land policy shifts through various land acts and the further development of the agricultural industry in Duhallow. Agriculture expansion was tied to British imports of Irish farm products, which meant increased growth in the 1860s when British demand was high; agricultural contraction followed, however, due to the effects of foreign competition, poor weather, and a brief industrial depression in the 1880s (Donnelly 1975). Donnelly cites competition with American crops as the reason for this decline, a shift in production that resulted in about 70 percent of cultivated land in County Cork being pasture or hay (as opposed to consumable or export-oriented crops), an amount that increased to almost 85 percent by 1891. Throughout this period, Duhallow uplands farms remained relatively small and focused on dry stock and dairy, butter, and calves.

Increasingly complex ties between farm production and outside markets were occurring, while various land acts (five between 1870 and 1909) were reshaping the structure of landlordism and peasant rights. Donnelly (1975) is perhaps the best local source on the impact of landlordism on the Duhallow region during this time and on the shifting rights of Irish farmers as they were first granted the security of tenure and compensation for improvements through the 1870 Land Act to the Land Purchase Act of 1903, which provided a scheme through which tenants could purchase their own farms. The nature and size of small holdings, often emerging from a landlord system, were a common issue in broader debates about the hopes for an independent Ireland and what its economic focus should be. Tony Varley (2004) points to particular tensions around western land congestion in Ireland, where high numbers of holdings with small land sizes sat uncomfortably against few numbers of farms with large holdings in areas with rich soil. The mechanisms through which Irish farmers could become owners of their own land, or sometimes failed to do so before and after Ireland became an independent state in 1922, are beyond the scope of these pages. This simplified description here instead emphasizes the degree to which local contemporary farmers traced their farms back to specific moments in Irish history and how outside powers consistently regarded Duhallow as needing developmental intervention. Naturally, a colonial power intent on establishing control of the populace and increasing economic gains would be interested in developing and modernizing agriculture. What is significant here is that the same narrative about the region has persisted for the better part of two centuries and, I suggest, misses the broader picture of what is occurring both socially and environmentally.

Post-Independence and State-Led Agricultural Development

For much of the twentieth century, upland Duhallow remained somewhat defined by the same descriptors prevalent during the previous century: relative isolation, marginal land, small farms, and limited local development. Although Irish landlords still held 80 percent of the land, which was often the most fertile (Cullory 1986), increasing local ownership and a shift in the local economy meant some positive changes for land users post-independence. The price for cattle slowly rose, and butter became an increasingly profitable enterprise. Commercial dairying also increased, and north and northwest Cork became central to the industry (Cullory 1986). In 1938, a local group of farmers and suppliers formed the Newmarket Cooperative Creameries Ltd., which eventually stretched from Ballydesmond to Freemount (Allan 1973). In addition to the milk industry, turf continued to be a significant local commodity. In 1940, the Turf Development Board (later called Bord na Móna) began cutting and selling turf on 600 acres of bogland, today called Barna Bog, which remained open until 1984 (Allan 1973).

The *Journal of Cumann Luachra*, a small publication local to Duhallow, contains many everyday life stories from the early and mid-1900s. Local accounts include visiting shops, attending church, and eventually transitioning toward technologies like radio, television, and tractors. Such stories emphasize rich local culture and healthy communities with vibrant social networks. This period of relative growth and limited prosperity overlaps with Conrad M. Arensberg and Solon T. Kimball's well-known anthropological work *Family and Community in Ireland* (1968), a richly detailed account of Irish rural culture considered by many in the following decades as a stable point for community comparison. Yet placed in the historical context even briefly outlined here, it is clear that these decades were representative of a stable life about to be shifted not through the winds of modernity but by those of ongoing change and adaptive livelihoods emerging from and living in tumultuous times.

For many farmers, the 1930s marked a shift as the new Irish state began to emphasize self-sufficiency in food production and stringent control in the home market (Gillmor 1989).[1] Desmond A. Gillmor, in his comparative political analysis of Northern Ireland and the Republic, draws a clear picture of the ways Irish state political priorities shaped farms, the results of which include, among other things, the total area under arable crops and tillage declines as farms shifted to pastoral farming and dairy production. While the state increased its role in farm decisions, Irish farm organizations struggled to unify their voice in representing farms' interests, in part because they were unable to overcome the "economic, social, political, and cultural differences between the western smallholders and the 'lords of the Pale'" (Moser and Varley 2012, 144), referring to large eastern farms. As a result, and in addition to the complexity of small holdings and the nuances of farm ownership post-independence, the creation of corporatist state-farmer relations occurred more slowly than in some other European countries. Peter Moser and Tony Varley point out that "agricultural modernization can be seen as subordinating farmers as

---

[1] Gillmor (1989) expands on early trade isolationism as it corresponds to an economic dispute with Britain as the Irish government discontinued land annuity payments and Britain enforced retaliatory duties and quotas on Irish imports.

a group" (139); to this end, how many farmers during this time began to see themselves as increasingly subject to the needs of urban centres with little option but to conform to their role as producers of cheap food (140)?[2]

The significant changes in agricultural communities attributed to the mid-twentieth century were partly a result of this increased state interest combined with the use of mechanized farm technology and new fertilizers. The latter increased farm efficiency and output throughout Ireland, resulting in fewer farmworkers overall (Gillmor 1972). Mechanization also led to other changes in farm structure, including the decline of horses from 6.3 percent of livestock in 1960 to 3.0 percent in 1970 (494, 496) and falling consistently in the decades after (Walsh and Horner 1984, 97). The Duhallow region likewise experienced a consistent population decline starting around 1946 that did not stabilize until the second half of the century (Dhubháin et al. 2009). The results of mechanization and increased pressure for farm productivity also mark a shift in human-environment relations, wherein various species adapted to low-intensity farming became vulnerable to new, more intensive methods.[3]

In contrast to bucolic accounts of Ireland in the early twentieth century, political and technological changes resulted in narratives of regional decline in the second half of the century. This is Nancy Scheper-Hughes's (1979) and Hugh Brody's (1973) research period, both of whom conducted ethnographies in rural southwest communities. Although distinct pieces, each found rural decline, demoralization, and despair while falsely resting on an illusion of prior prosperity in terms of the economy, land, and culture. Scheper-Hughes, in her examination of mental health and farming culture, predicted the decline of rural Ireland and an eventual impossibility for cultural survival altogether. Brody lays what he sees as the breakdown of communities, the devaluation of traditional mores, and the weakening hold of older conceptions over the minds of young people at the feet of increasing mid-century capitalism.

Yet while the mid-twentieth-century period did bring extensive change and instability, peripheral livelihoods have long been one of the few consistencies of so-called marginal areas—mirrored by constant political upheavals on the national level that included in the preceding century colonialism, famine, landlordism, hard-won independence, civil war, and economic depression. Certainly, many of Brody's and

---

2   Although not discussed in detail here, Patricia Wood (2017) offers an excellent breakdown of early Irish land management in relation to the continued marginalization of the Irish Traveller population, including the ways Travellers were increasingly controlled and partitioned to select locations.

3   Some species that benefited from traditional farming systems in the past, like the corncrake (*Crex crex*), disappeared completely from Duhallow within a generation and have become almost extinct in Ireland. Other species, like the curlew (*Numenius arquata*), are in steep decline but hanging on as breeding species in Duhallow.

Scheper-Hughes's observations do reflect material truths; demoralization, problematic inheritance patterns, and difficulties of thriving in challenging spaces were and still are considerable. Yet their calls of rural demise have not materialized nearly fifty years on. This is because their position was not witnessing anything as exciting as an ending but instead was focused on the far more mundane experience of one moment in the ongoing flexible livelihoods of people getting by and adapting to recurring difficult times.

Entry into the European Union

The idea that rural Ireland has undergone and is undergoing change is a common theme in writing over the last century, succinctly summed up by Carles Salazar's (1996, 25) observation of farmers in County Galway: "Everybody agrees that rural society is no longer what it used to be and, furthermore, that it will be no longer what it still is now." Nevertheless, there is little doubt that farming's cultural, political, and economic role in Ireland has dramatically shifted over the last fifty years. A watershed moment in this shift was the Republic of Ireland's entry into the European Economic Community (EEC), later to become the European Union (EU), in 1973. In particular, entry into the EEC firmly connected Irish farming to the Common Agricultural Policy (CAP), which provides a framework of economic support for farmers while promoting the priorities of production, efficiency, and scale. The CAP drastically reshaped the relationship among farmers, their land, and their communities.

While the impact of the CAP has been varied, one outcome for many areas was increased farm consolidation, sometimes to the detriment of communities in smaller rural areas that could not keep up with expansion. Others have argued that increased debt and declining farm self-sufficiency were other outcomes. For example, Mark T. Shutes's (2015b) ethnographic account of farming in County Kerry details how Ireland's entry into the EEC produced dramatic changes to milk subsidies, grants and low-interest loans—which effectively transformed a two-tier income system based on milk and cattle into a single-tier system based solely on milk. Shutes's work outlines in detail the mechanisms through which the near doubling of milk price subsidies per gallon farmers received between 1973 and 1986 forced local farmers to reduce cattle herds and replace them with milking stock. This shift led to a dramatic increase in farm equipment, racking up debt that produced a debt cycle few farmers could avoid, particularly in the context of later 1980s milk quotas. Thomas M. Wilson's (2013) work in County Meath details the enormous changes ushered in throughout the 1970s, including massive periods of economic growth coupled with increasing debt and a devastating economic downturn in the 1980s. In another example, Salazar's (1996) ethnographic work in County Galway points out that for many farmers, increased mechanization and farm modernization during this time also meant less farm self-sufficiency in terms of production diversity when the energy farmers put into growing food crops such as potatoes and corn for their own use shifted to growing fodder for animals.

Duhallow farmers were subject to these broader trends, with a specific consequence that debt amassed during these times also led to the expansion of tree plantations. As discussed further in chapter 5, the 1970s through 1980s saw increased state purchases of marginal farmland for afforestation. In this region, the debt cycle meant that many poor farmers sold off sections of their farms to the state during economic downturns for a onetime payment. In turn, the state could shift apparently underdeveloped land to what it saw as productive use by expanding the forest resource sector. Subsequently, in Duhallow, the 1970s and 1980s were marked by a slow aesthetic and material shift in the landscape at the same time agriculture was declining in national economic importance.

In 1993, with the support of IRD Duhallow, a survey of 600 farm families was undertaken titled "Duhallow Farm Families: Challenge and Prospect" (O'Donnchadha and Ni She 1994). At the time of the report, agriculture accounted for 38 percent of employment, manufacturing for 20 percent, and service for 42 percent. The low percentage of farm employment is representative of fewer primary farmers, the inability of small farms to take on extra labourers, and the necessity of many farmers to seek employment off-farm. The 1993 survey paints a stark picture: Duhallow had high emigration (4.3% population decline during the period 1986–1991), an aging population (with 25% of those over sixty-five living alone), a 19 percent unemployment rate, less than 50 percent of family farms with dependents under eighteen, and 30 percent of farms with no identified successor. Like those who had come before, the report's authors concluded that the future of farming in the region looked grim, particularly with smaller families, more family members working off-farm, a lack of consideration of non-farm enterprises, and a lack of succession planning.

Current Context

Nationwide, the economic significance of agriculture has been steadily declining since the late twentieth century. Between 1985 and 2005, for example, the number of farms fell by almost 40 percent across the nation (Mahon et al. 2010). The shifting shape of farms can account for some of these declines. For instance, while the total area of agricultural land has remained stable (around 64% of the state's land area), between 1991 and 2000, the average farm size increased by 21 percent

(Crowley et al. 2004). Yet despite this amalgamation, farming's economic significance dropped from 10 percent of the GDP in 1989 to less than 2 percent in 2005 (Hubbard and Ward 2008). In 2021, agriculture, forestry, and fishing combined accounted for around 1 percent of GDP.

National development schemes such as the Farm Modernisation Scheme of the late 1970s and the Farm Improvement Programme (1986–1994), EU programs through various iterations of the Common Agricultural Policy (CAP), and smaller programs that targeted regional and local levels were meant to bring Irish farmers into modern Europe. However, despite these efforts, Ireland is still seen as a country with less developed and less intensive farming compared to other European countries and with a continuation of farm systems based on small to medium-size family farms (Wood 2017). More broadly, Marie Mahon and colleagues (2010) have pointed out that structurally, Irish agriculture reflects multiple constraints, including small farm size, continued low levels of consolidation, an aging farm population, low incomes, and increasing numbers of farmers who work off-farm to make ends meet. In other words, the measures taken to bring Ireland's marginal areas into favourable comparison with the rest of the nation parallel long-standing efforts to bring Ireland into Europe's modernity.

Today in Duhallow, dairying is the dominant farm enterprise, although upland farms follow the same historical trend of having more dry-stock cattle than the lowlands (smaller and wetter fields provide less grass than is needed for large dairy operations). A profile of the Duhallow labour force (including all of the barony) between 1991 and 2011 showed trends of out-migration and increasing numbers of residents working outside Duhallow (O'Keeffe 2012). Jobs in agriculture, fishing, and forestry declined extensively in the late twentieth century (a reduction of nearly 41 percent from 1991 to 2011), with jobs in manufacturing and construction growing. An earlier study also indicated that 36 percent of farmers in the Duhallow area were considered "in poverty," with the average farm size owned by such impoverished farmers twenty-eight ha (Frawley and Hickey 2002). The same study also showed that those most at risk of poverty were dry-stock farmers who farmed less than twenty ha and those who operated hill farming—precisely those I worked closely with during my research. According to the 2022 census, in the Local Electoral Area of Kanturk, which covers much of the Duhallow uplands, around 15 percent of the labouring population worked in agriculture, forestry, and fishing. In Duhallow, the majority would have been in farming. However, as I point out later, this statistic does not account for the large number of people meaningfully connected to farms beyond labour.

While I argue in upcoming chapters that complete farm abandonment, although long predicted, is unlikely in a strict sense, it is still a concern locally and across

Ireland. Eileen O'Rourke (2019) offers a case study of the drivers of land abandonment in southwest Cork, emphasizing this issue's place-specific and context-specific nature. Her work highlights the fundamental reality of small farms in marginal areas: there is a poor fit between what the land can produce and what the globalized market demands. Consequently, it is increasingly difficult for farmers to stay on their farms. O'Rourke also highlights another significant feature of Irish farming—the provision of environmental services.

This last point is one of the most significant changes farming has faced in the last few decades, a change in the conversation about what contribution farming makes to the state. At the EU level, the status and function of agriculture and how much support it should receive are increasingly linked to other non-agricultural concerns, including regional food security and environmental sustainability (Mahon et al. 2010) as well as the multifunctional model of agriculture beyond mere production (Feehan and O'Connor 2009). In turn, the potential role of farming in Ireland beyond food production is increasingly important, especially for small, marginal farmers. Over the last few decades, many important changes in Duhallow can be traced back to this shift—for example, the establishment of an SPA in the region, a new push for afforestation, the expansion of wind turbine networks, and an increased national and EU interest in environmental outcomes such as biodiversity improvement through funded schemes.

IT'S TROUBLESOME GROUND: MARGINAL LAND AS STRATEGY

Within the last decade, the nature of marginality has taken on an alternate persona, particularly with the increasingly recognised role of small-scale farming in providing environmental services. This shift is reflected in payment schemes meant to support low-intensity farming across Europe and in the concept of high nature value (HNV) farming. HNV farming is an EU-recognised positive connection between low-intensity farming and biodiversity outcomes, and it reflects contemporary anxieties about the state of the environment. The reality that small farms could benefit biodiversity even if they are not strong economically is apparent in their overrepresentation in SPA-designated areas. The HNV farming narrative, in some ways, disrupts the story of underdeveloped upland farms in need of modernization that has been dominant in this region for over two centuries and replaces it with an appreciation for the environmental sustainability of small-scale farming. In other ways, however, this discourse relies on the same marginal narrative as a convenient mechanism to direct external priorities toward less valuable lands and populations.

While, as outlined in the previous sections, marginality is a long-standing political discourse, it is also a material descriptor. In upland Duhallow, saying that the area is marginal reflects a material truth of land type recognised in EU funding schemes. Upland soil holds moisture and is difficult to work with, and higher elevations mean shorter warm seasons and increased precipitation. Recognizing the added challenges of making a living under such constraints, the EU Areas of Natural and Specific Constraint (ANC) Scheme, often locally called the disadvantaged lands scheme, offers financial support for farmers working in difficult areas (defined in part by altitude, steepness, excess soil moisture, and limited soil drainage). I've heard Duhallow land described as shit, poor, marginal, disadvantaged, troublesome, heavy, or often just bad. While a farmer will admit to having some such land and will take advantage of schemes meant to support it as a strategic decision, these descriptors often apply to the upland area more generally or as an unspecified burden farmers must carry. When asked to elaborate, farmers discussed a combination of soil type, weather, seasonal timing, and agricultural rules that further limit already narrow windows of action. Thus, marginality is locally framed as a combination of a challenging environment, risk of governmental interference, and, at times, a strategical advantage by building on this confluence to create a new income stream through schemes.

After meeting a farm adviser who had been contracted to assess farm potential for a marginal lands scheme, I had the opportunity to walk a farm as it was being evaluated. "Have you ever seen such shit ground?" the adviser asked repeatedly as we trudged through the fields in our wellies. His steps were sure as he neatly navigated the field, heading downslope toward the riparian zone we were there to assess. As much as I tried to follow his precise movements, I found myself trailing behind, stuck in the mud, at times with water threatening to slosh over my boots.

Fields like these will either be "improved" or "reclaimed" through careful drainage and planting (mostly grass) or be left idle and seen as a combination of mismanagement and bad luck while also supporting a small number of grazing cattle when the conditions are right. However, schemes that provide money in exchange for protecting or enhancing areas of natural value offer new ways for marginal land to be productive. In this case, the accompanying adviser looked unsuccessfully for the presence and quantity of flora that would indicate the desired habitat type. While wet, the fields we were walking in this instance had been overly "improved," reducing their habitat value. Manure from uphill cattle drained down, providing overabundant nutrients for the fields below (a violation of regulations), and the area had clearly once been drained and planted in the optimistic hope of good yields, only to be left wet again when the effort proved fruitless or required too much work. Subsequently, while some desired plants were present, the land scored low on the adviser's rubric. He told me this put him in a tight spot; while the ground is not biodiversity-rich, if it can't pull in scheme money, the farmer may be tempted to use it more intensely—doing little good for the stream that runs below, whose protection is the object of the funding scheme.

After over an hour of walking, we climbed the sloped fields, searching for the farmyard and farmer. Invited for tea, I disinfected my boots in the boot bath found in dairy farms (I had not brought alternate footwear like the adviser had), washed my hands thoroughly, and soon sat in the sparsely furnished home with a cup of Irish tea. Advisers often see rule infractions while visiting farms, but to build good working relationships, farmers must trust them not to cause unnecessary trouble. An adviser's work, therefore, begins with a disadvantage; as their job is to inspect and evaluate farms and farming capability, few farmers feel comfortable with advisers on their farm. Aware of this, advisers must build relationships, turn a blind eye toward issues that do not affect them directly, and humbly suggest room for improvement.

After a good while spent discussing common acquaintances and inquiring about my background and family, the conversation turned to the farm itself. Farm maps were procured and laid out on the table, serving as a focal point for the exchange as I sat back and listened. As I found was common, both men were quiet in manner and polite. Their discussion circled the central topic; the fields scored lower than the farmer had hoped, but improvements were possible. Throughout the conversation, they discussed the core components of poor land: It has been extremely rainy, and more runoff is heading to the stream below than is preferred; cattle have been in wet fields when they should not have been allowed to be there, and their heavy gait has torn up the fields; further drainage in that area won't lead to better grass, but redirecting uphill runoff and keeping cattle out might improve the habitat. This is how the value of marginal land was negotiated: in the spaces among advisers, farmers, farm regulations, and the opportunities made available by short-term schemes directed at changing farm behaviour; around tables in sparsely furnished rooms with ample tea, biscuits, and freshly scrubbed hands.

As this case shows, farmers and farm advisers might take advantage of the cluster of programs surrounding marginal land to financially support low-income farms. In this sense, the concept shifts from an externally applied and often vague label to a savvy technique with precise, place-based requirements. However, much like this farmer's fields, Duhallow is often not marginal enough. When marginality is reframed as low impact, that is, closer to nature, the region's sluggish development can be framed as too much. Indeed, in a 2016 report (Hill 2016) on HNV farming in Ireland, the authors deliberately left the Duhallow uplands out of their data set despite meeting upland criteria mainly because, I was led to believe, forest plantations were too pervasive. This undeveloped region was too developed.

LIAM'S FARM: MARGINALITY IS LIVED

The idea that history resides in the everyday lives of people who live in its wake and shape its story is a truth much evident in Ireland. Uneven political interest in marginal areas has manifested in patchy personal trajectories and landscapes. Ruins of prior efforts and initiatives shape fields, farmyards, and life stories and remind people that they are living the decisions and events that came before this moment.

Near the beginning of my second visit to Duhallow, Maeve, an IRD employee and local resident who often allowed me to tag along during her work, introduced me to an elderly, widowed gentleman farmer. Liam was a university-educated man who was raised in a city and moved to Duhallow with his young wife nearly fifty years ago. After meeting a few times on IRD business, I asked if I could spend a day with him, and he warmly agreed. On the appointed day, I came to Liam's large, rambling home, surrounded by outbuildings in various stages of use and disrepair and bordered on one side by a once-loved garden. Like many solitary individuals I would meet, his home's interior had a feeling of passive neglect as corners and edges of rooms and counters became filled with shadow, dust, and unused objects. We began our day drinking tea and sitting in a comfortable room with windows that looked out on the fields below.

The farm we looked out on was less than 30 hectares and had a total stock of six donkeys. On our left, we could see the large section of plantation forestry that was part of a 100-acre sell-off early in his residence at the farm. In front of us was a series of small fields bordered by hedges, and to the right were a few of the resident donkeys and a cluster of outbuildings. Liam inherited the farm through his wife's side of the family. At its origin, it had been a single farm dating back to 1841, when the family members were tenant farmers on a much larger estate. The first family members who were complete owners were brothers who gained fee-simple ownership in 1932 when the nation scrapped payments to landlords and set up the land commission to give farmers ownership rights. The brothers divided the original farm in two, and one had belonged to Liam's wife's grandfather. The granddaughter had moved to Dublin and married Liam, and her brothers had moved to the United States. The brothers' absence left her as the sole heir to the Duhallow farm on which she, her father, grandfather, and great-grandfather had all resided. Consequently, when the time came, she and Liam moved to the farm of 179 acres and made a go of farming and raising their children.

The couple tried different farm arrangements: pigs for a time with a barn built especially for them, dairy cattle, and suckler cattle, although the land was never big enough for them and the grass never abundant enough to make a good living. Eventually, they sold a large portion of their land to the state for forestry during a

Figure 4. Donkeys in Liam's fields graze among the rushes. Author photo.

challenging time. The return was minimal, but they felt little else could be expected in such a marginal area. In the late 1970s, Liam took a job in the city to support his family, and the money he earned allowed minimal farming to continue. They also rented out land to their neighbour (a distant relative who traced his line to the original two brothers) until Liam's pension kicked in. I asked about their inability to make a go of the farm, but it was no real surprise to him; when he and his wife originally moved in, it had only supported seven cows.

We continued to drink tea, and Liam showed me the two-foot-thick walls of two interior rooms that were once the exterior walls of the original house. The rest of the rambling two-story home was added over the last 150 years as families expanded and houses modernized. The year his wife died, the farm was transferred to Liam. Since he counted as a new occupier, a farm adviser informed him that he qualified for two farm schemes that would provide some income as long as he kept the minimum required stock. Donkeys meet the requirement, are hardy creatures, graze each of his fields in succession, keep him company, and give him something to do (figure 4). With his children leaving for better opportunities, Liam lives in the large home much as his in-laws had when he and his wife first moved in to take over the farm.

Finished with our tea and biscuits, we moved outside, climbed into Liam's small SUV, and toured his farm. As we drove, Liam explained that he would plant twelve acres of his remaining land into forestry if not for the SPA designation. He hates the trees and tells me that forestry "neutralizes everything" and that everything in the trees is dead, that you can't so much as take a walk around them. Nevertheless, planting would have provided an income. Driving around his land, he counts out loud twenty-six bachelors, a few spinsters in the area, and one abandoned farm. He says it is sad; he likes to see a good pasture with animals, although few upland farms ever supported abundant livestock. Liam's entire farm is designated as an area of natural constraint, and much of it is SPA. He says that even if he wanted to, he cannot plant new forests, remove ditches or hedges, or remove bush; further, he has been unable to subdivide and sell a portion of his land because he was denied planning permission.

Throughout the day, Liam showed me how marginality manifests in material infrastructure, in the shape, texture, and pattern of the physical environment, and in his own decision-making. Like the previous farmer discussed in this chapter, Liam met with farm advisers who informed him of his land's quality, value, and options to make something of it. Much like the many generations before him, Liam's decisions shifted in response to the local economy and to international political events such as Ireland's entry into the European Union, and his choices continued to adapt to the various schemes available. After I left Ireland, donkeys were excluded from the species that counted as livestock; Liam would have to find other low-maintenance animals or stop grazing his fields and pull out of the schemes.

It is important not to romanticize marginal livelihoods. While many Duhallow residents speak of their past with nostalgia, most also underline those stories with ones of intense hardship and poverty. Many older residents in particular remember Ireland before it entered into the European Economic Community and well before the booming Celtic Tiger era of the 1990s. While these stories often tell of tighter communities and more frequent neighbourly collaboration, the hardships of daily existence are also evident. As should be apparent by now, Liam's difficulties are not new to his generation. The exact nature of the challenges he faces and the solutions he finds are unique, but the ongoing work of upland livelihood remains consistent. Liam's farm is also unlikely to disappear after he passes away. Instead, the intense social pressure to maintain family farms will likely result in one of his children moving back, much as his wife did; if that is not possible, a nephew or cousin may inherit the farm. If that does not occur, it is likely to be amalgamated back into the neighbouring farm—the owners, distant cousins, reuniting what was once a single holding.

TROUBLESOME LAND AND CURATED PLACES

The government encourages intensification, Teagasc too.

Teagasc needs to be aware of climate change; they are advising farmers to increase numbers and it's a problem.

We need farming but farming as non-intensive not as promoted by the EU or Teagasc.

The exodus of non-intensive farming practice is the greatest threat [against the hen harrier].

IRD Duhallow Survey Responses

The pressure to intensify farming was a common theme discussed during interviews and surveys with farmers. This feeling was grounded in the idea that small farmers *should* intensify their practices, rationalize their farm operations, make better use of marginal lands, and expand farms. The quotes above are from the IRD Duhallow survey I helped with, which asked farmers what they felt threatened the local landscape. Teagasc, the state agency that provides agricultural research, education, and farm advice, was often singled out as an organization promoting expansion and efficiency outside the small farmer's comfort zone. Beyond specific organizations, there was also a sense that progress and success in the community were tied to farm expansion and intensification, even in areas where such practices could be less economically viable and perhaps more environmentally detrimental—good fields are productive fields, after all. Increasingly, farmers felt they could no longer, or were unwilling to, keep up with the demands placed on them or their farms. In turn, various government workers reported that Duhallow farmers refused to expand farms, plant trees, transfer farms to younger generations, and change farm practices to the degree desired; their arguments at times closely mirrored those of nineteenth-century state agents who felt more could be made of the area. From the development perspective, the people were not fully cooperative in efforts to save them from their own marginality.

In my view, farmers' refusal to intensify or adjust farming techniques as often or consistently as desired is representative of an inherent problem with scalability—scalability is the ability of a project or business to change scale smoothly without any change in project frames. Scalability is a core feature of the global capitalist model wherein production and distribution can increase, perhaps globally, while maintaining uniform and reliable outputs. The plantation system within and beyond Ireland is an excellent example of scalability. However, such models are oblivious to the complexity and unpredictability of encounters and, put simply, they do not always work. As Anna Tsing (2015, 42) argues, "The challenge for thinking with precarity is to understand how projects for making scalability have transformed landscape and society, while also seeing where scalability fails—and where nonscalable ecological and economic relations erupt." In Duhallow, efforts to streamline agriculture to something more akin to an industrial model are not smooth in part because the landscape cannot easily be simplified; the ecology is uncooperative and as members of the landscape, locals who depend on the land can occasionally be unamenable to intensification. I qualify this with "occasional" here because as I have shown, at other times local farmers can strategically embrace schemes or projects, although often only partially.

Of course, the perceived pressure to intensify contradicts a parallel discourse regarding conservation and the environmental importance of so-called marginal ground. The area's Special Protected Area status, discussions around high nature value farming, and funding schemes meant to support small-scale farmers are collective indicators that marginal farmland—the right kind of marginal land—has ecological value. However, this recognition does not replace pressure to develop the region further. Instead, it adds yet another layer of expectation. Subsequently, in Duhallow, marginal status (which is an invitation for outsiders to develop or take advantage of the land) has resulted in an oversaturation of material and symbolic demands on the land and its various inhabitants. This oversaturation results from competing economic and conservation goals—neither of which scales well in this region—and a failure to address their well-acknowledged contradictions. Depending on the narrative, Duhallow—like Liam's farm described above—can claim low-intensity upland farming, green energy production, forest expansion, and large-scale species conservation as primary features. Some narratives may also draw on the language of HNV farming and traditional family farms. In the meantime, Liam tries to make ends meet and navigates these pressures the best he is able while seldom meeting the expectations of the state or farm professionals who have a stake in his behavior.

What I hope has become clear in this chapter is that marginality is not a simple story of rural decline or failure. As Thomas M. Wilson and Hastings Donnan (2006) point out, there has been no golden age of rural Ireland but instead a string of struggles, successes, and lives lived. As a political strategy, the idea of marginal land sanctions a discursive practice in which vacancy, waste, and poor adaptation are undisputed descriptors of place and justification for targeted change. In such areas, agricultural intervention, forest plantation expansion, green energy expansion, and extensive conservation zones make intuitive sense.

Certainly, this framing is not unique to rural Ireland and is a noted strategy in numerous nations. For instance, development scholar Anthony Bebbington (2000) traced similar discursive dynamics in Ecuador's highlands, where the government language of non-viability describes Campesino livelihood and justifies neoliberal development models. Dennis Gaffin (1997), in an in-depth case study of hazard placement in the US, detailed how rural areas are discursively emptied and made more viable for development and land seizure through narratives that use waste and ignorance as justifications for their actions. When marginality is understood as being behind someone else's baseline, it becomes more of a conceptual resource for political rhetoric and planning than an accurate descriptor. Much like the way the rural is synonymous with unharnessed potential for growth (a sentiment repeated in the 2015 Organisation for Economic Co-operation and Development [OECD] Rural Development Conference [2015]), the marginal interpretive frame establishes the conditions for potential and lays the groundwork for the conceptual, discursive, and material curation of such areas to meet the needs of more powerful others.

At the core, marginal areas are labeled as such because they cannot be easily incorporated into national or global production systems. In terms of the physical environment, this may be because the area lacks the required resources or predictability necessary to scale up, and augmenting it is too expensive or impractical. Many marginal areas around the world are found in such uncooperative environments. *Uncooperative* is a term I use deliberately to invite contemplation of non-human agency into this equation. Soil, water, temperature, stone, pests, plants, and other living creatures can be more insistent in such areas and difficult to fold into a simplified, reliable output. Historically, this has typically led to delays in colonial and state settlement and control. In Duhallow, wetness, incline, weather, and soil type were the features farmers (past and present) most often had to contend with. The idea of uncooperative extends world-making agency into the non-human realm, bringing attention back to what it means when farmers say this is difficult land, not as a metaphor but as a statement of fact and relationship. The short stories scattered throughout this book represent a few examples of how animals and plants move beyond what is expected, making worlds in their wake heedless of human plans.

In turn, many local farmers are likewise unpredictably unamenable to the requests placed on them. In chapter 3, I explore how family farm inheritance patterns in Ireland are problematic for the state, which wants to cultivate predictability within the agricultural sector. A 2013 report created in partnership with the Irish Farmers Association found that a lack of land transfer between farming generations stifles Irish agriculture. The authors argue that the lack of land mobility prevents young, "enthusiastic" farmers from accessing productive assets (Bogue 2013), indexing, of course, old and unenthusiastic current landholders. Since the dominant form of land transfer in Ireland is farm succession, this is a barrier to progress in the state's view. Duhallow farmers, like many others, can also be unamenable when it comes to planting their land. In chapter 5, I explore farmers' hesitancy to plant forests. Many farmers report feeling that forest plantations do not fit within the Irish agricultural landscape (Dhubháin et al. 2006), and they refuse to plant forests or insist on planting small, poor-quality portions of their holdings (Kearney 2001). With only half of Ireland's target goal afforested between 1996 and 2006 (Duesberg et al. 2013) and most expansion occurring on private lands, convincing farmers to plant is a priority, and their refusal to do so as expected is an ongoing source of frustration. More broadly, upland farmers can also be unamenable in their insistence on pragmatic responses to farm opportunities and their occasional resistance to programs meant to "better" either their farms or themselves (usually both at once). Chapter 6 explores flexible livelihoods wherein Duhallow residents draw income or engage in agricultural schemes in unpredictable ways. Throughout all of this, the failure of farmers to comply as requested is an outcome of the flexible economies that have sustained upland regions over centuries and is well matched to a likewise uncooperative landscape. This is the context of the quote at the beginning of the chapter—"We need to decide as a nation what to do with unproductive land. Is the land ever going to be profitable? Do we want to keep people on the land?" Those in a position to shape the Duhallow landscape and its population have asked these same questions since the early nineteenth century, as both the environment and its population resist complete incorporation into scalable national enterprises.

Abundant Travelers

One of the unexpected things that emerged during my fieldwork in Duhallow was how much of my time was occupied with weeds. Anthropologist Anna Tsing (2019, 34) argues that weeds "shout challenges to stability, [and] show us transformations in which landscape assemblages come together and fall apart." In Duhallow, where so much attention is given to controlling plants and animals (namely grass, cows, and trees), weeds offer an essential reminder to pay attention to those things that cannot be contained.

I became acquainted with national efforts to eradicate invasive weeds through a project in which locals scoured waterways and roads for targeted species.[1] Japanese knotweed (*Fallopia japonica*), Himalayan balsam (*Impatiens glandulifera*), and Rhododendron ponticum were the plants I had the most contact with. These are not just weeds but invasive non-native species that are one of the leading causes of biodiversity loss worldwide. They are auto-rewilders, referring to the independent movement of non-human species into landscapes where they were previously

---

[1] Many of the actors were employed through one of two local work programs. One of these is the Tús program, in which an unemployed person who qualifies can work 19.5 hours a week on local projects for a wage. Another is the Rural Social Scheme (RSS), explicitly aimed at local farmers and fishermen/women who are receiving social assistance. RSS and Tús are meant to add income in exchange for services that benefit rural communities, and organizations like IRD Duhallow can be one of the sources of such work. One IRD project was aimed at tackling a variety of invasive species, and it seemed to me that tagging along was a good way to get to know the countryside and meet people.

absent, often doing so in surprising or unexpected ways (Clancy and Ward 2020). Auto-rewilders bring potential to disturbed places through their capacity to thrive where others might not, but they also tend to out-compete native species.

Japanese knotweed is an invasive perennial of concern for Ireland. It can grow two–three metres in height and form extensive woody rhizome networks (roots), any small piece of which can rejuvenate the plant. Native to Asia and brought into domestic gardens, it is now a significant species of concern across Europe. Knotweed is an efficient plant; its height shades out competitors, and its hardy root system allows the plant to overwinter and emerge again the following spring. More so, it cannot be trimmed, cut, or chipped, as each piece has the potential to create a new plant. Because of this tenacity, tackling knotweed is not an easy matter. Knotweed must be sprayed with herbicide, most often Roundup, at the right time of year (local trials were favouring September and October) and with just the right amount (too much spray would shut down the circulatory system, and the poison would not reach the roots), with subsequent treatment needed in the following years.

A portion of the IRD team had been trying to treat knotweed as part of a landscape project on building healthy ecosystems and corridors (figure 5). On more than one occasion, I spent an entire day driving back roads to find stands the team had treated in previous years. We measured each stand, noting its length and health; took pictures from a similar angle as in prior visits; and placed a new sign that indicated to passers-by that this was Japanese knotweed, cautioning people not to cut or trim it. I was in charge of our map, a worn and folded document that had numbers and codes indicating knotweed stands dotted along its routes. We would navigate to known stands and mark new stands along the way. Maeve had been on the team for some time and was vocal in her frustration over how trimmers (machines that cut hedges on the sides of roads to ensure they did not overtake roadways) still trimmed knotweed. We also visited a gravel pit used by road crews where knotweed was growing in gravel piles that would be used in the entire district; calls were made and assurances were given that this would be noted, and with little hope from the team that anything would change, we moved on.

On another occasion, I had the opportunity to treat a stand with a longtime farmer in the region who was making extra money by doing side work with the RSS program. He was a kind, quiet man, and I asked questions about his farm and his life while we drove up to the stand in question. Once there, we dressed in protective gear—including a plastic body suit, goggles, mask, and gloves—and then proceeded to spray the stand (not too much). Once finished, we carefully disrobed, checked our map, and moved on to the next stand—again while I asked him about his farm work. I eventually caught on to his somewhat exacerbated glances that suggested the obvious—I was missing the very work I was asking about.

Figure 5. A summer student on a work program examines the regrowth of a chemically treated knotweed stand near a roadside gravel pit in Duhallow. Author photo.

Mapping knotweed stands was one of the ways I came to know the web of Duhallow roads, and it showed me how involved my routes of travel between farms were with this species. We visited farmyards of houses whose residents I had interviewed weeks before without noticing the large stands beside a barn or on the edge of the drive. The knotweed project wasn't meant for private property, but when the location was right alongside a more public stand, it was difficult for the team not to extend (with permission) the treatment. Yet knotweed was of little concern to most farmers I spoke with. None mentioned it during our conversations, and the team that worked most directly with farmers was frustrated at their lack of initiative and concern; among the things farmers were worried about, this uninvited guest was far down on their list.

Japanese knotweed and Himalayan balsam are active travelers. They move primarily along roadways and waterways, colonizing local landscapes and reshaping their makeup. These are feral landscapes, emerging with human-sponsored landscapes but not in human control ("Feral Atlas" 2022). They show us how human-made infrastructure like roads and altered waterways has feral effects and highlights the ways upland development is a more-than-human event. This feral landscape is not just made with balsam and knotweed; it has many contributors.

While conducting interviews at Killarney National Park, my attention was directed to Rhododendron ponticum, an exotic invasive shrub with stunning flowers that moved from garden to forest. Its spread shades out other species, including new tree growth. Called a disaster by the *Irish Times* (Woodworth 2019), the park has an extensive network of volunteers, students, and staff trying to tackle the spread of Rhododendron ponticum and the correlated destruction of some of Ireland's few remaining deciduous forests. Other problematic species in the area included the Zebra mussel (*Dreissena polymorpha*) and the Eastern Grey Squirrel (*Sciurus carolinensis*), among others. In 2014, the EU enacted a regulation on the prevention and management of the introduction and spread of invasive alien species (European Union 2014). This led to, among other things, the 2017 horizon scan for invasive alien species in Ireland (Davis et al. 2017), wherein a person can find the top ten and top forty invasive alien species likely to reach Ireland in the coming years. Such motivated travelers are challenging to stop, and they thrive in areas of human movement and disturbance.

Coordination around invasive species measures is scattered at best. Most people engaged in conservation were directly concerned with invasive entanglements, whether in streams, fields, roadways, or forests. At one stage, I had the opportunity to sit in on an Environmental Working Group meeting trying to develop an Invasive Species Response Plan. Eight of us were present, including some involved in local eradication efforts and representatives from Inland Fisheries and the National Parks and Wildlife Service. The discussion produced more questions than answers: What was feasible, where was the authority to finalize plans, how could different departments coordinate, who would actually enforce these plans and how? The frustration was palpable for those trying to create wildlife corridors in Duhallow, and such moments were a reminder for me that landscapes were constantly being made, just not always in the ways people intended.

3

The Family Farm

Conducting ethnographic fieldwork in any area means tapping into local networks where you can meet people, be introduced to others, and figure out the best way to get around and navigate local systems without making too much of a fool of yourself. By collaborating with IRD Duhallow and its existing research team, I was introduced to numerous upland farmers, in part through Maeve's outgoing friendliness and knowledge of, it seemed to me, everyone. The IRD project was farmer-oriented but naturally leaned toward those keen to undertake new farm projects. I wondered what the best way was to meet others who might be outside these networks. Just showing up at someone's house and introducing myself was more likely to create problems than new connections. Yet as it turned out, I needed only to pay more attention to what was around me.

As should be clear by now, in Duhallow and I suspect much of rural Ireland, farmers are everywhere. For instance, partway through one field visit, I received a tick bite on my stomach, and its head lodged in my abdomen—a nasty business. Following local advice, I reached out to a town doctor. During our conversation over the offending critter and its decapitated head, I learned that my physician had grown up in the region and had a small farm himself. We had an interesting conversation that shifted between treatment for my affliction and his thoughts on the Special Protected Area (SPA). Shortly after, I went to meet a farm adviser, and on my drive I contemplated whether my work was becoming overly bureaucratic. It seemed that I was meeting with and getting to know many managers, advisers, and other farm industry professionals far more than I was farmers themselves. But like the local physician, the adviser had grown up in the region and was a small farmer. Indeed, farm advising was his chosen profession because it allowed him the flexibility to dedicate time to the home farm. Similar to many rural regions worldwide, the lines between farm and community were murky—even more so when I opened my inquiry to include those not employed through farms but who had a farm in the family.

This chapter interrogates the roles associated with the family farm as I encountered it, outlining the gap between the family farm as a symbol and as lived experience. As a symbol, the family farm is a homogeneous, often romanticized concept that travels easily and encompasses a value-laden production system. The lived experience, on the other hand, is often far more complex and heterogeneous. To better understand how farmers navigate the family farm as both a symbol and reality, this chapter explores the inheritance patterns that are part of Irish farms and, in doing so, touches on gender dynamics, familial expectations, and the work of landscape. This context is integral to understanding the connection between people and land and the intense certainty of many locals that the family farm will continue despite evidence to the contrary. Broadly, I explore what the family farm means in this context, the expectations placed on the people who inherit such farms, the off-farm labour of women who cultivate on-farm opportunities, and the ways the family farm as a symbol provides a rich setting for the political curation of rural livelihoods and environmental subjects. Ultimately, exploring the dynamics of the family farm and what it means in different contexts is a central component of understanding environmental decision-making in Duhallow, as well as the opportunities available to small farmers detailed in the upcoming chapters.[1]

Two broad themes run through this chapter. The first is that the family farm is less an economic unit than an expression of a network of relationships that sits outside the strict divisions of work/home, nature/culture, and economic rationalism or irrationality. Indeed, it is among the few spaces where such relationships and their complexity can exist somewhat undisturbed. More so, the forces that locals see as threats to the family farm, such as industrial agriculture and land investors, are precisely those mechanisms that deny these relationships and seek to cleanly divide the private from the public and kin from land. Second, reifying the family farm as a symbol leads to poor representations of farming reality. This is important because as

---

1 This book works with binary gendered identities because that was the sole reference from all interlocutors. Trans or queer individuals, while present in the community, were discursively absent from discussions of landscape. Likewise, most relations were spoken of as male/female, and the few gay individuals I met were living in Ireland's larger cities. This is not to say that such individuals were absent but more that the dominant discourse and social pattern excluded them—an exclusion I was unable to breach.

a symbol, the family farm can be used as a discursive shield against the creep of intensification, biodiversity loss, and further enclosure. It becomes a fragile and romantic concept representing future hope (low-intensity, homegrown, traditional values) and loss (rural depopulation, economic non-viability, empty countryside). As a symbol, family farms risk falling short of an abstract ideal that reflects contemporary anxiety and sociopolitical ideology more than actual lived experience. It is the symbol of the family farm that is most commonly invoked in environmental planning, and the lived reality is where any contradictions of that symbol must be negotiated.

After well over a century of warnings of rural demise, small family farms are still around—although certainly in fewer numbers. I consistently heard from farmers and other community members that the family farm would continue, although I did not have the impression that those commenting thought the situation was unchanging. The presence of family farms is neither the romantic tale so easily inspired by its symbolism nor as desperate as economic reports and population assessments attest. For all its ease of reference as a discrete entity that moves through generations, the concept mutes tensions that result from its actual enactment. As before, today's small farm(er) is a tangle of guilt, obligation, attachment, joy, and the labour of many. There are nuanced strategies, means of getting by, and gendered negotiations that constitute rural areas and through which environmental decision-making manifests and landscapes are enacted.

DRIVING WITH MAEVE

Maeve is an Irish woman who was kind enough to befriend me during my visits to the area. A small woman with impressive strength, she is good-humoured, energetic, and talkative. As an employee of IRD Duhallow, I would often accompany Maeve on her daily work throughout the county. Shifting among manual labour, working on the farmer survey, doing outreach, organizing volunteers, and running errands, it was clear that Maeve's knowledge of the area and its residents was locally invaluable. Raised in one of the country's smaller cities, she loved céilí dancing, her horses, being outdoors, and her children. As a boots-on-the-ground employee, I often spent my days accompanying Maeve on whatever task she was performing that day. It seemed to me that she knew most people we met, and we often stopped in the middle of the road to chat with a passing vehicle or pulled into a farmyard to talk with someone.

In her fifties, Maeve was a single mother of adult children and had a small piece of property where she could look after her horses and board those of other individuals. She had renovated houses in the past, intending to sell for a profit; at one time she was caught up in a house that did not have fee-simple ownership and had difficulty selling what was, in effect, a centuries-long lease with no known owner.[2] On top of renovating her home and property, she was not content unless she was busy, and she found endless ways to contribute to the community. Her kindness extended to me, taking me on long drives to some of Ireland's more isolated mountainous roads and to a céilí where the speed of spinning and twisting footwork was beyond my awkward potential. To their delight, she also invited my children to ride her horses and play with her newborn puppies.

Strongly independent, Maeve was also aware of the gendered dynamics of rural Ireland and worked to ensure that we included women's voices in our survey. Regardless of this intent, we ran into consistent problems in achieving gender diversity among survey respondents. While Maeve suspected, and I was inclined to agree, that the farm women were very knowledgeable, most of them hesitated or refused to answer our questions, suggesting we wait until their husband came inside or, when the husband was present, deflecting most questions his way. Time and time again, women insisted that they had little knowledge of the things we were asking—questions mainly relating to the type of farm, their knowledge and opinions of the SPA, farm schemes, and so on. Trying to find a female farm operator was even more challenging; among the few we found, their views were meekly stated, and they often claimed an inability to respond at all. "I'm sure I wouldn't know about that" was a typical response.

As time went on, it seemed to me that Maeve's energy and forward manner of speaking were out of step with many farm women in the area, a point confirmed to me on more than one occasion when a male farmer would confide in a disapproving tone that they thought she was rather "bold." I met similar barriers on my own when I worked to include female voices and quickly learned that the farmer's wife constitutes a category of labour and behaviour with clear expectations and where deferral to the husband's knowledge is expected. During one interview, a woman who was the sole operator of her farm referred to her deceased father's opinions when asked about her views on the local environment and farming. She had lived and worked on the farm her whole life and, having no brothers, had inherited it from her father and was working to keep it operational, although she had recently sold most of the cattle. My direct questions about her experience as a farmer obviously caused her discomfort, and so I ceased my queries, disappointed by my inability to step away from the male-dominant representations in my work and convinced that I was getting something wrong. I am not saying that Duhallow women are incompetent farmers; all my observations led me to believe that farm women are highly skilled and knowledgeable about farm work. Rather, my challenge was the norms around how farm work is framed and discussed.

---

2   Ireland's property system is still working through the echoes of landlordism. Because of this, property entanglements like the one described here are somewhat common.

Yet this tendency toward evasion and deferral did not extend outside farmyard interactions. Outside of farming, I met women in various town offices, as teachers at the school, as owners of cafés, running local B&Bs, or sitting on various volunteer boards who were happy to share their thoughts. Women fill all the upper positions in IRD Duhallow itself, and most of its workers are likewise female (often farm daughters or farm wives). While accounting for individual differences in personality, such women were often outgoing, talkative, and articulate in sharing their knowledge and opinions. Yet I found only a few women running farms or, other than Maeve, talking about farm- or land-related topics in any detail. Sharing their knowledge of the local community, broader environmental or social concerns, and rural development was not a problem, but the specifics of farming usually led to a dead-end or a suggestion that I speak to any number of men they knew. As it turns out, this experience is typical of rural Ireland and is part of a pattern other scholars have noted that places enormous pressure on farmers to be successful and take the lead in all farm affairs. Yet the contradiction for me also lay in the work of Maeve and others at IRD Duhallow to create on-farm opportunities and spaces of representation for the very farms most women hesitated to speak about in detail.

THE BIG PICTURE

The family farm, where the agricultural holding is managed and operated at the household level and more than 50 percent of regular labour is performed by family members (Eurostat 2019), rests at a curious intersection of political, economic, and community interests. Such farms are intimately regional as centres of familial, social, and economic production while also part of national and international flows of goods, capital, people, and ideas. On the local level, the family farm is part of a cultural and economic model that is upheld by an assemblage of tradition, social pressure, and norms. Entwined in this are national and European interests in sustaining an economic system that is, even in the face of industrialization, the foundation of European agricultural production (Davidova and Thomson 2014; Matthews 2013). John Gray (2009) traces the common ground necessary for the negotiation of the Common Agricultural Policy in part through multinational agreement on the importance of preserving the image of rurality and the family farm as central to preserving rural society. In 2016, 95.2 percent of European farms were family-run (Eurostat 2019),[3] and family farm succession continues to be a significant concern for the EU more broadly (Anguiano et al. 2008; Burton and Fischer 2015).

Family farms made up 99.7 percent of all farms in Ireland in 2016. In raw numbers, of the country's 137,500 farms, only 400 were not family-run (Central Statistics

---

3 However, while non-family farms represent only roughly 5 percent of agricultural holdings at the EU level, they cultivated just over one-third of total farm area in 2016.

Office 2018). Farm holders were dominantly male (88%), and farm holders and their families made up 93 percent of all farmworkers. Over a quarter of those working on farms (71,700) were female, yet only 16,100 (less than 25%) were holders on the farms they worked. Drawing from the nine "small-area" census regions where I conducted most of my interviews, a similar picture emerges.[4] There were a total of 124 people working in agriculture, forestry, or fishing in this area in 2022 (while the Central Statistics Office clusters these employment categories, agriculture is by far the most dominant among them, with fishing almost nonexistent and employment in forestry minimal). Of those 124 people, 107 were men and 17 were women. Looking at the larger region, in 2022 the local electoral area of Kanturk (which includes but extends farther south than my research area) had 993 men (87%) and 146 women (13%) working in agriculture, forestry, or fishing. When also considering that in 2016, 71.7 percent of Ireland's total land area was dedicated to agriculture and that almost 43 percent of farms were less than twenty hectares in size, such statistics paint a clear picture of small-scale family farms, which are predominantly male-owned and managed.

This is not to say that larger-scale operations are absent or that labour dynamics are unchanging. Large agricultural operations are often found in lowland areas of Duhallow and Ireland more broadly. In particular, the region of the country known as the Golden Vale, a rich agricultural area in the province of Munster in the southwest, is well-known for large-scale farming. There are also some indicators that the male-dominated farming structure is slowly shifting. Peter Cush and colleagues (2018) argue that models such as Joint-Farming Ventures (JFVs)—where two or more farmers jointly operate a farm without necessarily co-owning it (such as spouses or children and parents)—enable women to gain increasing recognition on the farm, crystalizing their hard-won agency. Similarly, Sally Shortall's (2014) work with farmers in Northern Ireland has shown that the dominant patriarchal discourse around family farms obfuscates significant changes that have already occurred in women's labour and their roles as income generators.

Beyond the local and practical components of actual livelihood, as a symbol the family farm is often taken to represent an ideal community, economic organization, and political organization. Despite significant material differences in family farms (based on size, type of farming, location, and shifting labor dynamics), the model is widely understood to contribute to food security—ideally providing an uninterrupted supply of diverse produce, supporting the rural economy, and prioritizing long-term interest in environmental care (Davidova and Thomson 2014). Family farming is also associated with mitigating rural poverty and depopulation (Balaine

---

4 2022 Census, Small Area Codes: 47043002, 047267006/047267004, 47161002, 47161001, 47098001, 47098002, 47225002, 47225001, 127112002.

2019) and is understood to represent local culture and values. As a national or international object, family farms become abstract but culturally potent symbols that reduce extreme heterogeneity into an easily recognizable and value-laden symbol for which society and government hold particular expectations.

Because of its central role in agricultural production, the decline of the family farm model in Ireland has been a public point of concern since at least the mid-twentieth century and was a central component of the nostalgic and fatalistic accounts of rural culture mentioned in this book's introduction. The same concerns raised then still stand today. The farming population is aging. Those below age thirty-five represent just under 7 percent of farmers, and more than half of holders are age fifty-five or older (Central Statistics Office 2020b). Ensuring not only farm succession but an early transfer of farms to younger, presumably more modern next-generation farmers is a priority for the state and can be seen in tax policies and transfer programs meant to encourage early farm transfers.[5] Young farmers are understood to be more efficient and innovative, and some have argued that an imbalance of older farmers generally limits the agricultural industry's prosperity (Conway et al. 2017). Shane Francis Conway and colleagues' study argues that older generations contribute to a form of symbolic violence by insisting on maintaining land control and that younger generations are conditioned to accept their domination as legitimate and a matter of course.

All this is to say that the family farm is simultaneously deeply personal for those in Duhallow, as well as a material and symbolic unit of economic and social integration and a powerful organizing principle and point of political interest. As in the historical narratives in chapter 2, the family farm is a central component of local livelihood that is both materially lived and discursively and politically constructed. The tension between what is expected of farmers and their families and what actually occurs is a point of stress that shapes rural livelihoods in this region.

INHERITANCE

In the farm families I worked with in Duhallow, most daughters and older siblings had plans that led them away from the family farm, and the farmers I worked with were sons (usually younger) whose siblings worked elsewhere. Many of the women

---

[5] For example, the Irish government encourages early transfer of land to the younger generation by granting exemptions to stamp duty to those who start farming before age thirty-five and have recognised agricultural education. Likewise, agricultural relief can be claimed against the capital acquisitions tax. As of 2015, there has also been financial help through the CAP, where a 25 percent top-up on Basic Payment Entitlements can be paid to qualifying young farmers for up to five years (Teagasc 2020).

I met had full-time jobs and were farm daughters themselves, and while they felt connected to the family farm on a personal level, they had no role in its operation. Within this general trend, however, diversity was also present. As mentioned above, I did meet some female farmers or women living on their own on a small piece of land who enjoyed having a few horses or donkeys. Inheritance also took many forms, and farm transfer from uncles to nephews was common. For instance, Oisin, a schoolteacher discussed later in this book, inherited his farm from an uncle who had no children. Perhaps because Oisin has worked full-time off the farm for most of his life, his children enjoy the family farm but feel a limited obligation to continue to own it, leaving it an option for a nephew to inherit. In another case, an older physician I interviewed (also discussed later in this book) had a father who had inherited three farms (from his father and uncles); subsequently, each of his three sons inherited a farm. In turn, the physician's son inherited the family farm but had no sons of his own. However, through marriage, he had a dedicated son-in-law who would work to keep the farm running. All of this is to say that flexibility in apparently dominant patterns is one of the reasons upland farmers feel so confident that farming will continue in the region. A strong sense of familial responsibility, combined with the norm of including extended family and non-consanguineal kin, means that potential inheritors are somewhat varied, though overwhelmingly male. While farm studies suggest that both men's and women's positions are undergoing alteration and showing increased ambiguity (Byrne et al. 2013), there is also consensus that previous generations of farm labour and inheritance are likewise in flux.

Because the family farm model is dominant in Ireland, inheritance is virtually the only way to become a farmer. Indeed, in 2020, only a quarter of 1 percent of all agricultural land available in Ireland was exchanged on the market (Central Statistics Office 2020a). My observations in Duhallow align with a broader Irish norm, where inheritance typically follows a pattern of impartible patrilineal inheritance. Partible inheritance occurs when a farm owner divides their assets among multiple children. Ciaran McCullagh (1991) traces the development of stem-family inheritance, or impartibility, back to the Great Famine. He describes how before this time, when a male family member was married, the farm would be subdivided to give a portion to the newly married son. Because families were large and landholdings relatively small, the piece of land inherited became increasingly smaller. McCullagh points out that by 1841, half of Irish farms were less than five acres. At best, such farms could sustain one staple crop, often potatoes; thus, farms were particularly vulnerable to crop failure. This system, among other political features of the time, magnified the impact of potato crop failures in 1845 and 1846, when upward of one million died of starvation and related illnesses and another one million people emigrated. After this time, the stem-family (impartible) pattern became more dominant, wherein a single son would inherit the entire estate and the other children were encouraged to find their futures elsewhere.

Donna Birdwell-Pheasant (1992) outlines five elements central to the impartible system: unitary inheritance, son inheritance, heir marriage, the three-generation household, and sibling dispersal, most of which were present to some degree in my observations. However, in her anthropological case study examining historical inheritance patterns in County Kerry, she finds that differentiating between rigid and loose stem-family models is important. In the rigid model, the impartible, or stem-family, system firmly positioned the father as a powerful figure who ultimately decided which son (only one) would inherit the farm. While early inheritance patterns favoured the eldest son, it was certainly the father's right to choose a different heir from among his children. Historically, the son considered most suitable for inheritance was not provided with an education, meaning that the only alternative to remaining under the father's influence on the farm was to take unskilled, often poorly paid labour jobs, usually in the city (Harris 1988, 429). Birdwell-Pheasant's understanding of a loose impartible system allowed for multiple inheritors; however, her work and mine found this exception to be a trend usually encountered only with much larger farms. Overall, the impartible system continues today in Ireland, where it is common for a single heir (often, though not always, a younger son) to inherit the family farm.

While there are no specific legal barriers to women inheriting land, the patrilinear cultural norm is dominant and few women are farm owners. Female farm holders in Ireland make up only 10.8–12.0 percent of farm managers compared to a European average of 28.4 percent (Eurostat 2019). Many of those who wholly own farms have inherited them from their husbands with the intent of passing them on to a male heir when appropriate. More broadly, women are less visible in Irish agriculture, have less farm-related training, and are less likely to be the primary owner of a farm, resulting in what Shortall argues is occupational closure (Shortall et al. 2020). Indeed, in her study of gender dynamics on farms, Shortall found the dominant underlying feature shaping women's farm occupation was patrilineal land inheritance patterns that acted as an interactional social closure mechanism, in effect closing off farm occupation for many women—a finding that originated in Scottish research and was later extended to Ireland (Shortall 2001). Shortall has argued that this dearth of female farm operators should be of greater concern for a nation fixated on the continuation of family farms and the lack of inheritance plans among many aging farmers. While I tend to agree, I found only minimal national focus on this subject and no interest among locals in discussing this point.

The specifics of the inheriting son have received important academic attention over the years. Some have argued that historically, the inheriting son was a form of captive (McCullagh 1991) or the subject of community and familial manipulation (Scheper-Hughes 1979). More recently, scholars have examined the tendency for fathers to delay farm transfers, suggesting it is a form of symbolic violence that denies respect and legitimacy to adult children waiting to inherit (Conway et al. 2017). McCullagh (1991) has highlighted an essential lesson in all of this, arguing that the lines of fissure in nineteenth- and twentieth-century Ireland were not exclusively along class lines as is often claimed but were located primarily within the family itself. More specifically, he argues that land conflict within and between families, the dominance of the stem-family system, and the exploitation of family labour led to considerable and under-recognised tension. In my view, this argument is particularly significant because it recognises that the ideology of family was one that both denied and displaced conflicts created within the family system; that is, the profound importance placed on family and inheritance obfuscates the family dynamic as a source of conflict and dysfunction.

As much as the myth of prior rural stability selectively ignores consistent socioeconomic and political upheaval, McCullagh (1941) points out that family farms and their impartible/stem inheritance systems have always been strained. To this point, in Birdwell-Pheasant's (1992, 216) examination of historical inheritance patterns, she found that "despite a clear preference for a son as heir to the family farm, failure of son inheritance did not emerge as a strongly charged issue." Instead, she suggested that transfers to daughters, nephews, or nieces were not uncommon and that as much as 18 percent of farm transfers might have gone to someone other than sons in her case study (though of those, 41.5 % were then transferred to sons at a later date [221]). Birdwell-Pheasant argues instead that the rigid stem-family model became entrenched in Irish academic literature and equated with Irish peasantry because it fit the needs at a certain stage in the development of anthropology "when functionalist analysis and the 'ethnographic present' were standard fare" (229). Clearly, while the act of inheritance is a central feature of the family farm model and often does rely on sons to inherit, alternative patterns have historically existed and still do exist.

Nevertheless, while not exclusively relying on sons, the patrilineal and single-inheritor system is held in place and normalized by a broad network of people and practices that deserve further attention and are highly relevant for understanding the experiences of many farmers I encountered. Irish family farms should be understood as a network of connections that includes not just inheritors but also children and extended family members who do not inherit but continue to have deep ties to the family farm (Cassidy and McGrath 2014); this includes the practice of rearing children with very particular expectations and experiences in mind. For example, Anne Cassidy and Brian McGrath (2014) have worked extensively with Irish farm children who attend a university, most of whom do not expect to inherit the family farm. They found that a considerable degree of conditioning shapes the expectations of farm children. Such conditioning typically includes exposing or denying children hands-on farm experience, cultivating a sense of independence and feminist liberation among girls that helps move them toward education and off-farm living, and building intense farm experience, responsibility, and (limited) choice among boys (Cassidy 2017; Cassidy and McGrath 2014). Farm children, Cassidy suggests, are able to live with the paradox of their particular situation (girls raised with an eye to liberation and feminism but unable to inherit a farm due to their gender, boys given the idea of choice but heavily socialized with the responsibility to family duty) by shifting their social scripts as they move among home, university, and community life. Importantly, this socialization positions non-inheritors as farm supporters by building an intense attachment to place, family history, and sacrifice. In such a way, many non-inheriting siblings support and pressure the inheriting sibling to stay on "their" farm—one that belongs to the whole family. The following two sections weave these observations into the lived realities of what it means for farmers themselves as they navigate inheritance and the expectations of running the family farm.

THE STORY OF DARRAGH

As an example of farm inheritance in Duhallow, I turn to Darragh. I was introduced to Darragh through an acquaintance who thought we should meet because he and his wife were community-engaged, multigenerational farmers. After introductions, Darragh invited me to tour his farm one afternoon, suggesting I connect with his wife another day because she was busy. Darragh's farm is on the productive edge of lowland farming, south of the upland region where I spent much of my time. His farm was larger than those I had visited in other parts of Duhallow, and the drier land was immediately apparent to me in the extensive, even green fields extending neatly on either side of the road as I drove up to his house, with few rushy and rough areas visible. Darragh was welcoming and generous. I was invited into his home, plied with tea, and invited to ask any questions I liked. Our visit lasted the better part of the afternoon, as we spoke first in his kitchen and then spent some hours walking and driving throughout the farm. The following week, I returned to visit Mary, his wife, and some of her friends from nearby communities.

The oldest of three sons, Darragh was nearing retirement. He had a fairly large dairy farm that ran between 60 and 120 cows, and he had dedicated his life to its operation. Darragh's inheritance story was like many others I had heard. The farm had been in the family for over 150 years through his cousin's line. Darragh's father had often worked on the farm as a child, and at fourteen he started contributing most of his energy to helping the farm prosper. There had been financial difficulty with the cousin's line, and Darragh's father's people had helped them out. Subsequently, Darragh's father inherited the farm while still a very young man.

Darragh and his brother eventually inherited the 200-acre farm, split into 120 acres that he inherited when he was eighteen and 80 acres for his brother. A third brother left and found work elsewhere, as did his sister. While working actively on the farm, he completed his education at the local school and spent two years at a technical school working on a farm certificate. Darragh told me he would have liked to have finished his education before returning to the farm, but it didn't work out as planned: "Obviously, I would have liked to have worked outside the farm, but my father didn't allow me." His father had hired farm help in his son's absence, but when that help was no longer available, Darragh was obliged to quit school and come home, lacking only final exams to complete his technical certificate: "The workman left, and it was difficult to replace him, so I was pulled out of school the last month. I didn't do my exams. I stayed at home then because the workman left, and I had to come home. It was silage at the time, and there was work to be done. That is how my education got a quick end." The two brothers ran the farm as a single unit for fifteen years, with Darragh, his brother, and his parents still living on the home farm. Eventually, Darragh married and built up his section of the farm, building the house he now lived in. His parents continued to live on the home farm with his brother, who managed the business of his portion until the parents passed away; he never married or had children. When I met Darragh, both brothers were full-time farmers running separate operations, though Darragh's land was split by his brother's, making access sometimes difficult.

Darragh had two sons, one of whom was apparently content to take on work elsewhere and move away and the other, the older, who would inherit the farm. I found out later that he also had a daughter who was educated in the city. Darragh was under pressure to pass on his farm within the next few years, as the Irish government provides tax incentives to transfer farms on to the next generation before the farm owner turns sixty-five. In asking how he felt about the transfer, he stated that "it is a bit of a shock all right," but if he does not do so, he will have to pay €80,000–€90,000 in tax rather than €10,000 by his estimate. Like his father, Darragh imagines he will continue to do much of the farmwork after the transfer. When asked how his son feels about it, Darragh responded "he loves it, he is delighted to take it over," though I was unable to confirm this with the son himself. Darragh's older son completed his education and is a manager in a local industry. Darragh expects he will stay at his work and farm part-time because as large as the farm is compared to others, it may not be enough to support a family. While they were renting a house off-farm at the time of our conversation, his son and daughter-in-law had recently gained a permit to build a new home on the farm property—although Darragh was clear that it took a lot of work and time to get final approval and he had been frustrated with the process. While we did not discuss it, Darragh's brother, with no children himself, will likely choose his nephew (Darragh's son) as the farm inheritor, uniting the original farm once again—although it is certainly possible that a farm-oriented cousin might inherit instead.

Thus, the farm moves between family members, sometimes switching lines within the same family and with the exact details of what this looks like worked out between family members, sometimes in creative ways. The romanticism that was once historically abundant in Irish farm accounts—and that still sneaks its way in on occasion—rests on the assumption that family and farm are distinct units rather than shifting relationships among family members, land, and labour. Only by paying attention to diversity in patterns can a more accurate picture of farm life emerge.

THE POISONED CHALICE

My conversations with farmers often covered the pride of place, the value of farm labour, and the ongoing anxieties and regrets embedded in a farming livelihood. I felt that many farmers who took the time to speak to me were jointly occupying the spaces of satisfaction and the deep fatigue caused by difficult living, both proud of their labour and their farm while exhausted and anxious about their futures. The emotional toll of such tensions is intense, and I believe it deserves full recognition as one of the many contradictions navigated by small Irish farmers—a contradiction equally woven by the threads of inheritance systems, familial expectations, and, increasingly, the expectations of governments and society who feel they too should have a say in the nature of the family farm.

For most, upland farming is not, and never was, a consistent source of financial abundance. In terms of farm type and economy, many farmers told me a story that went something like this: Many of the local creameries closed during the mid-twentieth century because farmers were able to bring their milk greater distances and eventually to have large trucks occasionally visit their farm to pick up the milk rather than having to drive it themselves. Subsequently, the upland economy shifted, as having just a few milk cows was no longer worth the work and the cost of transportation. Most upland farmers eventually moved to suckler cattle because grass-fed beef was more likely to bring returns on their small fields and they could more easily participate in off-farm work when milking cows no longer consumed their days. However, farm income did not rise with, and sometimes fell against, the costs of housing and farm expenses. At the same time, many residents wanted more for themselves and their children than they had had as children. Comfortable transportation, the internet, entertainment systems, travel, and children's extracurricular activities all became a part of the rising cost of living and the expectations of what a good life should look like.

Despite these well-acknowledged financial challenges, those who inherit are under enormous social and familial pressure to keep up or improve the family land while increasingly being put in the impossible position of making doing so economically viable. As I was told on more than one occasion, "I don't want to sell because it was my father's and his father's before him." A local office worker who did not inherit but who comes from a farming background reflected on the future of upland farming, stating: "They'll always farm it . . . they might go off and get another off-farm job, but they will still keep cattle. But, you know, in a lot of cases, upland farming, it doesn't make any economic sense to actually do it. You know, if you—particularly if your cost is your own time and labour, but that's not the point. You know, it's what they identify themselves as." The farm inheritance pattern is thus internalized through desire but also obligation, social pressure, and cultural norms that influence desire. In exploring this pattern, Roisin Kelly and Sally Shortall (2002) have gone so far as to suggest that inheritance is akin to a poisoned chalice.

This pressure was apparent in many of my encounters with Irish farmers. For example, I was deeply affected by my meeting with Cormac, a farmer on the edge of Duhallow who had young children. I had originally met Cormac through Maeve, who was sure he had been part of the original survey group but he had not. We had a good visit that day, and I was invited to visit again. We met later at his house, with his young children roaming around and sneaking biscuits out of the tin as we sat and talked over tea. The difficulties he faced in trying to build what he saw as a good upland farming life were clearly taking an emotional toll. More than once, he asked what he was supposed to do, a question we both knew I could not help him answer, although the weight of it settled in my bones and is still with me today.

Cormac knew the story of his land going back to his great-grandfather, although it had been in the family longer than that. His great-grandfather was one of a family of ten children. His grandfather, who would eventually inherit, was a servant boy to another farmer and worked both farms until he was old enough to take over the home farm. He had many children, and Cormac's father was the youngest. Of those who left the farm, most of them made money in England. He told me that "people left Ireland because they were hungry in one way or another, they had basic needs. Though people left with a plan to come back, the love of the land for the Irish will always be there. Love, the desire to come home, expand the land, grow on the land." Cormac was good at farming and inherited the land rather than his siblings. His wife works full-time, and he now works full-time while trying to expand the farm and build up its capacity after his father let it go in his later years: "When I was young, we had cabbage, hens, and cows to milk. It's the whole way of life." In aiming for something similar, he admitted that he doesn't have a farm that will ever make money and that it would be impossible for him to do so if he did not work elsewhere.

Having grown up in the area, he has seen the view change. We stood at his window, looking out over the valley as he recounted the history of the farms and fields in our view. His house sat in the shadow of conifer plantations on one side and a valley stretching out below him on the other. Most original farms were now only minimally used, and he pointed out the change in the colour and texture of a field being grazed versus one that had gone fallow, now beige with rushes. At a crossroads where reductions in farm use are evident, he finds it depressing to live in the shadow of tree plantations and unused fields and buildings. He worries about the impact of afforestation in this area but also noted that Coillte, the company managing the plantation, is at least easier to work with than private forest owners. His childhood school lay empty just down the road, and he spoke about how difficult it is for his children to get to school and that they will need cars to get into town when they get older. He does not necessarily want them to take over his land, but at the same time, he can't see it leaving his family. He told me he felt that for himself, as a young person, change is easy enough but that he feels bad for the older farmers who need to adapt to survive.

As we spoke, I was struck by Cormac's earnestness. He loves his land and by his own words couldn't imagine why anyone would not want to farm, even if just part-time. When I asked if there was anything else he wanted to tell me, he responded "I want people to know what I have said, that is what I want." His struggles to keep the farm operational were apparent, as was his deep sense of obligation to and love for the farm. He and his wife work to support the farm and raise their children, a farm resting in the space among the shadows of growing Sitka spruce, richly grazed fields, and abandoned homes. Cormac's honest expression of the impossible place he inhabits, with both joy and exhausted defeat, stuck with me, and I knew it mirrored the experiences of many farmers. Some were having an easier time of it, and others were more openly bitter about the lot they had inherited and intended to continue to carry.

For some time now, it has been clear that inheriting the family farm can be an obligation and a burden as much as or perhaps more than a boon. This difficult space of identity and farming has drawn the attention of those who see concerning trends in suicide rates among male farmers. An early study on masculinity in rural Ireland and the pressures inherent in "staying behind," conducted by Catríona Ní Laoire (2001), accounts for high rates of suicide among men, particularly those who are unemployed and those threatened with unemployment—a category that includes many small farmers. Reasons offered include the combination of intense familial pressure, the perceived or real inability to leave, the stress of work itself, and strict narratives of masculinity and traditional values. The more I learned about this pressure, the more I understood and respected women's reticence to speak of farm matters and their insistence that I acknowledge and talk to the men who are most often the primary farm holders.

A 2018 Health Services report on men's suicide (O'Donnell and Richardson 2018, 108) notes that farmers are among the nation's highest groups of concern for committing suicide and that some farmers and rural, isolated men feel "left behind," adding that vacant homes and closed businesses are visible scars of a recession rural areas still grapple with. One of their research participants noted that "it always seems that we [west of Ireland] get left behind. It just gets accelerated with this recession. Dublin has picked up and has moved on, but there is nothing happening down here . . . It always seems every time something happens the West seems to get left further behind." The report includes personal stories, one from a farmer trying to grow the farm and his realization that his children would not want to take it over; this failure to continue to own the farm had been internalized as a personal failure. Clearly, the intimate connections among people, place, and social expectation are central to the ways farmers engage in rural livelihood and internalize their capacities, value, and future within it.

In deliberately recognizing such challenges, I believe the romantic depth and steadiness of the small farm as a symbol can be shifted to embrace the tensions and conflicts that McCullagh (1991) and Scheper-Hughes (1979) remind us have long existed. This is important to remember because as intimate as these observations are, the productivity of farms and farmer is also immensely political, a point I take up more thoroughly in the following chapters. State and international apparatuses are structured to support and value certain forms of labour for different political purposes, and ideologically, the small-scale work of the family farm is often culturally reified and nurtured in funding mechanisms that ask farmers to labour in support of the state's shifting green goals (e.g., plant trees, fence riparian zones, keep stocking minimal) or economic benchmarks (increase milk production or pasture, for example). Beyond the farm family, there is a political and social expectation that land should produce value, and farmers are encouraged to intensify and rationalize their output, ideally passing on their farms to those who are younger and more educated. In all of this, the desire for the right kind of productive environment comes with landowners who work hard and in the right way, as perceived by their communities and the state.

The expectation that land and farmers can be so many things simultaneously results in intense discomfort for many who try to meet these demands. Yet beyond discomfort, what was most apparent to me were the contradictions of people's lives and the subsequent importance of not smoothing out or explaining away things that don't always easily make sense. To that end, I will finish this section with the following brief encounter:

One afternoon, I had the opportunity to speak to a younger farmer who has a job in town that allows him to keep farming. His father transferred the farm to him some time ago, but to keep "everything sweet," the father was still the boss on the farm. When we spoke of the area's future, he responded that it was all "very sad." Like many others, he talked about school buses that are no longer full and sports teams that cannot easily continue for a lack of people. But then he added that "the reality of it is that people only survived before, they didn't have a living and you can't force something out of something that's not there. It's sad, but you either sit at home and wallow . . . or you get up and do something. And doing something, for the majority of people, that involves leaving." When I asked about his plans for his children, however, he said he would absolutely like for them to take over his farm, "I'd love it if they kept it going," adding that he would not like them to be too isolated but would love it if they could find a way to survive. In fact, he felt younger farmers might have an easier time because they are more adept at navigating the farm grants system while also working off the farm.

WOMEN'S WORK

During my discussions with (usually male) Duhallow farmers, I often heard what I came to call "the count of women," an assessment of the number and location of local women young enough to marry or, more specifically, bear children. This assessment would usually begin with a discussion of community decline, often along the lines of low school or sports team enrollment, and would shift to a geographic survey of women of child-bearing age in the region. Starting with the hills and valleys surrounding the farm and extending outward, this description invariably reported only a handful of youngish women living in the area. "Gracious," one part-time farmer said after detailing the women in his region. "Three. Are there really just three and all over forty?"

At first glance, such statements fit well with mid-twentieth-century ethnographies detailing the decline of rural culture and society that drew heavily from the concept of anomie. In their review of Irish ethnographies, Irene Ketonen-Keating (2021, 24) relates Irish anomie to eight central features consisting of feelings of hopelessness, a devaluation of farming, low rates of marriage, low rates of cooperative work, high rates of emigration, high rates of mental illness, and the loss of both the Irish language and traditional art forms. Ethnographies earlier in the century emphasized an absence of women and their disinterest in marriage when present (Brody 1973; Fox 1978; Scheper-Hughes 1979), ideas heavily criticized in later decades as predictions of the demise of rural Ireland were replaced by changing, rather than ending, cultural traditions. However, taking a closer look at 2022 census numbers in the nine small census areas where I did most of my interviews,[6] while 55 percent of men of marriageable age were single (including men who were single, divorced, and widowed), a comparable 54 percent of women were also single. In terms of age, 25 percent of the total female population was between twenty and forty-five (my own choice as an age range for women who might be likely to have children); men by comparison constituted a very close 26 percent. While these numbers are for the entire area, not just the on-farm population, there appear to be more young women and women overall than many of the men I spoke to could account for.

Where does this leave us? Bachelor farmers appear to be common in Duhallow, and many men told me of their difficulties finding marriage partners. At least half a dozen jokingly asked if I was available. "Nobody wants to be a farmer's wife," one middle-age farmer told me when detailing how difficult it had been to entice his girlfriend to marry him and move to his farm. Moreso, as earlier ethnographers reported and as the stories in this chapter attest, many of the farmers I spent time with were exhausted and felt socially isolated. Yet theories of declining communities are only so helpful—Duhallow families continue to farm and get by, and by their own account, they are not leaving anytime soon. My goal then must be to record these difficult aspects of local livelihood while also accounting for the ongoing creative presence of upland farms, how such presence is part of a multidimensional landscape, and the ideas of labour and family embedded in these reflections. Rather than a death knell, I understand this count of women to raise questions about the gendered dynamics of landscape as well as deeper patterns in the ways families are organized, what is expected of children as they grow older, and the gendered nature of inheritance and work.

Community and cultural vitality are linked to the presence of the family as a farm unit, and local anxiety over a lack of women and associated children is connected to the family farm model and the economic challenges of operating small farms. Yet this is not a simple rural decline story. I often heard from locals that the future holds the likelihood of more forests and fewer farms, that communities are getting smaller, that there are fewer children in schools and on buses and

---

6   2022 Census, CSO, Small Areas Codes: 47043002, 047267006/047267004, 47161002, 47161001, 47098001, 47098002, 47225002, 47225001, 127112002.

fewer people on sports teams. Most also felt that running small farms can only be a part-time occupation. Indeed, the count of women reflects concerns about the gender dynamics of rural depopulation. Women in their twenties *are* more likely to have moved to urban areas, and there are generally more men than women running and working on farms. However, the overall difference in the male-to-female ratio is primarily significant in the forty-five to seventy-nine age group (Central Statistics Office 2016), and many small villages in north County Cork have more women than men. Moreso, as much as men expressed a concern about the lack of women, most also felt there would always be farming in the area (as discussed above, creative inheritance through the extended family is part of that). Likewise, while some might be reluctant for their children to farm because of its inherent difficulties, there is significant social pressure to ensure that the farm continues in the family, a trend seen in other areas of rural Ireland as well (McCarthy et al. 2023). Focusing too much on the "lack of women" narrative risks missing what else is going on. Women are present, do important work, and make culturally informed choices. Rather than focus on numbers themselves, I think the count of women raises questions about the role of women more generally. While the full scope of this realization can only be touched on here (Covid limited my capacity to conduct follow-up research in this specific area), I believe far more research is needed on women's labour—including the extension of farm work to include off-farm positions that cultivate on-farm grants through farm schemes.

At the very least, focusing on women's work can help unravel certain farm dynamics. Farm women's under-recognised participation in the labour market, especially as contributors to the farm itself, has been pointed out for decades (Gasson 1992; O'Hara 1998; Whatmore 1991). In general, women provide significant on-farm labour when they are present, although official accounts of farm work often overlooked this work in favour of that performed by male farmers until the late twentieth century, and they still do on occasion. Such labour dynamics, perhaps never stable, shifted dramatically in the late twentieth century as women increasingly accepted work off-farm. As economists, academics, and governments failed to extend agricultural analysis beyond the boundaries of the farm and the primary farmer, this work again went largely under-recognised. Today, however, women's off-farm labour is often considered a central component of farm viability (Shortall 2014), although simultaneously it is culturally placed as secondary to the family farm, even when women's income exceeds or often subsidizes farm activities.

This "helper" role, putting aside the more prestigious "farmer" position (Price and Conn 2012), is an important source of farm income and family support and can be central to keeping the farm in the family. Researchers have examined the implications of women working off-farm for decision-making power, the restructuring of familial duties, and women's independence (Cush and Macken-Walsh 2018; Cush et al. 2018; Kelly and Shortall 2002; Shortall et al. 2020). Yet such studies consistently find that women's full engagement with farm work, ownership, and decision-making groups is still limited despite their increased economic power.

For instance, in 2001, Shortall completed a study of the gendered dynamics of farm organizations, concluding that women's participation in these generally male-dominated groups and the establishment of women's farm organizations did not significantly produce gendered inclusion. In this study, Shortall lists a series of Irish farm organizations that in 2001 were run by a predominantly male board. While some improvement has been made since then, a quick check shows that most committees of the Irish Farmers Association (IFA), Ireland's largest farm organization, are still predominantly male, except for the Farm Family Committee, which in 2022 was almost entirely women-led. In another example that relates directly to my experiences in Duhallow, Shortall's 2014 work found that to reaffirm their husbands' role as farmers, many women spoke little about their off-farm work and downplayed their success in the workforce. I see this pattern repeated in the way Duhallow women actively deferred to the men when I asked about farm details. "I wouldn't know about that," they told me, directing me to a male colleague or family member, even on subjects of which they clearly had extensive knowledge and experience.

The farm needs to be examined from a household level rather than an individual position (Kelly and Shortall 2002), placing women's labour as a central component of the family farm. This is important in terms of recognizing income streams but also because keeping the farm in the family requires the compliance and effort of the majority of those in the wider kinship circle surrounding a family farm (Price and Conn 2012). I would like to draw attention to the fact that the small family farm takes effort to run beyond just the primary farmer (sometimes through applying pressure on them). In particular, I want to extend the notion of off-farm labour to be more directly entwined with farm survival beyond a woman's income and to include the products of her work.

I am particularly interested in the notion of women's off-farm work as long-term and creative farm support, even for those who no longer reside on the farm. Working from the perspective of human-environment relations, my interest in farm women's labour is less in the fact that women work off-farm and more in that for some, their labour is part of the farm in unexpected ways. This observation extends from my work with IRD Duhallow and the recognition that many of its employees are farm daughters and wives who work to create on-farm opportunities and healthy communities while no longer residing on or being immediately connected to the farm itself.

IRD Duhallow is a Local Development Company (LDC). There are thirty-five LDCs across rural Ireland and fourteen in urban centres. Each is meant to support communities from a ground-up perspective and operates on a partnership model among industry, government, and local volunteers. Such a model works in the social economy sector as a way to fulfill community demands the market cannot fully meet. LDCs operate in this economy as social enterprises, "which refer to initiatives involved in the production of goods or services but with social, rather than purely profit-making or commercial, goals" (O'Hara 2001, 150). Social enterprises emerged out of the 1980s shift to Ireland's social partnership model, which acknowledged that a centralized approach to welfare was ineffective in tackling persistent issues of poverty. A focus on local development through LDCs was meant to be a place-based model to tackle social and economic problems. However, the exact nature of this model has shifted over time, with some arguing that they are becoming increasingly top-down and heavy with restrictive bureaucracy (O'Keeffe 2015) or that their power in funneling EU funding can challenge traditional structures of power (Collinson 2005).

One of the best-known programs delivered by LDCs is LEADER,[7] an EU-funded local development method that targets rural areas. In Ireland, under the LEADER Programme for 2014–2020, €250 million was available to support local initiatives and businesses, often funneled through LDCs. IRD Duhallow is an LDC that draws on LEADER as well as other funds to cover a range of social programming, including child and elder care, meal deliveries, infrastructural improvements to homes, support for local businesses, recreational opportunities, and core skills training. The environment is also one of its focus areas; the organization applies for various grants that can be administered locally. LDCs also support labour scheme opportunities while facilitating small-scale environmental change through the Tús and Rural Social Scheme (RSS) programs (through which I volunteered to pull invasive species from riparian zones, for example).

These community organizations, which, at least in Duhallow, are overwhelmingly staffed by women, fulfill significant social reproduction work. Through such organizations, paid and volunteer community members engage in the work of visiting isolated elderly individuals, delivering meals, organizing the "tidy towns" initiative, managing several local advisory boards, and establishing and manning local childcare centers, among many other things. They also work on finding,

---

7 LEADER is an acronym for the French phrase "Liaison Entre Actions de Développement de l'Économie Rurale," which translates to "links between activities (or actions) for the development of the rural economy."

applying to, and managing a variety of rural funding schemes that support the local economy—especially for small farmers. Farm subsidies for small-scale farms are often a central element of farm viability, and the cultivation of creative ways to work with the various programs that result from subsidies is taken on enthusiastically by organizations like IRD Duhallow, whose employees are often farm daughters, sisters, and wives. Through such initiatives, EU funds through LEADER but also through LIFE (a funding instrument for the environment and climate action)[8] and Farming for Blue Dot Catchment (a Department of Agriculture, Food and the Marine and EU effort for agricultural sustainability), as well as for hen harrier research, are locally channeled and increasingly central to farm viability.

Subsequently, women's off-farm labour provides new opportunities for farms in this increasingly mixed economy, not only through direct income for those living on farms but also through engagement with extra-local opportunities that can generate farm income. Their work creates opportunities for farmers to take advantage of the economic possibilities of schemes; in doing so, they work to shape the environment and people's relationship to it. Certainly, this was part of the intent of the partnership and local development model. Yet, for my purposes, I want to point out that in terms of farm support, this effort occurs less because of the impeachable integrity of the family farm institution and more because of the intensity of social anchors that persist and will continue to find a (sometimes creative) way of continuing. The full economic impact of such labour is beyond the scope of this research, but given that women are far more likely than men to work in administrative roles across rural Ireland and given the economic importance of such schemes, it is an area worthy of further investigation.

CONCLUSION

My intent in this chapter has been to highlight the challenges of the family farm model while signposting some reasons for longevity. The tension between continuity and change is important because in its focus on the family farm and supporting small farmers more generally, the European Union often positions the family farm as a shield against the creep of intensification, biodiversity loss, and further enclosure. This shield, however, was always cracked; the small family farm is and has always been a fraught collection of social and economic practices that isolate some and privilege few. This is not meant to undermine the important work of such farms or their role in local ecology, only that to understand the implications of policy decisions and green initiatives, an honest understanding of complex relations

---

8   LIFE is an acronym for "L'Instrument Financier pour l'Environnement," which translates to "financial tools for the environment."

is necessary. Holding up a romantic notion of the family farm as a symbol provides easy discursive space to further green goals (e.g., instituting high nature value farming, protecting riparian zones, reducing biodiversity loss, protecting important ecosystems) while creating the potential to proliferate impossible expectations for farmers who are left to navigate cultural, familial, and state tensions and overlooking the labour of those off-farm, who do their best to translate such expectations into financial gain. This mix is as likely to lead to blanket afforestation as to low-intensity farming unless the core contradictions between the rural development model and conservation goals are meaningfully addressed.

Itinerant Residents

Directive 79/409/EEC, otherwise known as the Birds Directive, was adopted in 1979, making it the oldest piece of EU legislation on the environment. The directive is considered by many to be one of the EU's cornerstone pieces of legislation. It aims to protect all of the 500 wild bird species currently found in Europe and to better the circumstances for the 32 percent currently not in good status. Recognising that because birds are often migratory, they can only be protected through cooperation across borders, the Birds Directive ideally ensures cross-border compliance. As habitat loss is one of the most serious threats for birds, the directive emphasizes habitat protection and created a Special Protected Areas (SPA) network for this purpose. Since 1994, all SPAs have been incorporated into the Natura 2000 network, a coordinated network of protected areas that includes SPAs and Special Areas of Conservation. Annex 1 lists 194 bird species that are particularly threatened and demands that member states create SPAs for their habitat. This legislation led to the Stack's to Mullaghareirk Mountains, West Limerick Hills, and Mount Eagle SPAs within and beyond Duhallow and meant to protect hen harrier habitat—one of the birds listed in the Birds Directive. This SPA is one of the numerous sites that protect habitats across Ireland and Europe that may be ideal for the hen harrier.

My encounters with the hen harrier took place primarily through a computer, as the IRD environmental team members tracked hen harriers that had been tagged and were kind enough to show me the newest tracking data when I was in their office. Maps would appear on the screen with jagged lines indicating the flight path of a tagged bird that wandered throughout Ireland and beyond. With such data, various research and community groups can get a general sense of where birds winter, how often they return to the same sites, and what their general journeys entail. When a tagged bird fails to move for too long a time, the data also provide an opportunity to investigate its probable death.

The monitoring of mobile species like the hen harrier is complicated. Groups such as the Irish Raptor Study Group, BirdWatch Ireland, the Golden Eagle Trust, and the National Parks and Wildlife Service collectively coordinate a monitoring program. In Ireland, national surveys were undertaken in 2010, 2015, and 2022. For the most part, monitoring involves extensive teams of volunteers physically being in known or suspected sites long enough to be likely to see a hen harrier if present. Each monitor has a "square" assigned to them that they are in charge of. Monitoring typically happens during the breeding season (March through August) when an aerial food pass between males and females makes the birds easier to spot. My hours spent looking skyward, recounted at the beginning of this book, were part of yearly monitoring in the SPAs. However, my most intimate engagement with the hen harrier was unexpected—at least for a social scientist who knew very little about birds.

I returned to Duhallow in the fall of 2019 to share some research results and took the visit as an opportunity to visit farms and get out on the land. At the end of one such day, a local monitoring team invited me to head out to Barna Bog and look for hen harriers. Barna Bog is a four-km cutover bog in Duhallow with no special protections, much of which had been owned by Bord na Móna for more than sixty years. Bord na Móna is a semi-state-owned company that has been developing peatland since 1946, selling peat for home heating and electricity generation, although more recently it has expanded away from peat development. Barna Bog was a Bord na Móna site for decades, but operations had long since halted. Since that time, it had reestablished itself with local groups as a wildlife hub in hopes that it would become protected, wind farms had developed around its edges, and various court cases had tried to halt the expansion. I had visited Barna within my first week of coming to Ireland, searching for signs of owls, falcons, or merlin. I had spent hours carefully walking through the bog, failing miserably in my attempts not to fall in its wetness on numerous occasions and being instructed on how to locate something that would indicate a plucking post—a space where a raptor might pluck and dismember its prey, leaving behind the unwanted pieces for us to find and note.

However, this visit was different. Two teams arrived at the bog in the hour prior to dusk. One team went to the far end of the bog along its lone central vehicle track, and I stayed at the end near the entrance with two others. Binoculars in hand, I prepared for what I had come to know as an uneventful few hours with eyes drawn to the sky. Yet within a half hour, hen harriers began to arrive in the dusky sky. After so many fruitless attempts to see the controversial bird, I could hardly believe my eyes. So many birds were arriving that the teams would radio each other as they appeared, ensuring that each team was not noting the same bird by describing its arrival and direction.

This was a winter roosting site. Outside of the non-breeding season, hen harriers regularly form communal roosts, with multiple birds settling in at one site during the evening. Barna Bog was the local site of choice; birds seemed to care little for human-defined boundaries of ideal habitat type.

In 2001, there were 34 confirmed pairs of hen harriers and 19 young in the Stack's SPA. The population has dropped by a third since 2005, and while the overall population loss has halted, the numbers of fledged young are still declining. Fifty-one fledged from 17 confirmed pairs in 2019, 33 fledged from 13 pairs in 2020, and 19 fledged from 34 pairs in 2021 (Hen Harrier Project 2021). Nationwide, there were 62 confirmed and 7 possible breeding pairs of hen harriers in the SPA network. In 2015, the last national survey published, an estimated 108–157 breeding pairs of hen harriers were recorded nationwide—including those outside of designated sites (Ruddock et al. 2016).

The hen harrier continually drew my attention, not only because of the policy implications of conserving habitat areas for farmers but because their configurations defy attempts at human control, persisting in their mobility and not producing in the "right" way or the "right" place, for example. Hen harrier movements as tracked on computer programs, witnessed by monitoring teams, and occurring in the absence of watchful eyes are happening in the fields and skies of Duhallow. Like invasive weeds and sneaky foxes that travel where they will, such species are part of the landscape, stubbornly uncooperative in the eyes of humans who urge them to behave in ways that better suit delineated land categories.

4

Containing the Unruly

Life as Told Through Incentives, Regulations, and Calendars

As in many rural areas I have worked in, frustration with regulations, government structures, and administrators was typical among Duhallow residents. Farmers told me that working between departments to ensure cross-compliance was difficult and that there was too much "muddy water" to make sense of anything; that common sense was no longer part of farming, as regulations mandate actions that don't always make local sense; that there were contradictions between departments and nobody working in an office had "the authority to change anything"; and that getting through to any office was a "bloody nightmare." While it may be tempting to understand such sentiments as typical complaints—I have encountered similar feelings among farmers in rural Canada, for example—doing so misses an opportunity to take the entangled relations of farm and government procedure seriously. Over time, I came to understand such references as highlighting the ways regulations and bureaucratic structures are materially, discursively, and conceptually woven into ideas of place, work, and belonging. The overlapping domains of farm regulation, species and landscape protection, forestry regulation, protected areas legislation, and rural development plans mean that farms must be explored in conjunction with the bureaucracies that aim to inform their shape. To this end, this chapter provides a sketch of such entangled rules as well as a view from the people whose careers orbit Duhallow farms.

Considering bureaucracy as a component of upland livelihood and environmental relations is necessary because as much as farming is a physical and material practice, it is also intensely political. Central to my conversations with every farmer I spoke to were the various regulations, training requirements, schemes, scheme requirements, *potential* regulatory changes, and interactions with various types of bureaucrats and farm professionals. Decisions such as when farm activities can occur throughout the year, what needs to happen (or not) and where, and what possibilities might subsequently emerge are only partially in farmers' hands. While it might seem contrary to the hard work of any single farmer, as an industry, agriculture is a social more than a solitary enterprise.

This chapter highlights the reality that bureaucracy is part of upland livelihood and is one of the mechanisms through which environmental discourse and change occur. I use the term *bureaucracy* loosely, broadly understood here as a government structure within which services and competencies are defined by law and regulation, hierarchies of authority and decision-making are clearly defined, standardized processes and procedures are the norm, and clear work divisions and high specialization are standard. Unstable, imperfect, and hiding under the guise of rational efficiency, the bureaucratic machine is more a cyborg, less a thing than a set of ongoing and constantly renegotiated relations between different parts incorporated into a loose whole. However, I am less interested in the exact nature of bureaucracy[1] than in how land users engage with bureaucratic tools, such as defined departmental reach and guiding documents, and how government employees—often themselves from farm families—understand and navigate the rules that shape human-environment relations.

At the broadest level, all landscapes are bureaucratic—ecology is political, politics are ecological, and regulation and associated bureaucratic structures are one mechanism through which the political is affirmed and materialized. But what does this acknowledgment mean for people and places, how do we understand it, and how do we talk about bureaucracy without allowing bureaucratic ideals to predetermine the analysis? First we must recognise that many farm professionals, though fleshy cogs in a political machine, are people who navigate and negotiate the shifting terrain of policy, regulation, authority, and paperwork. I understand government actors as an active part of the landscape on at least three fronts. First, materially—office workers live *somewhere*, after all; second, they are an active part in the sense that landscapes are at once material and discursive and that discussion around and documents pertaining to place matter in specific and intimate ways; and third, that the work and agency of government employees should not be overlooked when tracing

---

1 With acknowledgment that the conception of bureaucracy as entwined with the rationalization of society (Weber 1978) and the role of rationalization in attempts to control otherwise difficult environments and manage their complexity (Clegg 1990; Touraine 1988) are certainly relevant for this book's wider argument.

on-the-land decision-making. On this last point, I turn to Tania Murray Li (2007), who reminds us in her examination of how the assemblage of community forestry is held together that it often takes the work of many dispersed individuals just doing their daily jobs to keep up the structures that shape and regulate the environment. Following Colin Hoag's (2011) analysis of the role of anthropology in unraveling bureaucracy, we must recognise the creative and informative role of many bureaucrats. Moreover, as Sune Wiingaard Stoustrup (2022) and others (Singh et al. 2013) have pointed out, "Policy developments should not be understood as 'texts,' travelling from those in power down to local levels unhindered, but as a complex process wherein values, rationalities and ideas are constructed as common sense, and which then acquire particular response locally" (Stoustrup 2022, 2475). The translation work that leads to local response is carried out in part by the voices and decisions of office workers whose job it is to interpret the rules and regulations emanating from policy. In the end, upholding strict divisions between local and national, farmers and bureaucrats, public and state perpetuates a false sense of clear boundaries and political stability.

Through interviews with employees of the National Parks and Wildlife Service, the Department of Agriculture, Food and the Marine, Teagasc, and a farm adviser, this chapter explores bureaucracy and regulation as a central element of farm life and government workers (not all of whom would identify as bureaucrats) as important actors within that life. An assemblage of individuals, organizations, departments, and documents works with and across each other on any number of human-environment interactions relevant to farmers' day-to-day lives. Spanning high to local levels of government, research, industry, and organizations, people engage in place making and nature building by constructing and reinforcing conceptual frameworks that feed down to manifest as material differences that farmers negotiate, cultivate, avoid, and ultimately enact upon the landscape. In the stories below, I aim to draw attention to the increasing bureaucratization of farming, the forms of professionalism that emerge within this increase, and the spaces of agency that government workers and farmers carve out for themselves. Ethnographic research must be attentive to these components of Irish farming, as they define more and more aspects of daily farm life.

A BUREAUCRATIC ROADMAP: A CONVERSATION WITH A NATIONAL PARKS AND WILDLIFE SERVICE EMPLOYEE

The mechanisms that create and oversee a state's rules and structures are confounding in part because they rest on an ideal vision of order and objective truth that never fully matches or is specific enough to fit local realities (Hoag 2011). Messiness stems from this gap between ideal and lived experience and the interactions of multiple actors, influences, and oscillations in state making through time. In Duhallow, this includes things like European Union (EU) priorities, the specific manifestation of neoliberal practices, a centralized government, contentious local governance patterns, and the material practices of daily life. This section introduces bureaucracy in Duhallow by detailing some of the components that influence farmers, outlining the broad political context, and drawing from the experience of a longtime government employee.

I met many people who worked in and around the National Parks and Wildlife Service (NPWS) while I was doing fieldwork. As the NPWS is deeply involved in Special Protected Areas (SPAs) and Special Areas of Conservation (SACs) and implements various EU mandates around environmental protection, many farmers reference the NPWS as an organization they often come in contact with. Declan has worked with the NPWS for some time, and after talking with and interviewing other individuals in the organization, he likewise agreed to meet with me and discuss his work.

"So it's just a little bit messy in terms of government departments," Declan said when I asked him to describe where the NPWS fits in relation to other departments. He added that every time there is an election, the NPWS gets "shunted" around, "not being a huge priority at the moment." Working from a printed schema of government structure laid out on the desk between us and adding notes, arrows, and lines as we spoke, Declan outlined the departments, pieces of legislation, community groups, and industries he worked with most often. As we spoke, he detailed the history and implications of the various interdepartmental shuffling, changes in government leadership, and changes in international priorities. You have to understand, he told me, "that the name over the door changes, but the work and relations of the people doing the work stay somewhat stable regardless of where NPWS rests."

At the time of our meeting, the NPWS was in the Department of Culture, Heritage, and the Gaeltacht. In the recent past, it had been part of the Department of Environment. Declan said the prior arrangement had been a natural fit, as the NPWS aligns with heritage in theory but with the environment in the practical workings of what it needs to achieve. However, the Department of Environment had been split during a prior shuffle and become Housing, Planning, and Local Government, with some sections moving to the Department of Communication and Climate Action. As Declan spoke, I tried to keep track of this system's various inner workings, which are integral to so many, while feeling sympathy for farmers who often needed to navigate the system.

Declan told me that the Department of Housing, Planning, and Local Government was still responsible for things like water quality issues but also included climate action, "which of course, relates to biodiversity generally." Housing and Planning was also responsible for environmental protection because it was the parent department of the Environmental Protection Agency—"with whom NPWS also has close synergies"—as well as Inland Fisheries and the Sustainable Energy Authority, including Petroleum Affairs and Renewable Energy. NPWS also needed to work closely with the Department of Agriculture, Food and the Marine, which is divided into three areas: "It divides into much more than three, but from our point of view, the key players are agriculture, forestry, and fisheries." Beyond these departments are private and semi-private organizations of note, including Coillte (Ireland's semi-state-owned forestry company), Bord na Móna (which deals primarily with peat), and Bord Pleanála (Ireland's national independent planning body, which deals with planning applications and appeals on planning decisions).

Internally, Declan also broke down work divisions in the NPWS, although most individuals work "across stream" to support each other. Outlining the work of the scientific team, licensing, regional operations, division managers, and so on, Declan stated that "on the scientific side, a lot of what we do is reporting to the EU every six years on the status of all of the habitats and species that we have to protect, which is a huge job," adding that the team is also responsible for zoo inspections under the EU Zoos Directive, "which is weird." He noted that "a bit of government is missing there because the Department of Agriculture have the vets, but NPWS have to do zoo inspections to see that they're consistent with the Zoos Directive." He added after a pause, "All of that is not about nature; none of it is about nature."

It is necessary to note that the political structure within which Declan and his colleagues work results from broader political ideology, organization, and relationships between nations and between public and private interests. As an employee, Declan is not working in isolation but is subject to various rules, hierarchies, and mandates that make up his job. Below, I outline some of the context within which both Declan and farmers work before returning to our conversation. For my purposes, what is important to remember is that the push for Irish austerity, profit-driven development, highly centralized government, and privatization occurs in parallel with intense government oversight and EU initiatives meant to support the environment and provide social support to small farmers. Furthermore, as abstract as some of these work divisions are, they often track onto shovel-in-dirt decisions.

Today's mix of government oversight combined with increasing privatization of social services and profit-driven development goals is part of what neoliberalism looks like in Ireland. Neoliberal policies and practices are not a homogeneous force; instead, they manifest within multiple shifting local contexts. Noel Castree's (2010) breakdown of neoliberalism might be helpful here. While emphasizing the importance of local context, Castree broadly breaks down neoliberalism as a worldview that emphasizes money-mediated markets and individual liberty, policy discourse (including privatization, marketization, deregulation), and policy measures (including limiting government borrowing, removing obstacles to competition, building human capital, and so on). To understand Ireland's unique manifestation of neoliberalism, Rob Kitchin and colleagues (2012) suggest the inclusion of numerous local influences such as Ireland's colonial history and subsequent intense relationship with ownership and property, localism, conservatism (resulting in less of an ideological divide between political parties than is seen in some nations), and a transition to an open economy after decades of inward-focused development and status as one of Europe's poorest nations.

Declan's work also takes place in the context of Ireland's astounding economic rise in the second half of the twentieth century and its equally impressive fall post-2007, which led to Ireland being one of only three EU nations that required an International Monetary Fund (IMF) bailout. All of this manifests politically as a combination of the increasing privatization, public-private partnerships, low corporate taxation, and light regulation that are hallmarks of twenty-first-century neoliberalism but mixed with European socialism—including welfare safety nets, EU regulations, and high indirect taxation.

Of particular importance is the increasing interconnectivity with the European Community that has been developing over recent decades. The term *Europeanization* refers to the various processes involved in the fundamental reorganization of the way politics are structured by EU member states and the shifting relationships that stem from it. Europeanization studies pay particular attention to the domestic-level impacts of EU structures and how European political discourses, strategies, institutions, and policies have led to political change (Graziano and Vink 2013). Europeanization is also entwined with ideas of identity, belonging, and culture and the extent to which Ireland's interconnectivity with the mainland produces changes therein. While some have argued that this influence is perhaps overestimated at times (Girvin 2010), the relationship demands an ongoing examination of the degree to which processes of integration at the macro-levels of society, politics, economics, and culture in Europe trace onto specific locales (McCall and Wilson 2010).

A specific example of Europeanization is the fact that farming in Ireland is heavily shaped by EU priorities as expressed through the Common Agricultural Policy (CAP) and how the CAP has shaped Irish agricultural development. The CAP is the agricultural policy of the European Union, which has undergone various iterations since its introduction in 1962. The iteration of the CAP during fieldwork covered the period 2014–2020. The next reform began in 2023 and is scheduled to extend through 2027, with an interim agreement reached to bridge the two programs. With the CAP, in the broadest sense, funding is divided among rural development, income support, and market measures. The CAP is split into two pillars; farmers, planners, community workers, and most others in Duhallow were aware of and often referenced these pillars and their various programs.

The first pillar of the CAP is direct payments to farmers, which comprised seven multipurpose payments at the time of fieldwork, each with specific objectives. These include a basic payment per hectare (Single Farm Payment), a greening component that offsets the cost of providing environmental public goods, a young farmers' payment, a redistributive payment whereby farmers may be granted additional support, additional support for areas of natural constraint, coupled support for production under particular circumstances, and an optional simplified payment plan. Some of these are compulsory for member states (such as the basic payment scheme), while others are voluntary. Cross-compliance between schemes is mandatory, as is following EU rules on public health, animal health, the environment, and animal welfare. On the broader level, the meta-narrative is intended to support small and medium farmers by recognizing their economic, social, and environmental importance.

The second pillar of the CAP is the EU's rural development policy designed to support rural areas of the Irish Union; it is more flexible than pillar 1. The key priorities include fostering agricultural competitiveness, ensuring sustainable management of natural resources and climate action, and creating balanced territorial development. These include such things as a focus on knowledge transfer through training and information campaigns; advisory services; investments in farm infrastructure; development of farms; village revitalization; investment in the development of forests; payments to the Natura 2000 and Water Framework Directive; payments for forest, environmental, and climate services and forest conservation; and support for working groups of the European Innovation Partnership for Agricultural Productivity and Sustainability (EIP). Of particular importance for Duhallow has been the LEADER Programme. LEADER has evolved in tandem with the "European model of agriculture," which emphasizes the multifunctional nature of the countryside and advocates incentivizing and enabling farmers to protect and promote the rural landscape, biodiversity, and countryside access (Feehan and O'Connor 2009). LEADER and EIP are central funding sources for various Duhallow development projects in which many farmers are engaged and to which the NPWS often has connections.

Back in Declan's office, we moved away from discussing various departments and individuals he worked with and started to review key pieces of legislation that shape his mandate. On the edge of the map of departments now crisscrossed with lines and names, he began to write out acronyms for the various programs, documents, and pieces of legislation that most influenced his work. "I should do this more often," he said with a laugh as he started going through his list.

At the time of our conversation, the Heritage Bill had lengthened the time when farmers could burn the hills (under certain conditions) by a month and allowed cutting hedges for a month longer and a month earlier than before. News of this potential change had been mentioned by a few farmers, but they were unclear on the details and what "certain conditions" meant. Declan added that this change was particularly controversial "with the NGOs [non-governmental organizations]" because certain bird species that nest in hedges could be negatively affected. Moving down the list, he mentioned that the NPWS relies heavily on schemes managed through the Department of Agriculture, Food and the Marine. For instance, the hen harrier scheme is contracted out to a private firm with oversight from the Department of Agriculture, Food and the Marine EIP (pillar 2). The scheme directly impacts the SPAs, which are under the NPWS mandate and from which they often field queries from farmers. Moving on, Declan mentioned the EMFF (the EU Maritime and Fisheries Fund) that included deep-sea corals, which fell within the NPWS mandate—an inclusion he felt was bizarre. Likewise, invasive species legislation was important for Declan's work, as was the Birds Directive, which included around 190 species of birds (this directive eventually led to the establishment of SPAs in Ireland). The NPWS is likewise responsible for international conventions, such as the Nagoya Protocol (which Declan describes as creating access and benefit sharing), CITES (the Convention on International Trade in Endangered Species), climate change legislation, and the Prioritised Action Framework for Natura 2000 (PAF), which relates to the Natura 2000 sites in which SPAs are found. Declan also spoke of site-specific conservation objectives (SSCO) for each of the SACs and SPAs, where his department was trying to move from generic descriptors to something more specific for each site, "so there's a heck of a lot of work in that and we're kind of two-thirds of the way through."

The list continued. In response to a question about how much progress he felt was being made, Declan said "making progress can be tricky." He pointed to the Hen Harrier Threat Response Plan as an example. The plan has been stalled for over a decade, partly because the NPWS had problems getting agreements across sectors in a reasonable time frame. The delay in this plan had been mentioned by farmers, foresters, and community workers—all keen to see it completed in a way that would be favourable to their needs. Declan did not anticipate its completion anytime soon.

Consultations and knowledge sharing are mandatory components of many EU and national programs and, therefore, part of Declan's work. However, as both EU and Irish programs work within particular political and funding cycles, the space for meaningful consultation is often compressed. This means that if the time between an announced funding cycle and the application deadline is too short, applicants may be unable to consult as much as they would like. Likewise, information can be lacking for those participating in the consultations and information sessions if only partial information about upcoming programs is available. Even the people involved or those who might be overseeing a program are not always made clear when information needs to be shared with the communities. Lack of information during meetings was a common complaint of many farmers when they spoke of the establishment of the SPAs and associated schemes. Locals complained that detailed and precise information was lacking; since schemes often work with time lines set by the CAP—which can be heavily reworked between iterations—it was not easy to get a clear picture of what impacts new programs might have.

Declan agreed that farmers were right to be frustrated when I brought up this issue, adding with a smile, "consultations with the community can be a bit savage. There's a blood sports element to that, you know. Being on the other side, it's entertaining. It's genuinely entertaining to see some poor official up on the stage with his good jacket on and his briefcase with slides, you know. But then afterward, people talk to you and you can have very civil conversations after a very hostile meeting very often." He recalled an occasion when he was asked to attend one such event early in his career, having drawn the short straw. He said locals were justifiable angry, as he had been given only slightly more information than the public had—"some things [are] coming down the line, but we don't know exactly what or when"— although he was able to have a civil discussion afterward over a cup of tea.

Speaking more directly about public confusion, Declan attributed it to numerous causes. Information sharing often comes in the mail in the infamous packet of information that is so dense and difficult to understand that farmers use it to start their fires in the evening. However, he also felt there might be some deliberate sharing of misinformation among community members, more for the drama and to express generalized frustration. He added that sharing information properly would require a level of resourcing that the NPWS is simply unable to provide, saying that ideally, you would go from home to home and have these conversations numerous times, although even then it would take a long time for community members to trust you. Declan emphasized that this was one good side of LIFE projects (such as the one I was involved in), as there was room for this depth of sharing. This reflection resonated with me as I recalled Maeve's and my home visits, where farmers would ply Maeve with all sorts of questions about hedge cutting dates and scheme regulations that she did her best to answer but otherwise tried to pass on later to someone with more knowledge.

In addition to a feeling of empathy toward those employees and community members who have to navigate this system, a few things stood out to me in our conversation. Ireland's bureaucratic context includes multiple layers of influence that range from international agreements and legislation to political arrangements within departments and working relations between individuals in departments. Those who work in this system are fully aware of the shortcomings and messiness of these structures and the pressure that shifting time frames and limited budgets place on their capacity to do their jobs well. Government employees navigate this landscape as farmers navigate theirs (not forgetting that many government workers have a family farm), each frustrated by the unwieldiness of such a system and varyingly committed to making the best of it. The combination of budget cuts and privatization over the last decade and a half, and the depth of intervention and oversight that result from EU funding and Ireland's intensely centralized government model, produce a particular landscape and particular relationships to the ecosystems within which people live. Declan is one actor among many in this system.

OCCUPYING THE GAP: CONVERSATIONS WITH A FARM ADVISER

Due to the intricacies and overlaps of landscape management on almost every level, regulation and its associated bureaucratic structure are part of farming in a tangible way. Many regulations originate in government departments whose jurisdiction overlaps with the farm, including through forestry, agriculture, parks, planning, and so on. However, because of the integrated nature of EU farming, farm incomes today are also flexibly tied to numerous and shifting funding schemes. Schemes mean that in addition to meeting land-use standards required for compliance as an EU member, farmers are subject to substantial additional regulation tied to agricultural programs, resulting in a particularly complex regulatory landscape. The shifting tangle of rules and obligations around farming is tricky for many farmers to navigate successfully, particularly those without agricultural degrees. While some rules remain relatively stable, others are likely to change between program iterations or with changes in government. Likewise, rules related to activities such as burning, cutting, spraying, and planting may alter as the state gathers and reviews new data. For these reasons and for some mandatory scheme requirements, farmers often need to hire a farm adviser or planner. One middle-age farmer explained the need like this: "You have to have an adviser—you see with me I have to because I'm not into internet and I have no—I wouldn't be well-read. A lot of farmers wouldn't be well read in—some people don't just [know]."

Advisers (who provide holistic farm advice) or planners (who supply case- or scheme-specific advice, sometimes also referred to as advisers) might also be mandatory for some schemes. For example, the farmer mentioned above hired a planner to score his fields so he could apply to the new hen harrier scheme (mentioned by Declan as the scheme contracted out to a private firm but overseen through the

Department of Agriculture, Food and the Marine). He paid a woman €550 to walk through his fields and evaluate their appropriateness. If accepted into the scheme, farmers can make more money by increasing the quality of their fields over time, so scoring is necessary many times during the program's lifetime. The farmer voluntarily added an extra €50 to help cover transportation costs. The cost of paying planners or advisers and paying fees for licensing, training, or applications is part of running a farm. This section reviews my conversations with Rian, a local farm adviser whose job is to help farmers with planning and decision-making.

However, before exploring Rian's experiences, I want to place his work and that of other farm professionals in a broader context. The regulatory complexity of farming is part of a trend wherein knowledge-based authority or the power to specify how food is produced has been diminished by the professionalization of agriculture in Ireland over the last century (Moser and Varley 2012). Indeed, Peter Moser and Tony Varley have argued elsewhere (2013) that this shift has resulted in the progressive subordination of farmers as a group to the will of those in urban centres. Just as important, however, farmers are often active agents in this process—a point John Gray (2007), in his extensive work with Scottish hill sheep farmers, takes special care to make: farmers are not simply subsumed in broader EU processes but can carve out their own niche of action and negotiation within them. Indeed, I argue in this chapter that farmers' ingenuity, or perhaps unruliness, is such that they may be farming grant programs as much as cattle. In any case, there is an increasing gap between farmers' own expertise and farm decisions, as seen in the quote above. This farmer is not "on the internet," is not "well-read," and therefore does not "know." Keep in mind that this man is running the farm he was raised on and has been the primary farmer for nearly fifty years. To contextualize this shift and the reach of regulation and professionalization in farming, I want to highlight a few examples of how regulation and farm practice meet in sometimes unexpected ways.

As Declan pointed out, actions such as when to cut hedges need to align with shifting policy. Hedges proliferate quickly in Ireland, and their extent can cut into the total farmland calculated in Single Farm Payments. I once spent a good part of a day with one elderly farmer whose total farmland calculated for payments had been reduced because his hedges had overgrown on all sides of his fields. When to spray slurry is another such activity that needs to occur with careful consideration of the rules. Slurry, the liquid manure created through dairy farming, is stored in tanks throughout the winter when the ground is cold or wet. Once fields are dry enough, farmers take tanks pulled behind tractors and spray the liquid onto fields as fertilizer—an activity with a particular olfactory announcement. Spray when the ground is too wet or hard and the manure will run off into nearby streams, causing environmental damage. However, in the meantime, farmers may still have full tanks and cattle housed in barns, with the ground too wet for them to grass-feed. Spraying outside of the season comes with hefty fines if caught and is a point of contention with farmers who feel they can judge the suitability of their land better than a bureaucrat "in some city." Set dates in regulation for spraying slurry or cutting hedges are part of what farmers refer to as "farming by calendar." These are blanket dates set by state institutions as to when activities can occur on a farm. From the farmer's perspective, such dates often fail to consider regional landscape, soil, and weather variations. In such ways, farmers' power and decision-making are reduced in favour of expert knowledge produced off-farm.

In the above examples, regulations determine what farming activities can occur, as well as where and when—not only because policy sets rules but because, as I will explore below, individual actors within the system variably uphold or prioritize some rules over others. However, policy and regulation are also heavily involved in shaping the perception of what good farming looks like among farmers. For example, the Agricultural Certificate, known as the "green cert," is a series of land-based courses that, when completed, meets the requirements of a qualified farmer for purposes of scheme revenue and Department of Agriculture, Food and the Marine programs. Advantages of the green cert include qualifying for such things as young farmer support schemes, basic payments, and reduced land transfer fees when the inheritor is thirty-five or under. Subsequently, many experienced farmers will need to complete their green cert at some point. Courses can cost upward of €3,000, although prices vary between providers and over time. Many of the small farmers I spoke to talked about the financial burden of inheriting a marginal farm, where the cost of the green cert, combined with the inheritance tax, makes the farm less viable for those who might inherit. In any case, as the state has a hand in the content of green cert courses as well as ongoing targeted training offered through Teagasc (Ireland's semi-state-owned agricultural and research company), such official mechanisms and farm pathways are an efficient means of shaping farm practices and priorities and are an example of intensified state involvement in a time of deregulation.

Advisers and planners sit somewhere between civil servants and private businesspeople. They should have expertise in all regulatory components of farming and an in-depth awareness of on-the-ground farm practices. Ideally, they also have personal contacts in government departments whom they can contact for clarification of questions or who might let them know when change is expected. Some advisers work directly for state or semi-state bodies, but many operate on a private business model. They may act at different times as middlemen for scheme procurement, may be responsible for assessing farm or farmland performance, and may also be expected to build a meaningful participatory relationship with farmers. Marie Mahon and colleagues (2010, 109) note that "the move towards a multifunctional model of agriculture and new consumption roles for the countryside means that advisory bodies are also tasked with becoming increasingly innovative in the way they conceptualise and respond to a changing agricultural landscape, to deliver advice and services that facilitate farm families to adapt and remain economically viable in an increasingly globalised and unprotected agricultural sector." The authors go on to argue that as expectations of what advisers are capable of increase, a variety of factors—including adviser positionality, contradictions between goals of growth and participatory consultation, client expectations, and complex bureaucratic systems—can hinder their work. I argue throughout this book that farmers, as those actually engaging with the land, are required to navigate and negotiate contradictions within the bureaucratic system surrounding agriculture. However, planners and advisers are perhaps next in line for fully experiencing the effects of a landscape oversaturated with others' expectations.

I now turn to my conversation with Rian, who was a farm adviser and a farmer, having grown up on and eventually inheriting his family farm (with some SPA lands). While he initially intended to take over his family farm full-time, Rian quickly realized that the nature of his farm's black and heavy ground, increasingly unpredictable weather, and the intensive labor requirement of expanding dairy farms meant his small farm could not compete as a standalone enterprise. Instead, he completed the training to become an adviser, moved his farm stock from dairy to suckler (beef), and now has around fifty cows at home while working full-time.

Meeting in his office during regular business hours, I explained to Rian the broad picture of what I was doing in Ireland and how my work with farmers increasingly included land policy. He laughed and said his primary job "is to make sure that their [farmers'] paperwork—which they're allergic to—is correct." We spent the next few hours chatting, often circling back to questions of how farmers get their information, confusion around schemes, the best (or most profitable) choices for farmers, and the potential spaces of contradiction between departments and regulations. Rian did not romanticize farmers as faultless but likewise took pains to point out the difficulty of upland farming. He described farming and farm planning from his point of view.

Some advisers work for the state more directly, such as those with Teagasc, or more distantly through private firms. Both, at times, are charged with scoring fields (evaluating according to a metric) and ensuring that appropriate rules are followed. Rian, for instance, took training in the new hen harrier scheme to score SPA fields in the program. Although seldom enacted, advisers also have the potential duty to report gross negligence. While they are likely to object to the term, I believe it is useful to understand planners and advisers as what Colin Hoag (2011) calls street-level bureaucrats. Hoag suggests that the most creative room for collaboration and creation within the system is at this level of bureaucracy. Street-level bureaucrats tend to have limited power, if any, but they represent the system to the general public and feed important information upward. More so, they are often antagonistic toward higher demands, and they sympathize with the population they are meant to influence. Hoag suggests that researchers, academics, and community groups pay particular attention to this level of bureaucrat, advocating, as I have here, that bureaucracy is embedded into people's daily lives and therefore should not be ignored or set aside as too governmental for place-based research.

Rian began by breaking down the scheme system as it stood at the time of our meeting, with revenues from Europe in the form of Single Farm Payments, paid schemes like GLAS (Green, Low-Carbon, Agri-Environment Scheme), and disadvantaged payments. Rian believes many farmers are "killing themselves" to make money. They think "the cattle have to make money for themselves. But they don't understand that for many of them, €15,000 or €20,000 will come in the post without having animals anyway." Rian is referencing a shift that occurred when the CAP payments were decoupled from production measures, partly because of European overproduction problems. With decoupling came the potential for smaller farmers to relax their farm efforts and focus less on increasing production by working more diligently within the system and less on the land, what some might see as a farming scheme (as opposed to farming the land or farming cattle).

When asked to describe his work further, Rian added: "We submit their [farmers'] basic payment, we declare what land they're farming for the year, we ensure that they have enough stock, that they qualify for the disadvantaged [scheme], we make them aware of every possible scheme that's there, try and get them into it, and try and get as much [money] coming in." He does this, he says, while hoping that the farmers eventually realize that the effort they put in to keep their land stocked as much as possible is not necessary.

With that said, Rian did express some hesitation with this approach. Specifically, he had concerns over how long it could sustain fields "in our side of the country"—where people need to top the land with manure and graze it to keep the desired flora abundant, too little grazing can be as much of a problem as too much: "Like, are you doing something probably that would have a longer-term effect? I'm not sure. But as you sit in front of me this minute, that's how I can get the most for the farmer at the end of the day." Another hesitation Rian shares are the fees attached to various payments. Speaking of scoring fields for the hen harrier programme, he stated "it's a pity that they have to pay the planner again, you know, that they pay us for the basic payment, they pay us for their GLAS and the hen harrier scheme," noting a prior scheme in 2009 that had higher than average uptake—probably because it had no associated fee.

Bureaucracy also comes in the form of boundaries and the rules that make boundaries manifest by shaping human action. Boundaries follow NPWS staff as they work in different regions and Coillte staff as they work with forest districts in Ireland. In my explorations with Maeve and invasive species, I understood how crossing county lines may mean that different services or offices are in charge of particular aspects of the human-environment relationship. We needed to work with two counties to ensure that signage was correctly posted and that proper rules were followed. For farmers, the clearest examples of boundaries raised were what areas fell within the SPA. As the conservation zone is a patchwork of areas, some fields may fall within the SPA while fields that border the same farm may not. Not all farmers were aware of where the divisions fell on their land or even if they did, but the designation did impact what schemes they could access and the activities that could take place on some fields.[2] Numerous actors, pieces of legislation, and requirements orbit something like SPA designation. Farmers and those working in the government need to incorporate those new features into their existing relationships and landscapes while aiming for integration. As an adviser, a trained planner in the new hen harrier scheme, and a farmer with some SPA fields, Rian had plenty to say about this feature of the Duhallow uplands.

He told me that while some farmers might be deliberately playing up confusion around the SPA, many others are genuinely in a tough spot. For example, he explained that farmers need to keep the ground in good agricultural use to meet the terms of the Single Farm Payment—for instance, through grazing (having animals feed in the fields), topping (applying slurry as fertilizer to encourage growth), or cutting. This work is necessary to keep rushes and bushes from taking over fields: "So what happens then is, like, if you have a patch of scrub, or if you have areas that are getting overgrown, you're technically supposed to keep that in such a way that it's eligible ground, so scrub and bushes is [sic] not eligible." However, contrary to that is SPA land on which scrub, bushes, and "poor" land are beneficial to wildlife, are encouraged, and cannot be removed when present. Such changes would constitute "improving fields," which farmers cannot do on SPA land. As a result, side-by-side fields of similar appearance and on the same farm may have a preference for or an obligation to get rid of scrub or rushes.

---

2 The establishment of the SPA itself is detailed in Sharon Bryan's (2012) account of establishing the Natura 2000 network in Ireland. Bryan outlines the bureaucratic work involved in delineating protection boundaries for migratory species such as the hen harrier. They argue that this network is an example of nature-society line drawing, pointing to the bureaucratic labor involved in boundary maintenance—something encountered by farmers as they try to navigate the what, when, and where of not only their farm as a whole but individual fields as well.

Adding to this confusion are the specific contexts of each farm. Speaking of the way areas became designated, Rian admitted, for instance, that most farmers have "a few good fields," and so it's possible that some farmers had a bad year "when the photos were taken" and had their good fields designated when they should not have been ("poor" fields are those that are better for the hen harrier). This would mean that their good grazing fields may have registered as scrub in a particularly dry year but that removing that scrub would be interpreted as "improving" the land.

Many farmers also confuse the rules associated with the SPA (which are few) with those associated with the payment schemes that may be drawn from but not necessarily attached to SPA land. For example, in the GLAS scheme, rushes need to be cut in a way that leaves diverse habitats. This rule results in a visibly striped pattern on many upland fields as farmers cut rushes back in strips. Farmers sometimes confuse this scheme regulation with an SPA regulation, which has no limits on treating rushes, only that they cannot "improve" fields (usually meaning draining, tilling, planting, and closing gaps).[3]

According to Rian, the most common complaint farmers had about bureaucracy was confusion about and contradictions between schemes—a point also made by Declan at the NPWS. Precisely what is involved in each scheme and how the different schemes interact are points of ongoing frustration for almost every farmer I spoke with. They often understood the various shifting requirements as nonsensical while also admitting that they had not thoroughly read the rules behind the schemes. "Only a lawyer could read that stuff," a farmer told me after I asked about the regulations. Again, farm advisers often help farmers with this process, but it is not free knowledge. Furthermore, there needs to be a good fit between adviser and farmer in terms of working style and priorities when advising on scheme regulations. Small farmers often suggested that advisers who work through Teagasc are more aggressively productivist than independent advisers, and they worried about the pressure to intensify when they intuitively felt the land could not sustain doing so. Such advice is very different from that given by advisers such as Rian.

Like Declan, Rian could understand and sympathize with broader farmer confusion. Rian pointed to the fact that farmers talk among themselves and spread inaccurate information: "You see, like, as I say, a lot of farmers are allergic to paperwork." He told me that a lot of the information they pick up is what they learn from someone at the shop or the pub, "or some fellow told them here or there, and, like, they don't—every time they join a scheme they get a terms and conditions for every scheme, that thing is used to start the fire that evening, it's burnt, like, I mean, it's just not even opened."

---

3   For instance, with SPA land, farmers can open up existing drains (clear out ditches) but not add new drains.

From Rian's perspective, confusion arises through misinformation spread among the farmers more than from anything else. However, he admitted that one tricky piece involves the various versions of schemes. For example, he pointed to dates as "a thing that constantly change[s]" and mentioned GLAS, which is part of the rural development program (pillar two) and offers upward of €5,000 (€7,000 in some cases) for environmental action. Rian explained that "with GLAS 1 there was no date for topping [cutting] rushes, you could top them. And then it came to GLAS 3 and you can't go near them until July 1. So, like, you have a farmer then who sees the neighbour who is in GLAS 1 and he's cutting away, and then he rings me—or maybe doesn't ring, which would be way worse—and cuts his rushes." So not only do the rules of schemes shift, but neighbouring farms can be under different versions of the same scheme.

For Rian, the confusion is understandable but also preventable. He added that "they [farmers] do not fully understand the schemes themselves"—tending to burn the details of the schemes the day their packet of information arrives in the mail. He did note that the advisers have courses they offer farmers to try to keep them up to date but added that "it's a pain in the neck for them to attend. It's torture, right." Rian stated that the information gets scrambled, and people take their own version of it: "This is the reason why advisers are there, so farmers can call and ask."

I do not believe Rian would see himself as a bureaucrat, and as an independent adviser and small farmer, he is probably correct in thinking of himself as less governmental. However, when Rian steps into the planner role and scores fields or works to initiate a new program or scheme, shares state legislation and best practices, or reports back to government departments on what he sees, Rian is a state representative working within a heavily managed, hierarchical system. While hiring an adviser is technically optional, it is, in reality, mandatory if farmers want to access many of the critical resources necessary to successfully farm in Ireland. As such, advisers are key actors in disseminating state knowledge and enacting state goals. The farm advisory system is one way the state can shape farming practices and attitudes. The work of advisers is part of the knowledge production and sharing that is central to upland farming. While this knowledge primarily relates to farm practice, it can sometimes include how best to farm the state—that is, how to work with policies in the most beneficial way for the least effort. Precisely what knowledge and skills are shared and what outcomes result depends on the adviser, the farmer, and the unique features produced by that joining.

KNOWLEDGE, NATURE, AND PRACTICE: CONVERSATIONS WITH AGRICULTURE AND FORESTRY EMPLOYEES

While employees' personal experiences, histories, and viewpoints matter in bureaucratic relationships, their actions still reflect and enact a broader ideology as they work within a system over which they have little direct control. For this reason, bureaucracy can help identify the ideological structures that shape the human-environment relationship and the tension points that emerge between ideal and real practices. To better understand how state ideas of knowledge and nature weave their way into material practice, this section draws on interviews with two land professionals, one in the Department of Agriculture, Food and the Marine's forestry section and one who works for Teagasc. In bringing these two conversations together, I explore objective knowledge and advice, the nature-culture dualism, and the objectification and alienation of nature as fields and farmers are transformed into a resource. These themes are central to understanding how such workers construct farmers as both a barrier and a resource, shaping the way many in government interact with farmers and interpret their actions.

Organizing and conceptually structuring the non-human world is part of the legibility process central to state making. James C. Scott's (1998) detailed account of the development of the forest industry stands as an excellent example of how states account for, organize, and regiment the natural world in such a way that the abstract idea of a resource replaces the specifics of any site or feature of the natural world: one that is tidier, delineated, and subsequently more straightforward to manage. While most nations, including Ireland, have, at least in principle, abandoned the tendency to radically simplify resource management (for example, sustainable forest management principles and high nature value farming ideally work with the entire ecosystem approach), the human-nature division that is central to this radical simplification is still a central part of the way policy and official discourse treat the idea of the environment. How the non-human world is organized through government departments is an excellent example of this.

For example, Keefe works in the Department of Agriculture, Food and the Marine in the forestry section. He has filled many roles in his government career, including acting as a forest inspector. His department is responsible for licensing, including almost every aspect of forest management, from planning to harvest. I met with Keefe in his office in the city. When I asked how his department fits into the broader scheme of the government, like Declan at the NPWS, he provided a genealogy of where forestry has historically been located. At one time, forestry stood on its own as the Forest Service; later, it was in the Department of Natural Resources and, after that, in the Department of Communication and Natural

Resources. When located in the latter, the budget was a large part of that of the overall department, which in Keefe's view made forestry an easy target for fiscal cuts. However, at the time of our interview, forestry was in the Department of Agriculture, Food and the Marine and constituted a small portion of a much larger budget, leaving its workers feeling more secure.

I asked if communication was good within his department, and the response was an immediate and firm "no." Keefe added that communication within the Department of Agriculture, Food and the Marine and between the various departments he worked with was challenging. For example, he pointed to collaboration with the NPWS, noting the lack of staff due to budget cuts: "I suppose the lack of personnel in Parks and Wildlife would be a ... constraint because when we send anything to them for consultation—and we consult with them, we're not just barging away—because they haven't got the personnel they usually send back an answer saying 'This isn't a[n] SPA.' That's it. And I go 'Oh, you don't want to do that. That's not why we sent it to you.'"

When asked about inquiries from farmers, he stated that farmers would be far better off asking Teagasc or their own farm advisers questions rather than try to navigate the departments in question. This confirmed what farmers had already told me as they detailed their experiences of being shuffled from department to department when asking a question.

The frustrating overlap and breakdowns between departments, also mentioned by Declan and Rian, are far more than bureaucratic inefficiency; they result from attempts to organize a landscape into neat categories that do not fit reality. The fact that advising, conservation, national parks, forestry, agriculture, and wildlife, not to mention invasive species, inland fisheries, and others, are scattered between departments is a symptom of an ongoing effort to rationalize an otherwise complex, interrelated world. Water, soil, fish, trees, plants, animals, and people interact in complex and changing ways that cannot be easily represented in a simplified bureaucratic structure. Given this, it is not surprising that every government employee I spoke with emphasized how difficult working between departments was, how challenging working within various rules and shifting schemes made their daily work, and how difficult it would be for a farmer to navigate departments. This departmental turmoil is not the source of tension but a symptom of a broader system that prioritizes efficiency and simplification over complex and entangled relations.

Yet the simplifications that shape bureaucratic structures *are* enticing. Anna Tsing (2015) writes eloquently about the allure of abstraction, its elegance, and the enticement of a simplified concept, object, or idea. Reducing complexity to its constituent parts has a long tradition in both science and government and is part of a rationalist tradition that makes things easier to keep track of from a large-scale perspective. My point here is not so much to address the political attempts at ordering nature, which have been well documented and explored by others, but the fact that these attempts have tangible consequences; they are lived. For example, cross-compliance is a technocratic solution to government-created problems that shifts the onus of navigating the misalignment between what is desired and what "is" to those working closest to the object of interest—that is, farmers and ground-level bureaucrats who need to make sure they align across various priorities. Very often, they cannot do so and instead shuffle meetings, priorities, schemes, and the like and do their best.

Another example of the tensions between what is possible and what is expected is found in the specific jobs each worker in the system is tasked to complete. For example, an often-mentioned point of tension with government employees (as well as farmers) was the challenge of navigating demands for productivity with environmental priorities. Part of Keefe's job is to support the increase of forest cover throughout the island, discussed in more detail in chapter 5. Keefe describes this goal as a push and pull among different government priorities and sees the SPA as a symptom of that tension. Summing up the designation process while we looked over a map of the region on his computer screen, Keefe reminded me that forestry was assumed to be beneficial for the hen harrier at the time of designation: "So they [SPA planners] really went around, they were looking for the grassy rush fields and forestry and then stitched it all together. You'll see, like, some of these are just grassy fields [pointing to the scattered squares not in the SPA], and that's all forestry [pointing to scattered blocks within the SPA]. So in general, they went for the grass rush, bog, and the forests." To me, the map looked like a patchwork quilt with distinct squares representing different ecosystem types field by field. Keefe and the map portray these landscape types as separate from each other, even though Keefe knows the map is often inaccurate at the field level.

For Keefe, much of the tension lies in EU versus national priorities. He stated that the first conservation priorities were "from the bloody EU," which cares less about economics and is instead more environmentally focused: "So to get it [new forestry] past the EU you'd have to have all these environmental controls ... 100 percent state-funded, but you still have to get approved from the EU, and you wouldn't get it past without these controls." While his job is to see forestry expand, various environmentalist groups in addition to the EU are also prioritizing environmental outcomes, "which is grand; you'd expect them to do that." But then, he adds, the IFA (Irish Farmers Association) and the industry push the other way, toward economic development: "And then you're trying to balance all of these ... while the government want[s] to form an industry; you have to listen to all that crap ... and then you have all the grants for people who do want to just focus on the environmental, you know, for planting broadleaves, you know." Keefe has limited confidence in the state's ability to expand forest cover substantially and attributes this to the various overlapping but incommensurable demands on the landscape.

The fact that the economy and the environment are intimately connected is well-known, but they are nevertheless framed in policy and planning as distinct features of society, an approach that tends to discursively transform people, places, and things into resources. Instead of being fully addressed in a broader paradigmatic shift in governance and planning, this disjuncture is left for those like Keefe and Rian to navigate. A lack of communication or good working conditions between departments is often found at these particular intersections, reflecting incongruity between deeper ideological ideas of ordered nature and the practicality of its enactment. This juncture also provides a pressure release valve, where the inability to produce sought-after outcomes can be placed at the feet of "inefficient bureaucracy," thus avoiding a deeper reassessment of what is possible in the first place.

The reality that the landscape cannot be all things at once is apparent in the ways departments knowingly navigate toward their goals while being fully cognisant that many of the various barriers in their way to success are other government priorities. This is particularly clear when discussing competition for resources across departments; Keefe labels land and farmers' attention as scarce resources for which different government departments compete.

For example, Keefe sees forestry as squeezed into a tight spot. He says dairy farmers are pushing into the poor land as they try to expand their already intensive farms: "You have the environmentalists coming down there and saying 'some of that's really important,'" adding that forestry is squeezed from both sides and gets pushed into the really bad land. Small farmers with poor land then become the focus, and Keefe acknowledges that they need to be incentivized to see the forestry option as enticing, especially as agricultural subsidies compete for their attention. He would like to see more trees on the landscape, not just as part of his job but also as part of what he understands as "good" land. For Keefe, "The only reason [small farmers] exist is because they get more grants from the EU," and they are very good at knowing what is available to them and how to get the most out of the system. Note how farmers, like the physical environment, are isolated and turned into resources through this perspective.

Others likewise mentioned this sense of competition for scarce resources, including Matt, who works for Teagasc. At the time of our meeting, Matt was helping farmers make decisions around forestry. He positioned his job as one meant to provide an objective opinion:

> I give them [farmers] independent and objective advice on what they're doing or what they propose to do. So, for example, if they're thinking about planting [trees],

> I will go through whether the ground is suitable for planting, whether it's the best use of the land, what are the impacts on other farming enterprises... what can you expect out of this in terms of what will happen to the land, what the cash flow will be, that kind of thing. If you have a forestry company, well, they're all going to tell it's a great idea to plant; where because we're a state agency and we're meant to be independent and objective, if I feel it's not a good idea, I'll tell you it's not a good idea.

Like Keefe, Matt also feels that farmers are particularly good at pulling the maximum amount of subsidy off of their land.

When asked about the expansion of forestry on farmland, Matt stated that larger farmers compete for better agricultural land, which displaces beef and sheep farmers who then buy, rent, or lease marginal agricultural land. The result is that "we're all chasing the same marginal agricultural land." As he understands it, this is why forest expansion has been stalling, as competition for land and—important—for farmers' attention is intense.

As outlined here, small farmers and their "under-used" fields are scarce resources on numerous fronts. In trying to navigate the space between what is expected and what is feasible to achieve, bureaucrats in numerous areas work to draw dedicated small farmers to their cause. The goals may be expanding forestry, increasing the uptake of an environmentally minded scheme, protecting a riparian zone, or changing burning practices; but each of these needs small farmers to buy into and see through their particular needs. This is partly because larger farmers and farms are already productive in a way recognised by the state—subsequently positioning those on the periphery as still up for grabs.

Both Keefe and Matt mentioned the need for farmers to think about holistic planning and to maintain up-to-date practices. Regarding training, Matt emphasized the green cert's positive role in ensuring that farmers can meet shifting demands:

> Like the green cert itself, I mean yes, farming is a vocation, but it's also a job, and you do need the skill level to do it, and you need—if you did any job you'd need qualifications, and it should be the same for farming. You know, it is a job, it needs some sort of professional expertise. Doing something because your father and grandfather did it that way, that's not a good logic for running a farm, and the reason why the green cert, the succession taxes, are there is to ensure that farmers or people that inherit land do have the green cert and that there is some baseline level of knowledge. And I think it is reasonable that it is so.

Matt is particularly frustrated by farmers who lack an overall operable plan for their farm, stating that he finds it "intensely annoying" when farmers move from scheme to scheme and enact a rotation of actions when whole farm planning would be a more rational approach.

In positioning small farmers as a necessary resource for departmental goals, land professionals formulate and enact ideas of what a farmer is and what their priorities should be. These views reflect the broader government ideology that has positioned small farming as both an asset and a barrier to progress (and to the department's expected work outcomes). Such discourse also further alienates farmers from their fields, transforming their livelihood and social reality into a scaled-up "problem" of marginal land and marginal farmers. In this way, we can see the construction of a second pressure release valve—where the inability to produce sought-after outcomes can be placed at the feet of irrational farmers, thus again avoiding a deeper reassessment of what is possible in the first place.

CONTROLLING THE UNRULY LIFE AS TOLD THROUGH INCENTIVES, REGULATIONS, AND CALENDARS

As the title of this chapter and section suggests, I aim to highlight the ways government priorities at various levels shape farm lives and local ecologies in non-linear ways, meaning beyond cause (a piece of legislation, for example) and effect (the landscape intervention). Many have noted that bureaucratic systems are less rational, objective, and detached than governments might wish, and Hoag (2011) argues that in recognizing this, we must write from the gap, looking for the space between what should be and what is. In this case, the gap includes contradictions or inconsistencies that result in departments competing for resources—including farmers' attention—and working toward land-use goals they feel will never be achieved (such as substantially increasing forest cover or fully protecting conservation areas).

Declan, Matt, Keefe, and Rian work in different departments in the government or are tangentially related to the state through the nature of their work and their dedication to enacting its structures. Each felt that farmers were often confused about the specifics of what should be happening on their land. All felt that some of the fault for this lay with farmers who tended to briefly skim or burn program regulations or draw on advice from neighbouring farmers rather than professionals. However, each also found good reasons for the confusion, particularly in terms of how different goals and schemes interact, compare with each other, and change over time and who would be the best person to reach about a particular issue. When unable to answer questions or offer solutions, those working in the government admitted to directing the public to departments they knew would redirect them back to their own office so they might initially have something to offer the person, however ineffectual it might be.

Writing from this gap also means recognizing the agency and situatedness of the various farm professionals who orbit farms—who, rather than passive government mimics, are often community members themselves, fully aware of and perhaps intimately caught up in the space between what is and what should be. This means that at times, the shared goal between actors is to navigate the system rather than enforce rules as intended. Navigating the system could be internal (for instance, sending inquiries to other departments) or external (such as helping farmers navigate schemes to achieve the most money with the least effort). Such compromises could occur at any level of governance, but I suggest they are more likely to happen when they are closer to the materiality of farms themselves. This means that low-level bureaucrats or farm professionals who are aware that the goals they are told to achieve might be impossible may do their best to get by while being resigned to the inefficiencies of the system. At this juncture, it is easy to suggest that the unwieldy machine of bureaucracy is to blame rather than the fundamental contradiction between competing goals. The belief that farmers should increase the production and efficiency of farm outputs, support goals for increased state forest cover, participate meaningfully in initiatives meant to support biodiversity, and maintain any previously existing low-intensity practices while also following and keeping up to date with shifting policy is an unrealistic—perhaps even impossible—expectation. Yet this tension is passed on to landowners in everyday decisions about their engagements with animals, plants, soil, and fellow humans as rural landscapes and their inhabitants are curated to produce desired results.

Permanent Residents

The Birds Directive is often spoken of hand in hand with Council Directive 92/43/EEC, otherwise known as the Habitats Directive, adopted in 1992 and transposed to Irish law in 1997. It lists over 1,000 animal and plant species and 200 habitat types as protected. Annex II species have core habitat areas designated as Sites of Community Importance (SCI) and are included in the Natura 2000 network. These sites can be designated as Special Areas of Conservation (SAC). The directive requires that member states take measures to maintain or restore natural habitats or species listed in the annexes, including habitats and species (National Parks and Wildlife Service Ireland 2013). There are dozens of SACs across Ireland, often clustered around waterways.

Two species within the Habitats Directive and Duhallow SAC waterways are the lamprey eel (*Lampetra planeri*) and the freshwater pearl mussel (*Margaritifera margaritifera*), both of which have been part of numerous monitoring and habitat restoration projects along the Blackwater River, which flows partly through Duhallow. The freshwater pearl mussel is a freshwater bivalve; its shell is in two parts that enclose the animal's soft body. Freshwater pearl mussel can live as long as 140 years—Ireland's longest-living animal—and can grow to between twelve and fifteen centimeters long. They live buried or partially buried along rocky river bottoms for much of their lives.

I had the opportunity to visit a pearl mussel SAC outside of Duhallow with the Pearl Mussel Project and two Duhallow scientists. Two members of the local team

Figure 6. A freshwater pearl mussel, centre, rests among the rocks of a stream. Author photo.

working to better habitat in the area had offered to show us some of their project sites, and we spent a lovely afternoon driving small roads and stopping to wander paths to reach the streams in question. I was lucky enough to see a pearl mussel roughly eight centimeters long resting among the rocks during our walk and was surprised to learn about the extraordinary journey of this rather sedentary creature (figure 6).

The life cycle of the mussel is astounding. Adult males release sperm that is inhaled by the female, resulting in fertilized eggs; the resulting *glochida* (developing larvae) brood in the female's gills. Adult female mussels later release one million to four million *glochida* during the summer months, although their mortality rate is upward of 99.9 percent. To survive, a salmonid fish—either Atlantic salmon or brown trout—must inhale the *glochida*, and the *glochida* must attach themselves to the gills where they remain for upward of nine months, following the fish along its own journey. The young mussels drop off the host fish the following summer but must land in an area with oxygenated sand or gravel. The juvenile mussel then buries itself in the river bottom, remaining covered for up to five years until it is large enough to withstand the force of moving water and stones of the river. The mussel then spends its life attached to the rocky river bottom, filtering up to fifty litres of water daily. Their work helps keep river systems vibrant.

Populations of this animal have declined by 90 percent across Europe over the last century. One of the main reasons for the decline is poor river quality, which can significantly impact the survival rate of the young. Some of the primary steps taken to support river quality within SPAs are oriented around agriculture and include improving the biodiversity of habitats (in fields near waterways and along the water's edge), fencing riparian zones to keep out cattle and sheep, maintaining riverside habitat (such as the work of the Rural Social Scheme folks I was pulling Himalayan balsam with), and improving nutrient management on farms to reduce nutrient runoff into rivers and streams. There are also forestry implications through restrictions on fertilization, harvest, and management around water courses. These implications include restrictions on aerial fertilization of forests because of concerns over phosphate enrichment in streams that might negatively impact salmonoids.[1]

The freshwater pearl mussel is a long-term Duhallow resident that actively shapes its ecosystem while likewise being impacted by human activities along waterways and changing land-use policies. Unbeknownst to them, in some cases this species is one of the direct reasons farmers are incentivized to fence riparian zones or encourage certain types of species growth. The freshwater pearl mussel moves in and out of bureaucratic and local focus as it is alternately the core of place-based, time-specific projects or assigned to the background behind other pressing matters. In either case, it enacts its full life cycle to the best of its ability while shaping the waters that flow through Duhallow. Of course, this is only one of many species that call such waterways home, flowing into and out of human interest over time.[2]

---

[1] The Draft Plan for Forests and freshwater pearl mussel in Ireland Consultation Document was released in 2018 and includes detailed measures that shape the relationship between forests and the pearl mussel.

[2] Another fascinating example is the Brook Lamprey (*Lampetra planeri*), which lives a comparatively short life of three–five years. The Lamprey is an eel-shaped fish with a sucker mouth part rather than a jaw. I first learned about the species through signage that was part of a prior IRD Duhallow program to improve local SACs. In asking further questions, I discovered that Ireland has three species of Lamprey, all of which share some curious features: They have no scales or bones and are among the least developed invertebrates. Each also has an extended larval stage during which the juvenile lamprey (*ammocoetes*) filter-feed on organic matter in riverbeds; for this reason, they are tied to the maintenance of healthy river systems, much like the freshwater pearl mussel. While Brook Lamprey remain in their rivers of origin, River Lamprey and Sea Lamprey migrate to the ocean for part of their life cycle. Because of this migratory feature, damns and weirs, in addition to water quality and habitat, pose significant threats. Lampreys are also engineers in their own right, often engaging in nest building during which they remove larger rocks to create clear areas of gravel access along river bottoms. In turn, this can maintain and expand spawning habitats for salmon and trout. While the Brook Lamprey is not considered a threatened species, it is at risk due to habitat degradation.

5

What Is a Forest, and Who Gets to Decide?

The National Forest Inventory defines forests as land with a minimum area of 0.1 ha under stands of trees 5 m or higher, having a minimum width of 20 m and a canopy cover of 20% or more within the forest boundary; or trees able to reach these thresholds in situ. The forest definition relates to land use rather than land cover, with the result that open space within a forest boundary either permanently or temporarily unstocked with trees, along with felled areas that are awaiting regeneration, are included as forest. (Department of Agriculture, Food and the Marine 2019)

"They'd get rid of their wife before they'd get rid of the land, they would, I'm not exaggerating." This statement was made by a manager working in the forestry sector. We sat in his quiet office near the edge of town and discussed upland farmers and the state's plans to expand forestry in Ireland. His work is part of an effort to expand national forest cover from 11 percent to 18 percent by 2046 (Department of Agriculture, Food and the Marine 2014a), although the exact target shifts along with policy. As forest growth needs to occur on private lands, small farmers' reluctance to commit to this land-use change is a point of frustration for him. However, making such a change is not a small decision because forested land must remain so in perpetuity under Irish law, where it is a criminal offence not to replant deforested areas within two years. In other words, if a field is planted with trees, it must remain forested for all future generations unless stringent requirements for an alternative are met (a rare event that often requires that land elsewhere be planted).[1] Forests and agriculture are intimately entwined in Ireland, and in Duhallow, more than 12 percent of agricultural land has been converted to forestry over the last three decades. Nevertheless, despite forest growth, the state's afforestation targets are consistently unmet, and for the forest manager above, the decision of upland Duhallow farmers to resist planting (and therefore impede planting targets) is irrational.

The establishment of the Special Protected Area (SPA) in this region, with its regulations and priorities, has brought many of the contradictions of rural land-use planning to light. In Duhallow, it is nearly impossible to discuss farming, the SPA, or afforestation without implicating the others. This entanglement results less from any inherent connection and more because of the tensions and inequities of land-use change. For example, when afforestation was halted in the SPA until the Hen Harrier Threat Response Plan could be agreed on and made public (a draft plan was released in 2021), the value of farmland within that designation was no longer propped up by forest subsidies. Farmland was suddenly worth far less than its neighbouring non-SPA fields—so little, in fact, that many farmers suggested that banks were uninterested in their farms as collateral against loans. No longer able to plant trees or place wind turbines, the lack of control farmers had over their land and the processes that are changing the shape of their communities became abundantly clear. While this loss of land value has angered farmers, at the same time, many farmers and non-farming rural residents fervently object to the shift afforestation has brought to the Irish landscape—including those who might themselves consider planting trees for economic reasons—making afforestation a tense political topic.

This chapter focuses on afforestation (planting trees where there have been none in recent history), specifically, the peculiar contradiction among private landowners who both detest and desire having plantation forests on their lands and the various mechanisms that attempt to guide them to plant trees. The questions of what a forest is, what it can provide, and who gets to decide are central to this, as competing economic, social, and conservation goals come to a head and are enacted on small farms through forest decisions. In all of this, I argue that in embracing the narrative of multifunctional forests, the Irish government is able to take advantage of green and community-friendly language to position planting trees as the best economic and most moral choice. Within this, I also trace some of the discursive techniques

---

1 However, the 2021 draft Hen Harrier Threat Response Plan does suggest that there may be room for some SPA-designated land to be deforested without penalty. How and when this would be allowed to occur is still unclear.

applied in policy and state-funded research that mute local complexity and experience. In taking this perspective, I hope that the inconsistencies experienced by landowners who are angry because they cannot plant their land with trees and yet see forests as an abundant landscape feature are understood as the natural outcome of a difficult situation—that is, an accumulation process that economically appeals to locals while simultaneously drawing them into a new human-environment relationship that alienates them even further from their land and communities.

In all of this, categorizing plantations as either "good" or "bad" is not my interest. Indeed, a simplified pro-con approach obscures the more complex, context-dependent truths of what plantations mean to those who live near them. Instead, I want to focus on how plantation forests are discursively framed throughout this dispute. To do this, I first introduce Irish forest history and the afforestation debate, then turn to two forest stories that exemplify state narrative and lived experience. In illustrating these stories, I find clear parallels between the long-standing drive to "develop" Duhallow, as is apparent in chapter 2, and this more recent push to forest Irish hillsides. I see this in particular in how this process reproduces long-standing power dynamics dependent on the idea of marginal land of little value, irrational local actors, and the prioritization of outside and "objective" knowledge. It should become clear that the question of to-plant-or-not-to-plant is insufficient without unpacking the assumptions behind these ideas—specifically those of development, progress, what is "green," and ownership itself.

WHAT A MESS?

Locals often reminded me that this land was hard-won through a long and challenging history and that landowners should have the right to decide what to do with their land. In discussing this topic, a resident gave me a farmer's name to contact. After I called him and introduced myself, Brennan agreed to meet in a local parking lot, where he picked me up on his way home from work in the city. We spent the early evening driving through upland Duhallow on the roads that circle and intersect his farm. Brennan repeatedly referred to the entire region as "a mess." Well over two thirds of his 140 acres are Special Protected Area (SPA), something he only became aware of after being refused forestry and turbine permits. The youngest of many siblings, Brennan inherited the farm and the expectation that it would be kept in the family. While his siblings had moved elsewhere and married, Brennan was a bachelor who looked after his elderly widowed father. They lived together in their family home while Brennan worked a full-time job in the city and kept the farm running. His father likely received news of the SPA designation when it was first established, but, like many, he may have ignored the notice. Brennan now spends his weekday evenings, weekends, and any other days off keeping the farm going with enough cattle to pull in Single Farm and Green, Low-Carbon, Agri-Environment Scheme (GLAS) Payments. At one point, he had ambitions to expand his farm operation by raising enough funds from afforestation and turbines to rent or buy better land in low-lying areas. While Brennan dislikes plantation forests, better land would have supported more cattle and perhaps allowed him to work only part-time in the city.

With those opportunities now closed to him, he stood with me on a road that overlooked the valley where his farm was located and surveyed the fields, hills, forest blocks, and turbine networks unfolding in front of us with what I interpreted as resignation. "It's like I'm a tenant on my own farm," he said in reference to the multitude of restrictions placed on him as a landowner. Below us, we could see forest blocks lined with wind turbines on all edges. His fields were between these blocks, marked by the pattern that comes from cutting rushes in strips, something required by the GLAS Payment scheme. Cutting fields in strips is meant to help local biodiversity by building diverse habitats. In Brennan's case, the fact that his patterned fields sit near monoculture forest plantations felt to me like a mockery. After an evening of driving and discussing his work and farm and driving through forest blocks that used to be active farms, Brennan took me back into town to fetch my car, as he had to get up early for work in the morning. Not for the first or last time, I was poignantly aware of the impossible position many upland farmers find themselves in.

Brennan does not particularly like forests; they don't look or feel good to him, and he correlates their spread with community decline. Yet he is not against planting forests on his land, and he can understand farmers who choose that path. Plantations, if not blocked by the SPA, would offer Brennan and his father an opportunity to better their lot in life by making an income that would allow them to purchase land in a lower-lying area. For many others, the associated subsidy payments plus even a minimal tree harvest return mean a comfortable retirement and the option of children inheriting the land. All of this is to say that it is not enough to discuss the meanings and values of a landscape, as this chapter aims to do, without also recognizing that livelihood is both embedded with meaning *and* fundamentally economic—something the government is well aware of in offering subsidies to plant land in the first place. As I discuss further in chapter 6, upland livelihood rests on flexible livelihood strategies that take advantage of multiple overlapping economic strategies, of which plantation forests are one.

A BRIEF OVERVIEW OF FORESTS IN IRELAND

Forests in Ireland have long been tied to land and population control, with the Tudor Conquest and Act of Union (1603–1800) period probably the time of most significant forest exploitation and decline. During this time, wood was used to build British ships, was burned for charcoal, and was cleared to make way for agriculture; forests continued to be removed to expose Irish rebels and secure land for the Crown (Neeson 1991). Indeed, clearing forests to expose Irish rebels was a central tactic in the ongoing experiment of British colonial control over at least 900 years of conflict between the two island nations (Rahman et al. 2017).

Because of this history, the term *plantation* is associated with both colonial expansion into Ireland and the use of Irish land for tree crops. Niall O'Carroll (2004), in their account of Irish forest history, cites sources from the eighteenth century onward who employ the term *plantation* in this dualistic way, denoting an area of densely planted trees for the purpose of wood production and a unit of colonial settlement.[2] During much of this history, marginal agricultural lands and their inhabitants have been consistent targets: first for deforestation and later for afforestation (Asselin 2022). The link is important to recognise, as forests and land control in rural Ireland have a long history wherein external forces and their social and economic priorities have worked to shape or curate a rural aesthetic and local behaviour. This pattern has cultivated mistrust of outside organizations and experts who would suggest forest-based land-use change (Flechard et al. 2007).

Although a long-established regional priority, Irish state forestry only officially began in 1906 with the establishment of Ireland's first forestry school on the Avendale Estate in County Wicklow. The first forest payment grants were introduced in 1922. In 1928 the Scheme Forestry Act included four pounds for an acre planted with forest, increasing to ten pounds an acre in 1948 and twenty pounds an acre in 1958 (Farrelly 2006b). Through sustained effort, forested areas grew from less than 101,173 hectares in 1922 (including Northern Ireland) to 404,695 hectares in 1991 just in the south (Neeson 1991, 4) and to 732,650 hectares in 2017, wherein the state reported reaching its highest level of forest cover in over 350 years (Department of Agriculture, Food and the Marine 2018). Once at an all-time low at an estimated 1 percent of the total national area, forests in Ireland today occupy closer to 11 percent of its landmass. Growth over the last century is the product of a sustained national effort to be less reliant on imported wood products while simultaneously building a forest industry from the ground up by creating a resource that has not existed in abundance for centuries. Throughout the twentieth century,

---

2 As a unit of colonial settlement, sixteenth- and seventeenth-century plantations saw the confiscation of Irish land by England and the settlement of this land by settlers from Great Britain. This technique was meant to control and subdue Gaelic Ireland.

official efforts to expand forest cover included legal protections of forested lands, penalties for cutting trees, various financial incentives to plant them, and the state purchasing agricultural land for large-scale planting, among other initiatives.

While a sustained effort to expand or protect Irish forests is long-standing, extensive forest expansion truly started in the 1970s, as it was in the last decades of the twentieth century that land purchases and incentive programs increasingly prioritized forestry as an economic opportunity worth aggressively pursuing. During these decades, initial forest growth relied on land purchases by the state. The quick purchase of apparently abundant, cheap land in marginal areas is remembered bitterly by some Duhallow farmers, who recall their parents' farm selling for very little while the family was desperate for poverty relief. However, the availability of land for sale was short-lived as, despite desperate economic situations, most farmers were unwilling to sell their land. Subsequently, the state government focused on incentive programs to encourage afforestation on private land. In 1981, the Western Package Grant Scheme was introduced due to the depletion of European Union (EU) forestry resources, making upward of eighteen million pounds available for private-sector forestry (Farrelly 2006b). Other programs were introduced in the 1980s and 1990s, including the Compensatory Allowances Scheme, which offered monies to farmers who had planted land and would potentially lose headage payments. In 1989, the state established Coillte Teo (the Irish Forestry Board) to manage state forests commercially. By 1990, the Forest Premium Scheme had also been introduced, which paid farmers who planted forests an annual premium for twenty (later fifteen) years. The premise of such premiums was to ensure that no cash outflow was required from the landowner, together with compensation for land loss while the forest grew (Flechard et al. 2007). Rates and years of payments were adjusted in 1992, 1994, 1998, and 2000 (I am sure they also include changes not listed here). Yet despite more recent scheme adjustments, private planting rates peaked in 1995, resulting in only half of the targeted area being planted in Ireland between 1996 and 2006. Since then, numerous studies and reports have focused on private landowners' hesitancy to plant trees on their land despite financial incentives—especially as the state's current (though shifting) goal of 18 percent forest cover by 2046 is unlikely to be reached based on recent planting numbers.

The Rural Environment Protection Scheme (REPS), introduced in 1994, is one of the many potential factors influencing a slowdown in tree planting. While there is no specific restriction on afforesting REPS land, farmers cannot receive payments from both schemes. REPS is a significant scheme in upland Duhallow, with most farmers I spoke to enrolled. The forest planner discussed in chapter 4 cited REPS as one source of competition for land, as have prior studies (Duesberg et al. 2013; Flechard et al. 2007). More broadly, however, as much as increasing forests depend on small farms, agriculture and forests do not mix on a practical level. In a 2001 COFORD[3] report on forestry trends and farmer attitudes, the author states: "The downturn in afforestation in 1996, while grazing livestock continued to expand, was indicative of increasing competition for land from agriculture, and with cattle production in particular beginning to have a restrictive impact on forestry. While the further reduction in afforestation in 1997 can be partly attributed to the timing of the review of the forest grant and premium rates delaying planting, nevertheless, it is likely that competition for land use with livestock was also a factor" (Kearney 2001, 2).

As of 2017, forest ownership in Ireland was 50.8 percent public (mostly Coillte-owned) and 49.2 percent private, with public forestry at a near standstill regarding geographic growth. Plantation forests are the dominant model in Ireland and heavily favour quick-growing non-native conifers as their primary species, although late twentieth-century policy changes mean many are now bordered by a deciduous boundary and can contain some diversity within them. As a landscape feature, plantation forests tend to be dense and linear and often include ditch or dike features to help drain the boggy land. Natural features such as large stones, hillocks, fallen trees, and canopy holes are actively discouraged through management. The non-native Sitka spruce remains the dominant species, making up nearly 40 percent of all trees in Ireland and over 50 percent of all stocked forests. The next-most-common species in plantations are the lodgepole pine (7.8%) and Norway spruce (3.8%), both non-native conifers (Department of Agriculture, Food and the Marine 2017). As a non-native conifer dominant in Ireland, the Sitka spruce has become a particular point of tension and for many is symbolic of the plantation forest model more generally. The aesthetics of plantation forests are important to emphasize, as their homogeneous, linear, and dark characteristics are key elements of local distaste.

FORESTS UP FOR DEBATE

As a Canadian growing up in the boreal forest and living in a lumber town, I had taken forests, what they were, and what types of debates surrounded them for granted. Yet as a fundamentally introduced land type, perhaps it is no surprise that forests are particularly controversial in Ireland for reasons that challenge the nature of forests themselves. Throughout the controversies of where, when, if, and what to plant are broader issues around the rural economy, the meaning of land, and the definition of a forest. In Duhallow, I was first introduced to this debate through the Irish Farmers Association, local members of which were vehemently opposed to the

---

3 The Council for Forest Research and Development (COFORD) is appointed by the minister of the Department of Agriculture, Food and the Marine to advise on forestry.

limitations on afforestation imposed by the SPA designation. However, I quickly learned that many were equally opposed to specific planting instances or even to afforestation altogether.

While Maeve and I conducted surveys with IRD Duhallow on hen harriers and SPA views and knowledge, upland farmers often discussed forestry, particularly in reference to upland threats. Locals described forests as green deserts and community killers, and on more than one occasion, forests were described as blanketing, suffocating, isolating the area, and forcing people out of rural areas. Comments included:

> Forestry has destroyed the country; you can't expand if you want to.
>
> You will not win land back from forestry.
>
> Forestry is all right for the first fifteen years, but there is no local employment from it, and it kills communities.
>
> As forestry spreads, the people have to retreat, like plantations of the sixteenth and seventeenth century.[4]

Similar sentiments have been expressed by rural Irish for the better part of two decades, with research in County Kerry (Carroll et al. 2009, 2011), County Roscommon (Flechard et al. 2007), County Cork (Dhubháin et al. 2006), and Ireland more broadly (Dhubháin and Wall 1999).

Part of the reason behind the "community killer" argument among farmers I spoke to was the permanency of forests. Because land once forested needs to remain so under Irish law, afforested areas were understood as permanently removed from the rural farming landscape. This legal protection meant that land use could not shift, but it also meant that "place" was no longer present. One farmer told me that before planting, he knew the area, the hills, and the glens: "If you showed me a picture, I would tell you where that was." However, after planting, a picture of the area could be one of anywhere in Ireland—the place's locality, story, and feeling were gone. In other words, for many, forests represent local erasure and the destruction of rural place more generally. This erasure of place existed in terms of belonging and feeling but was also more material—forests are generally inaccessible unless they are along forest roads.

The inaccessibility of forests is demonstrated by one story of a family I came to know just outside one of Duhallow's smaller towns. I had interviewed three generations of this family and one evening was sitting at a table with a father, his grown son, and his daughter-in-law. When I asked about the farm's afforested plot and

---

4 Also cited in Asselin and Mee (2019).

whether they ever go into that area, the father and son told me a tale of a missing tractor tire. The tire, I understood, was nearly as tall as a grown man and was rather heavy. It had been repaired after a mishap led to it going flat while out in a field. The father and son worked to roll the repaired tire out to the stranded tractor. All was going well until the two lost control of its forward momentum on a hilly stretch; the tire accumulated speed, moved beyond their reach, and headed downhill and into their plantation area. Because of the section's considerable incline, both were sure the tire's speed and momentum would take it through the trees, and they were worried that cars on the road or the small house below might be harmed. They quickly left the field, found their vehicle, and drove down the hill to the spot in the road where they deemed the tire had likely come out of their small forested section. Relieved to find that it had not emerged (no damage had occurred to body or property), they walked the edge of the forest where its trajectory may have taken it. After walking above and below the forest's edge, they determined that the only thing left to do was enter the forest. Walking and crawling, the two struggled through the dark trees, trying to find the huge tire. They searched the better part of the evening until one of them found the tire lying on the ground partway through the dense trees. The next monumental task was to get the mammoth tire back through the trees and up the hill, where they could once again attempt to move it toward the tractor. While they laughed at the story, the father stated in all seriousness that you wouldn't go into a forest unless something had gone wrong, and that is not something to look forward to, so the answer to my apparently absurd question was "no"—they never went "walking" through the trees.

As forests expand, Irish residents who object to their structure, presence, or implications have become more vocal and widespread. At times this has meant organizing against forestry in a public way. For example, Áine Ní Dhubháin and colleagues (2009) cite an action group on the Cork-Kerry border in 1993 challenging what it called "blanket afforestation." An intervention by a group in Rockchapel (a Duhallow community) resulted in a formal complaint sent to the EU and an investigative response by Coillte (Mahoney 2002). As detailed later in this chapter, a case in southern Duhallow resulted in one woman preventing nearby afforestation on the ground of centuries-old tertiary rights with both considerable support and admonishment from fellow community members. In a quieter way, farmers' sustained refusal to plant as desired is likewise an indication of protest.

More recently, the Save Leitrim group has emerged as a vocal opponent of forestry, gaining widespread media attention (Forde 2018; Save Leitrim 2021). Founded at a meeting held on January 1, 2018, in Drumshanbo County Leitrim, the group has held protests and petitioned governments since its inception. Its primary goals include stopping the further decimation of rural communities, schools, sports organizations, and businesses in small villages and towns; securing a future for young farmers who currently cannot compete with forestry companies to buy land; and, among other things, protecting the environment by stopping further habitat loss, which it sees as contributing to the terminal decline of many species of ground-nesting birds. As is apparent with these goals, the potential adverse environmental impacts of extensive afforestation are a substantial concern of local objectors, as is worry over non-locals or, at times, international investors buying land to plant for investment purposes. Locals and groups can also appeal forest decisions, including afforestation, deforestation, and building forestry roads. The Forestry Appeals Committee was established in 2017–2018; at first, appeals rose sharply, with 35 in 2017, 197 in 2018, 489 in 2019, and 874 in 2020. However, in 2020 the committee established a 200 euro fee for appeals; as a direct consequence, the number of appeals fell to 149 in 2021 (Forestry Appeals Committee 2021)—a figure that likely underrepresents cases of forest tension.

Certainly, this issue is not isolated to Ireland. Similar debates are also occurring beyond Ireland, where the impacts of the global timber trade and simplified forest management models are increasingly scrutinized (Hecht et al. 2014; Tsing 2015). Likewise, international greening programs and land grabbing (Borras et al. 2012; Delestra and Feydel 2014), the role of afforestation in mitigating climate change (Böttcher and Lindner 2010), and concerns around forest discourse in climate strategies (Winkel and Storch 2013) mean that forests and forestry are global issues of concern. As such, the Irish plantation model and its opponents are one strand in a broader debate over what forests are and what they might provide to humanity more generally. Whether they know it or not, small upland farmers are key actors in a global question of what forests mean.

FRAMING THE DEBATE: RESEARCH, FIRSTHAND EXPERIENCE, AND LAND-USE DOCUMENTS

Given this well-established debate, I am interested in how such local concerns are understood and integrated into a discourse specific to Ireland, particularly how Irish forest discourse shapes upland livelihood. To explore this, I touch on two particular areas: how forest research has framed locals and their concerns and how plantations have become synonymous with forest in this research. The importance of this last point was highlighted for me by local voices who insisted that such entities were not forests. Ultimately, I argue that the ways local problems with afforestation are officially framed not only mute farming (and others') voices but draw attention away from more systemic issues such as how afforestation contributes to a broader accumulation strategy and reworks the property relationship, often while hiding behind the morality inherent in green language.

In Ireland, one strand of afforestation literature has paid specific attention to whether afforestation benefits ecosystems. However, readers seeking clarity on this point will be disappointed. Far from reaching a clear consensus, most research finds that the impacts of plantation forests depend heavily on their surrounding context. A 2007 report prepared for Ireland's Environmental Protection Agency emphasizes such unclear consequences, reporting that forestry plantations can be beneficial to biodiversity in the landscape if properly planned and managed and can have a negative effect if not (Iremonger et al. 2007). More specifically, it reports that planting semi-natural areas results in an overall decrease in biodiversity, while planting improved land does not harm or actually improves biodiversity (19). These findings are also confirmed by Erika Buscardo and colleagues (2008) in their examination of afforestation impacts five years after establishment, which found that afforestation negatively affects semi-natural grasslands and can positively affect improved grassland. However, in marginal areas such as Duhallow, with a long history of both agriculture development and low-intensity use, the distinction between improved and unimproved land is tricky. In a literature review of thirty-six publications on plantations and biodiversity in numerous countries, Leah L. Bremer and Kathleen A. Farley (2010) found that tree species, previous land use, and plantation age determine plantations' biodiversity benefit. More specifically, they confirm that improved land can benefit biodiversity while concluding that older plantations are bad for biodiversity, especially in the "shrubland to plantation" and "grassland to plantation" categories, also noting that most specialist species are affected negatively by plantations. In other words, context matters greatly in determining the ecological impact of plantation forests, as do, I might add, the parameters in which ecological benefits are measured. Nevertheless, those for or against forestry often cite only one side of these findings and gloss over their contextual dependence, a tendency likewise noted in forest debates occurring in Germany and elsewhere (Winkel and Storch 2013).

REFRAMING LOCAL DISSENT THROUGH RESEARCH

The forestry problem in Ireland has resulted in a cluster of research that aims to explore the disconnect between state needs and farmer practices. I decided to explore this cluster as a phenomenon in its own right because such sources were cited to me by forest officials as the dominant academic voice in the forestry question and because this cluster of research aimed to explore and explain farmer opinions about forestry. My ongoing effort to make sense of this literature has been influenced particularly by two scholars who have worked to unpack complex forest relations and histories. The first is Tania Murray Li (2007), who provides a detailed analysis of community forestry as an assemblage within which managing critiques establishes cohesion in an otherwise complex network of connections. In Li's model, assemblage refers to the ways heterogeneous elements come together as a whole, often to address a specific need. In this piece, and others (Li 2014), Li works with a discursive conception of assemblage building off of Michel Foucault's (1991) exploration of governmentality and discourse. This approach is akin to Aihwa Ong and Stephen J. Collier's (2007) work, wherein heterogeneous elements are brought together through particular articulations. Such anthropological problems, Ong and Collier argue, are "domains in which the forms and values of individual and collective existence are problematized or at stake, in the sense that they are subject to technological, political, and ethical reflection and intervention" (4). Central to the idea of assemblage are the ways heterogeneous, contingent, unstable, partial, and situated elements are tied together.[5]

In considering plantation forests as an assemblage, I recognise that such forests are the product of a collection of trees, soils, practices, documents, voices, declarations, and rules that render such land use both sensible and governable. This model helped me visualize the complexity of forests as material, political, economic, and social structures while also complex organisms in their own right. The second influence is the seminal study of James Fairhead and Melissa Leach (1995, 1996), who in their retracing of false forest histories in sub-Saharan Africa detail the inaccuracies social science research can perpetuate through a failure to question underlying assumptions. This latter is important because, as I have argued elsewhere (Asselin 2022), the research surrounding planting hesitancy in Ireland constitutes a particular field of knowledge that, because of its focus on planting resistance, fails to adequately and seriously explore locals' problems with plantation forests.

In examining how locals are represented in such research, it is essential to note that the primary research and funding bodies investigating farmers' social hesitancy to afforest in Ireland are directly interested in forest expansion. These bodies include the Agriculture and Food Development Authority (Teagasc) and Coillte, Ireland's primary forestry company (state-owned). In addition, the state likewise supports research through the Council for Forest Research and Development (COFORD), appointed by the minister of the Department of Agriculture, Food and the Marine to advise on forestry issues. Indeed, it is challenging to find afforestation research on the views of farmers that is not connected to one of these bodies. Understandably,

---

5   This approach is somewhat distinct from that of Tsing, which I draw on in chapter 6.

such institutional bodies would have a vested interest in better understanding planting constraints, and all resulting research is clear about its limitations, priorities, and funders. However, as a collective, the studies outlined below obscure the potential for other queries and observations; thus, through the authority of their academic and institutional voice, they determine the shape of forest discourse in a decidedly limited fashion. This is because much published research on this subject aims to better understand and overcome planting resistance and, subsequently, often implicitly (or sometimes explicitly) frames farmers as a barrier to progress. Such a pattern is not an abstract academic query, however; the participants in these studies are taken to represent Irish farmers, including those of Duhallow. Through the authority inherent in peer-reviewed and published research, such studies shape the policies that impact rural livelihood. Below are four brief examples of the ways current forest research approaches Irish farmers.

First, the benefits of plantations are often an assumed starting point rather than a focus of investigation. While scientific studies have taken pains to outline the degree to which context is important in determining the environmental impact of plantation forests, this nuance is often simplified or ignored. Moreso, the presumed environmental benefits are conflated with social and economic benefits. For example, in exploring Irish farmers' intent to afforest, Stefanie Duesberg and colleagues (2014), funded in part by COFORD, started from the stance that new planting targets would support a range of processing industries, help farmers better diversify their businesses, and support carbon sequestration. Duesberg and Dhubháin (2019), whose research was funded in part by the Department of Agriculture, Food and the Marine, postulate how to balance economic, environmental, and recreational forest management goals; they assume that each is valid and equal, ultimately asking whether forest management could be intensified without causing further conflict. In another example, John McDonagh and colleagues (2010, 237), with Teagasc collaboration, examined why Irish farmers displayed reluctance to engage in forestry production and why "the promotion of a resource that delivers on so many of the EU's stated policy objectives for sustainable rural development generates seemingly little appeal" within the farming community. While each of these publications did solicit and present useful data on farmers' viewpoints, none seriously examined the benefits of plantations, which constitutes the core of hesitancy. Instead, farmers' perspectives were subtly contained in a frame of rural development and environmental progress—that is, these things are "good," so why are people refusing to engage with them?

Second, in taking the good of plantation forests as a given, farmers often become implicitly or explicitly repositioned as barriers within such studies. In a

COFORD-supported paper, Duesberg and colleagues (2013) argue specifically that Irish farmers' value system is a barrier to afforestation. The authors interviewed sixty-two farmers and cite "deeply rooted attitudinal barriers" as a problem, arguing that farmers are entrenched in a productivist model that has them failing to see the multifunctional attributes of forests. In another example, David Nevins, the chairperson of COFORD, wrote a foreword to Brendan Kearney's (2001, iv) review of studies concerning farmer attitudes toward forestry, stating that the government strategy for the forest industry sends a strong signal of the government's commitment to forestry and that "if the planting targets are to be achieved, farmers, as owners of the target land base for forestry, must be convinced of all the benefits of forestry." Similarly, in a conference paper published and available through COFORD, Niall Farrelly (2006b, 13) wrote that the lack of forestry knowledge among farmers and their unwillingness to conduct operations were obstacles that must be overcome for the full benefits of afforestation to be realized. In these examples, the seamless discursive transformation of farmers' views to barriers emphasizes the pervasiveness and normalization of plantation logic. My issue is not the claims that farmers are a barrier (from one perspective they are) but the researchers' refusal to acknowledge the legitimacy of local reasoning.

Third, if forests are an undisputed good, then anyone who questions their expansion is faulty, often due to backwardness, laziness, or a lack of knowledge. This particular approach already fits within a long-standing narrative that positions rural small farmers as barriers to progress, a thread that is centuries in the making and therefore easily invoked. Many studies cite a lack of farmers' knowledge or awareness. For example, Tomás N. O'Leary and colleagues (2000, 40), in their COFORD-funded study that aimed to introduce social dimensions into discussions around forest policy, suggested measures that could be used to "nurture a more positive disposition in the future." The authors stated that forestry's potential contribution was obvious to professionals (implicitly suggesting that anyone who fails to see this lacks knowledge) and argued that increased public awareness through a multifunctional "rural development–type" forestry was a solution. In addition to a lack of knowledge of forestry as a reason for hesitancy (also found by Collier et al. 2002; Farrelly 2006b; Savill et al. 2013), others have also suggested that the negative feelings that prevail around some areas of forestry seem to be an impediment. Dhubháin and colleagues (2009) researched stakeholders' perceptions of forestry, including a Duhallow case study. They found that a contributor to negative perception is the length of time forests have been in the region. Locals in areas with a longer forest history seem to more greatly appreciate forest affordances, implicitly suggesting that such affordances are present and only need to be recognised. Similar implications are found in research that suggests a lack of awareness of potential economic benefits (O'Leary et al. 2000; Vidyaratne et al. 2020).[6]

Fourth, the use of language that reduces farmers to targets is prevalent. In the study by Duesberg and colleagues (2014) mentioned above, researchers were able to change the minds of 16 percent of their survey respondents toward favouring plantations after providing further information. The authors concluded that past planters may be convinced to plant more through an information campaign and that, building on findings of a separate study (Sutherland et al. 2012), "employing such information campaigns after trigger events negatively affecting the course of the farm business could improve their efficiency" (Duesberg et al. 2014, 19). In other words, a study aimed at assessing local intention was geared toward directly addressing perceived deficiency and suggested targeting farmers in particularly vulnerable circumstances. The stated intent of a study funded by COFORD and Teagasc (Collier et al. 2002) was to find out why farmers were not taking up forestry and to make recommendations to address those reasons. Among other things, the study suggested that moving away from the general promotion of afforestation to "promotion targeted directly at farmers" (3) would better help reach planting goals. In addition, the authors propose solutions, such as more targeted promotions, and report that Teagasc (i.e., farm advisers) are better compensated financially by encouraging farmers' choice to afforest. This latter point is particularly interesting given that the farm advisers interviewed for my project actively recommend that their client farmers should not plant small or marginal fields because doing so does not make economic sense.

None of this is to say that valuable insight cannot be garnered from these publications. There is consensus, for instance—and this is very important—that locals feel that their communities see few economic benefits commonly associated with plantations (Dhubháin et al. 2009), that they feel "good" land is too valuable for forestry (Duesberg et al. 2013), that forests do not merge well with rural Irish identity and good farming practices (McDonagh et al. 2010), that plantations produce

---

6 Such benefits are not always certain. Many community members are concerned that planting subsidies have raised the value of land; as a result, locals are less able to afford land purchases (Crowley 1998; Dhubháin et al. 2009). Increased land prices are particularly challenging for farmers who want to expand their holdings or young couples who hope to build near family farms. In contrast, within SPAs, the inability to plant forests has, in effect, removed the state-subsidized selling price, making SPA lands worth considerably less than similar neighbouring fields—in some cases upward of £4,000 per acre less (Cadogan 2018). Others have questioned the forestry model's economic benefits, particularly for the numerous farmers with small holdings (less than ten ha). For example, the economic justification for hiring contractors to harvest and move the wood to market when timber prices are unpredictable is questionable (Farrelly 2006b).

a feeling of isolation (Carroll et al. 2011), and that there is a lack of planting consultation and an overrepresentation of conifer species, which have limited cultural value (Bonsu et al. 2019). But it cannot be sufficient to detail such findings while simultaneously creating the appearance that such opinions and feelings are misinformed, backward, or something to be mitigated. More than informants, study participants, or stakeholders, farmers in studies like those discussed in the preceding paragraphs, are targets for behaviour change, if not directly in the study then in its impetus. The impact of such collective works needs deeper consideration, not the least because it can be used to represent farmers' views while simultaneously undermining them. Such research has also produced a concerning self-citing domain of expertise wherein circular references further produce the appearance of agreement.

PRESENTING A DIFFERENT KIND OF STORY

Among the many reasons upland farmers are concerned about plantations, the language of blanketing, suffocating, erasing, and covering is a common one. These descriptions correlate to ideas of light, views, place connection, and movement. When taking these comments seriously and refusing to explain away or justify them, a different kind of story emerges that speaks to the things that make up people's everyday lives. Before returning again to official and academic discourse, I turn here to the idea of place, a personal and experiential connection to the landscape that is difficult to account for in policy-oriented documents. In presenting this material here, I aim to disrupt objective and sterile accounts of forests present in official documents and academic research through experience.

When locals talk about plantation forests as destroying the landscape, they are commenting on the character of places and communities that mean something to them. A lasting contribution of place scholar Edward S. Casey's (1997) work is a broad recognition that place is imbued with power partly through its connection to knowledge by way of lived experience. In Ireland, plantation forests materially and discursively create generic, measurable, and containable space that erases specific sites and the broader character of a place, severing the connection between knowledge and experience. Non-locals can likewise note and respond to this change. For example, the Irish Upland Forum, a collection of Irish upland stakeholders and researchers, left the region off of its 2018 upland report—despite the fact that it met the group's technical definition of uplands—because it no longer had enough *upland character* to qualify—further muting local voices.[7]

---

[7] Personal communication (October 2018) with two individuals in the Irish Upland Forum in response to my query.

Locally, we can see the change of place in other ways. For example, sightlines matter in Duhallow, and historically, landscapes have been mainly open, places where treeless bog and fields meant a person could see far to the next horizon. The capacity to see the twin mountain peaks known as the Paps of Danu was commonly mentioned as a landscape marker that is no longer possible to view for many.[8] More than once, when out on the land with farmers, they would stop in a high, open area and point out the Paps of Danu on the horizon. Just as often, a farmer would point in the direction where they would be visible if not for the forests that block them.

Beyond distant vistas is the capacity of plantations to erase particular and meaningful places altogether. For instance, the upland area known as Doctor's Hill in the Mullaghareirk Mountains is scattered with abandoned and broken homes closed in on all sides by dense conifer forests. Once a vibrant farming area, the region was progressively sold off and planted, with houses left standing because it was cheaper to plant around them than to disassemble them. "Why, just look at Doctor's Hill," farmers would say when I asked what they meant by plantations as community killers. With plantations, places lose character and become uniform. However, full acknowledgment of the impact of a lost place or landscape requires an in-depth examination of the specific and subjective aspects of locality and an appreciation for the aesthetic and emotive qualities of landscapes that are difficult to incorporate fully into scientific literature.

Sight is also relevant even on smaller expanses, for instance, where people find themselves living in unfamiliar darkness. The family I mentioned earlier with the missing tractor tire shared a story of one of their children coming home from the university after the trees behind their home had been harvested. Since they had not entered the empty bedroom in some time, she and the rest of the family were shocked by its brightness when they opened the door. None of them had realized how dark the room had become as the plantation had grown over the last decade. Forestry proponents know the concern about light, and regulations now manage how close trees can be planted to inhabited buildings. However, when I broached the subject with the manager mentioned at the start of this chapter, he stated simply that "people are not entitled to a view, they are not even entitled to light"; legally, he is correct. When recognised in plantation research, concerns about light or views are often quickly summed up in a single line or incorporated into a broader list of barriers. Yet the material truth about these changes to land and people is far more profound than any summary could provide.

Beyond sightlines and light, the capacity to enjoy landscapes through experience is also important. Indeed, this is acknowledged in land-use documents that point to

---

8 The twin mountain peaks are shaped like breasts. Danu (sometimes called Anu) is a goddess of fertility.

plantations' recreational potential. However, residents quickly pointed out the distinct differences between plantations and the mixed broadleaf forests in Duhallow, often negatively comparing them to a locally treasured deciduous forest that has multiple well-used walking trails. While Coillte promotes recreation opportunities in plantations, these walking areas most often amount to straight and monotonous forestry roads that cut through dense plantations in various stages of growth or along narrow-cut trails—usually where an existing popular walking path was intersected by planting. While some walking groups use these trails, most prefer those available in open land or in the few areas of mixed deciduous forests. The daughter-in-law in earlier stories pointed out that she would not feel safe walking in a plantation forest unless she were with others and even then, only in full light. She added her worry that plantations increased crime in the area by creating sufficient cover for criminals to meet without encountering neighbouring farmers' watchful eyes. While only a few people I spoke to associated plantations with crime, I did query a local garda (police) officer who confirmed that plantations are good meeting points for drug deals in his district. While not a significant point in this research, the worry about crime speaks to a changing sense of place and well-being that is worth noting.

Wanting to experience this landscape as much as possible, my partner and children and I accompanied local groups on multiple organized community hikes—only one of which included a section of plantation forests—and went on numerous walks on our own through Coillte plantation lands. On one occasion, we spent approximately three hours walking a popular upland circuit around a mountain in the southern part of the barony on an organized walk. While most of the hike was spent rambling through open upland fields and over fences and carefully stepping on stones in wetter areas while a gentle mist fell and soaked us through (we were woefully unprepared for what we thought would be a short ramble—my friend had assured me that even the elderly would do this walk), the final stretch of our walk was at the bottom of the mountain we had circled. By then, our group had spread out considerably, with faster walkers (many of whom *were* elderly) already waiting at the bottom of the hill with tea and cookies and those who were slower well behind our family. As our path neared the plantation at the bottom of the hill, it appeared as a tunnel into the forest. The darkness was immediately apparent as we entered, as was the silence. Dusk fell while we walked, and it became increasingly difficult to tell how far along the path we had come. On occasion, our children would yell out with delight when light appeared ahead because they thought it indicated the tunnel's end, only to find that one or two trees had died or fallen, allowing a beam of light to enter the otherwise dark forests. While we came out the other side happily enough, the idea that such trails would feel unsafe for lone walkers was immediately and materially apparent.

Safety, light, views, landscape markers, and the intricacies of knowing place are part of the things that make up everyday life. While each story told here might have only a small impact—a hill no longer visible, a place-based story no longer told, a bedroom imperceptibly turning to darkness over the years—collectively, these processes effectively disentangle, perhaps even alienate, people from land, farmer from field, and communities from landscapes. On their own, each of these complaints can be disassembled, pulled apart, rearranged, and sanitized. The gospel of efficient use, productive land, and mitigating impacts has no room for such subjective experiences; their complexity and messiness are unwelcome in scientific management's stark, factual space. All the while, forests continue to change the facts on the ground (Li 2014),[9] wherein specific assemblages materially shift the nature of the land itself and in turn create the empty and marginalized space necessary for forest expansion.

MAKING PLANTATIONS INTO FORESTS

Collectively, plantation forests as represented in policy, much academic research, and industry-related material invoke a meta-narrative that often rationalizes rural land use, fragments the landscape into distinct features, and naturalizes land-use decisions as common sense or irrational. However, within all of this is a subtle sleight of hand that I believe deserves particular attention: despite farmers telling me such things are not forests, plantations have become precisely that.

Because plantations are simultaneously materially and culturally produced, there is a distinct difference between the lived experiences of forests and those present in official discourse. When presented with descriptions taken from land-use documents that describe all that forests (i.e., plantations) can provide—including recreational value, biodiversity, and mental health and well-being—locals scoffed at the idea that their local collection of conifers can be understood in such a way (Asselin 2022). Given the gap between experience and official description and the importance of land-use documents in bureaucratically shaped livelihood, I explored the ways plantations were discussed in land-use documents. In a sub-study that reviewed eighty-six land-use–related documents at the EU and Irish levels and deeply analyzed nineteen of the most relevant examples (Asselin et al. 2022), my colleagues and I traced the logic whereby official institutions, as authors of important documents, discursively transformed plantations into forests by muting tensions between forest types. We argued that with forests, the failure to clarify how words are used produces ambiguity that favours the broadest and most positive

---

9 Li argues that one feature of assemblage to pay attention to is the way official processes materially change landscapes, changing the facts on the ground to suit existing and official narratives.

interpretations. This occurs because without further clarification, forests are generally understood as a good thing.[10] The polysemic nature of forest (meaning the term is fairly inclusive) often leaves interpretation up to the reader/listener unless the context of its use narrows the field of possibility. We found that many documents embrace forest as a deliberately open concept rather than reducing ambiguity.

Examples like the following are common, a phenomenon our small team came to call "forests as all things":

> The essence of the changes [of this new forest policy] lies in the expression of the public's understanding [of] and interest in the multiple benefits that forests can provide and in particular the range of environmental and social services, focusing on biodiversity, water quality, landscape, recreation and leisure, climate change mitigation and renewable energy. (Department of Agriculture, Food and the Marine 2014b, xi)

> Forests also make a positive contribution to the quality of life, providing a pleasant living environment, opportunities for recreation and preventive healthcare, whilst maintaining and enhancing environmental amenities and ecological values. (European Commission 2015, 9)

As a broad category, forests are associated with biodiversity richness, carbon sequestration, soil fertility, water filtration, recreation, mental well-being, and climate change mitigation. The broad language of forest avoids forest-type particularities while simultaneously skirting criticisms specific to the plantation model. We found that by taking this approach in forest-related documents, plantations can unproblematically inhabit viable economic and environmental space while dodging the necessary specifics of planting context that would otherwise be necessary behind such claims, subsequently appearing as an unmitigated good.

While many documents refer to forests and their affordances (those things forests provide) in the broadest way, we also found that when more detailed descriptions were present, language in documents moved seamlessly between the idea of what we called forests as an ecosystem and forests as a resource. Text that discusses "natural" or system-based forests (forest as an ecosystem) implies a collection of trees, plants, and animals not primarily managed for timber products. In Ireland, these passages index deciduous or mixed non-plantation forests and their related flora and fauna, although this was seldom clearly stated. In contrast, when texts referenced forests as a resource, timber production was the dominant feature; although rarely clearly stated, this most commonly implies forest plantations.

---

10 There have been many calls aside from my own for precise forest definitions in important land-use documents (Chazdon et al. 2016; Hecht et al. 2014; Neumann 2014; Winkel et al. 2013).

When referencing forests as a resource, the typical text focus narrows to the tree, wood, or features that directly relate to tree growth or lumber quality. Example passages include:

> Opportunities to increase volume production include the choice of faster growing tree species and the use of improved planting stock for the main conifer species. Improved Sitka spruce would result in an increase of at least one yield class. (Department of Agriculture, Food and the Marine 2014b, 4)

> Timing of clear felling, like thinning, depends largely on the species and the yield class, but is also determined by stocking rates, thinning history, previous management, plantation size, threat of windthrow, market price and distance from markets, and also economies of scale regarding adjoining areas for felling. (National Parks and Wildlife Service Ireland 2015, 21)

While such passages clearly refer to the plantation forest system, the documents did not clarify the forest type. Instead, they often moved seamlessly into descriptions that implied deciduous or non-managed forests without marking the transition. This material was of interest to us because of the unaddressed tension between forest referents and the failure to acknowledge the real-life differences in forest type on the ground. The people I was working with in Duhallow were clear that different types of forests were not equally valued, and my firsthand experience showed me distinct material differences. Yet most forest literature (within and beyond Ireland) failed to make this distinction. The semiotic ambiguity created in this process glosses over conflicting interests among forestry, conservation, and agriculture, in addition to other uses—implicitly suggesting that forests can benefit all at once. This discursive feature was most evident in text passages that list multiple and overlapping forest affordances as taken-for-granted truths. For example:

> The essence of the changes lies in the expression of the public's understanding and interest in the multiple benefits that forests can provide and in particular the range of environmental and social services, focusing on biodiversity, water quality, landscape, recreation and leisure, climate change mitigation and renewable energy. (Department of Agriculture, Food and the Marine 2014b, xi)

> Forests provide ecosystem services on which rural and urban communities depend, and host an enormous variety of biodiversity. (European Commission 2013, 9)

> Apart from the benefits accruing to biodiversity, leisure and recreation, carbon sequestration is by far the biggest non-production benefit and the role of Irish forests is key to the country meeting its international climate change targets. (Department of Agriculture, Fisheries and Food Ireland 2010, 55)

Forests also make a positive contribution to the quality of life, providing a pleasant living environment, opportunities for recreation and preventive healthcare, whilst maintaining and enhancing environmental amenities and ecological values. (European Commission 2015, 9)

Uncoupling the word *forest* from any particular type of forest facilitates broad generalizations. Subsequently, the core assumption apparent in such documents is that all forests can draw equally from this pool of affordances.

The language in such documents, often technical and authoritative, has another significant effect: It establishes a domain of expertise from which locals and their unique experiences are easily excluded. For example, the language around sustainable forest management is highly technical while also discursively disassembling forests into parts (e.g., water quality, soil structure, wood type). This technique— "rendering technical," to use Li's (2007) terminology—allows an unruly array of forces and relations to appear as a bounded arena in which calculated interventions produce beneficial results. By both discursively dividing the environment into parts and relying exclusively on a narrow range of expert voices, communities and problems are presented in technical terms as arenas to be investigated, mapped, classified, documented, and interpreted; in addition, their vectors need to be explained, and they are subject to calculated redesign (Li 2007). In this way, critiques of plantations' lack of biodiversity can be mitigated by a mandatory 10 percent inclusion of native species and buffer zones along roads and paths; concerns over the visual and biological effects of deforestation can be mitigated through rotational cutting; and observations by farmers that their water flow is changing on fields below plantations can be dismissed as uninformed and subjective. In much the same way, concerns over the environmental impact of Ireland's planned increase in dairy production can be mitigated by increasing forests and thus creating carbon sequestration opportunities to offset increased carbon production. To be clear, I am not suggesting that forest practitioners are being dishonest or that mitigation suggestions are not useful, only that in this domain, there is no problem that can't be broken into its constituting parts and mitigated by scientific expertise.[11]

There are too many diverse voices for me to argue that this process is deliberate, but I can observe that collectively, the discursive slippage that ignores the difference

---

11 I am certainly not the first to point this out. Geographer Bruce Willems-Braun (1997) provides an excellent example of this technique in my home province in Canada. He examined the 1990s Clayquate Sound dispute in British Columbia, Canada, and detailed the ways a forest company emphasizes rhetoric of accountability legitimated through expert management, consultation, and going above and beyond—including the self-made claim that it generously provides public access to (already public) lands. This strategy was shown to split off expert culture from the life-worlds of community members.

between forest types, the domain of expertise that purports to represent local voice but fails to do so, and the language of expertise around forest plantation have the collective result of producing a rational and moral land-use category and positioning those who resist its logic as irrational and a barrier to progress.

AT LEAST THE LAND IS STILL THEIRS: ACCUMULATION THROUGH AFFORESTATION

Acknowledging the gap between official forest discourse (how forests are referenced in documents and research) and the specific materiality of plantation forests is significant because failure to do so obscures a more profound truth: The plantation model sits on a foundation of mass production, an exercise in scalability that requires a predictable and controllable resource. Plantations are (near) monoculture crops that are designed to scale up. In this case, the scaling is on the national level, where the state can produce national forest cover statistics from individual small-holder plots of land that are perhaps ten hectares or less,[12] ideally producing predictable and reliable outcomes. In the remainder of this chapter, I will offer an alternative lens through which we might view Irish afforestation, one that by focusing on land and human-environment relations highlights some potential implications for upland farmers and communities that deserve more attention than the current mainstream afforestation debate is producing.

As a logic with global application, the plantation model has consistently involved a predictable set of actions that include exterminating or removing local people, plants, and wildlife and importing exotic species and labour. This process generates models of production that destroy local diversity and legitimize such destruction as improvement (Shiva 1993). Plantation systems are also associated with contained forms of knowledge production and experimentation (Rusert 2015) while representing a logic that is part of a broader economic and political system of settlement and control (Thompson 1959). Far more than a colonial practice relegated to history, contemporary plantations continue to have similar structures worldwide today—often noted in the Global South (Besky 2019; Li and Semedi 2021), although certainly also playing out in North America (see Tsing's [2015] exploration of American forestry)—with various degrees of private and public control. While each manifestation is distinct, such cases result in predictable consequences, including the large-scale separation of people and land, the drastic simplification of ecosystems, and often the introduction of foreign species.

---

12 The minimum area for conifers is one hectare, although premiums are higher for areas over ten hectares.

In Ireland, widespread afforestation has made more advances in making land productively cooperative than did waves of suggested improvement before it. I believe this is because of the particular human-environment relationship plantation forests demand. While land control in a plantation model often occurs partly by divesting people of common lands and enforcing a private property regime, it can also happen by redefining the property relationship while keeping the core ownership element intact. In the Irish model (and those in many other places, I am sure), plantation forests sever ties between farmers and their farms by indirectly reducing their access to and control over their land. First, forested land in Ireland must remain so in perpetuity (Department of Agriculture, Food and the Marine 2014a), a rule that also extends to naturally seeded trees older than five years (for example, those that have self-seeded into farm fields). This rule hinders owners' capacity to choose what is planted (beyond trees) and how land should be managed by current and future owners. Second, afforested areas require unique skill sets, training, and permissions to manage, harvest, and plant adequately—to the degree that many farmers often hire outside companies to manage their land and its shifting legal requirements. Subsequently, the material and legal requirements of plantations move the expertise necessary to engage with afforested fields outside many farmers' reach.[13] This shift simultaneously reworks labor regimes and ecosystems and weakens the farmer-field relationship to one of title only.[14] Third, the obligations to manage and replant are legally entrenched within the plantation assemblage, with fines and possible jail time for landowners who fail to fulfill their forest duties (Asselin 2022).[15] Finally, as noted above, plantations can remove land from farmers materially as forested areas become difficult to access in any comfortable manner after about a decade of growth. This remaking of what ownership means for those with forested fields is not reflected by rhetoric that reduces the forest debate to the issue of planting alone.

---

13 This shift has been acknowledged and cited elsewhere. For instance, see Dhubháin et al. 2007.
14 This has been acknowledged by Kearney (2001), who argues that farmers are ill equipped to manage forests. Likewise, Farrelly (2006a) points to the efforts required by Teagasc and the government to retrain, concluding that in many cases it may be best to educate farmers in their management options (i.e., hiring out the work).
15 On a summary conviction, a fine is leveled not exceeding €200 (US$232) for every tree removed, not to exceed €5,000 (US$5,800); imprisonment for a term not exceeding six months, or both. On a conviction of indictment, the fine can be as high as €1 million (US$1.2 million), imprisonment for a term not exceeding five years, or both (Forest Act, section 17, subsection 6). An owner who fails to comply with a replanting order can face fines up to €5,000 (US$5,800) for every period of thirty days over which failure to plant continues, with further fines possible.

In the long term, plantation forests uncouple people and their land, although in a more roundabout way than did plantations in the earlier colonial era. The fact that this has not been further examined in the plantation debate is concerning, especially because the encouragement to afforest is often attached to a culturally specific logic whereby appeals to ownership as a reason to plant are particularly salient due to the dominance of the farm inheritance system. On more than one occasion, when asked about the impact of afforestation, those who worked in the forest industry stated that "at least the land is still theirs," emphasizing that plantation land remains in the farm family. Likewise, I came across many cases of fields afforested "just to keep [them] in the family." Such a strategy may risk long-term dispossession while the state accumulates forest as a broad category.

Forests as state accumulation make sense when we consider a broader level of abstraction, specifically as they are increasingly integrated into international land-use policy through green language. For example, while forestry makes up roughly 1 percent of Ireland's GDP (Freer-Smith et al. 2019), the contribution of Irish forests is increasingly measured beyond the economic and the material. In particular, Irish afforestation helps the state meet EU-mandated emissions goals,[16] including the carbon sequestration that will allow Ireland to expand its dairy sector. In this frame, Irish forests are not limited to Ireland but are part of a global forest system, with benefits beyond the local population. Indeed, the 2022 Intergovernmental Panel on Climate Change (IPCC) considers afforestation/reforestation to be an important climate change mitigation strategy worldwide. Likewise, the European Forest Institute released a 2022 report on the potential of forest-based climate change mitigation in Europe and found that afforestation/reforestation similarly have a potentially important role (Verkerk et al. 2022). While the exact nature of this role (and the relationship between afforestation and reforestation) is still debated, there is no doubt that forests are now thought of in terms other than as simply raw material and local habitat.

In this light, a distinct feature of forest plantations is the commodity their establishment produces even before physical forest products such as wood are harvested. In the context of climate change, "forest" is an economic scarcity in Marxist terms. By this I mean that forests as a reducing global feature (however specific those spaces of deforestation are) create an opportunity in places that have not been forested for centuries, like Ireland. Forests can garner exchange value under the new conditions of created scarcity on a global level.[17] From the state's perspective, it is

---

16 The EU Climate and Energy Legislation for 2030 requires that all member states adopt national energy and climate plans (NECPs). Ireland's NECP, submitted in 2019, relies heavily on afforestation measures and forest and land management to help reduce emissions (Department of Communication, Climate Action, and Environment 2019).

17 I would argue that this fits with Neil Smith's (2006) observations that green capitalism has

increasing forest cover and all of the affordances, such as carbon sequestration, forests provide. From the landowners' perspective, they do not have forests on their land, only plantations. While there may be short-term monetary benefits and—for the lucky few with substantial land and good lumber prices—long-term income, for most Duhallow farmers and others like them, this process deepens the inequalities between urban and rural and poor and wealthy as small farmers are further alienated from their land.

In this entire process, marginal lands and people provide an opportunity for salvage accumulation. That is, the discursive placelessness created by the marginal lands narrative (and impoverished residents) encourages an ongoing rotation of development initiatives veiled as a benefit to locals while in reality they are better suited for the state or firms to take advantage of existing market scarcities.[18] Afforestation, whether to help fight climate change or improve the resource sector, does just that.

CONCLUSION

I hope this context has made it clear that there is no contradiction in farmers both desiring and detesting afforestation. Instead, such tension is the culmination of an underrecognised process of accumulation, packaged to both appeal to locals and deride them while also drawing them into a new human-environment relationship that ultimately results in land alienation. The framing of the forest debate as a question of whether trees are good redirects anger over the resulting inequalities and contradictions toward fellow farmers or nameless bureaucrats and away from the plantation system itself. Farmers like Brennan, discussed at the beginning of this chapter, who was visibly upset and frustrated as we toured his lands, are in impossible situations that they navigate and manage to the best of their ability, for better or worse.

And yet, as much as such a logic seeks to simplify land and all its relations by creating predictable and controllable spaces, this effort is never complete. Public pushback against the monotony of conifer forests has resulted in deciduous buffers along public roads. Within the forest itself, practices have shifted in recent decades, and plantations now include other conifers scattered among the spruce. Larch in particular is noticeable, as it changes to orange in the fall. This diversity does not undo but instead reduces the monoculture nature of plantations. Other practices do the same. Foxes and other predators are good at making use of forests to hide in, increasing predation for ground-nesting birds, which are unable to keep a watchful eye on what happens under the tree canopy. Likewise, hen harriers began to nest

---

become a major strategy for ecological commodification, marketization, and financialization.
18 Tsing's (2015) examination of salvage value is an excellent example of this process.

in young forests because their structure somewhat resembles heather in the first decade or so of planting. The fact that this bird would choose to nest in such trees was unpredictable and led to the formation of the SPA that is now so contentious. Multi-species ethnographer Anna Tsing reminds us to look in ruins for what occurs there, and certainly, these unexpected interventions rub uncomfortably against the complete control that is implicit in the plantation model. Even human technologies introduce disturbance in the homogeneous cover of forest blocks. Wind turbines, for instance, demand clearance around their structures. To meet this need and comply with Ireland's forest laws, trees are planted and cut in continuous short cycles—forever a forest and never really a forest. Further, as chapter 6 attests, people themselves often remain resistant, although in unexpected ways.

Farm Fields as Multi-Species Entanglements

Land abandonment is a significant concern in the European Union, where as much as 11 percent of agricultural land is at high risk of abandonment (Castillo et al. 2018). One concern with abandonment is that it could lead to potentially adverse economic and ecosystem outcomes. Despite this broad trend in Europe, I met few people, other than two vocal rural residents, who would answer affirmatively to the question of whether land abandonment was an issue in Duhallow. After a time, I realized I had asked the wrong question. Proper abandonment—leaving one's land altogether—was possible, although unlikely, in an area where the family farm was still central to many people's families. The question instead was one of intensity and appropriateness of use. When asked if they felt the land was used as fully as it should be, local residents' responses became fulsome discussions of once vibrant fields, now left under-stocked or planted with trees. While there was little consensus on what exactly "proper" use was, most agreed that it involved people and land in an interactive relationship.

This recognition speaks to the way farms, as multi-species assemblages, have formed through a long-standing relationship wherein farm animals, farmers, and plants shape each other's composition and various habitat types—including grasslands, hedgerows, woodland/scrub, field margins, and peatlands. Recall that land use in Ireland is predominantly agricultural. Of all of the land in Ireland, 4.9 million hectares (58%) are used for agriculture (although I have seen the amount as high as 65%), including 427,800 hectares of commonage. Of that amount, 4.1 million hectares are grassland (Central Statistics Office 2018). Of the total agricultural area, 71.5 percent is dedicated to beef through specialist beef production (56.5%), specialist dairying (11.2%), or specialist tillage directed mainly at cattle consumption (3.8%) (Central Statistics Office 2018). Economically, the cattle industry has been a central feature of the Irish economy since its independence (McCabe 2011) and had shaped local social systems and environments for centuries prior (O'Connell et al. 2016), although sheep are likewise an important farm animal.

As a result of long-standing multi-species entanglements in small-scale farming, many fields are places with complex dependencies between plants and the species that feed on them and nest in them. This diversity is often specific to so-called marginal areas, where monoculture and otherwise homogenized landscapes associated with intensive farming have not entirely severed multi-species relationships. For example, semi-natural grasslands often have over forty species in a two-by-two-meter quadrant, whereas improved fields often have one to two species. As a result of similar long-standing agricultural practices across Europe, approximately 50 percent of European species actually depend on agriculture (Kristensen 2003; Stoate et al. 2009). In this way, too little use is a concern along with too much use (figure 7).

For example, Molinia meadow is a type of wet grassland community listed in annex 1 of the EU Habitats Directive, commonly found in western Ireland. In such meadow, the grass *Molinia caerulea* is prominent but should not be dominant, and it is accompanied by several other characteristic plant species including *Succisa pratensis* (Devil's-bitscabious), *Cirsium dissectum* (Meadow Thistle), *Anthoxanthum odoratum* (Sweet Vernal-grass), *Filipendula ulmaria* (Meadowsweet), *Potentilla erecta* (Tormentil), *Juncus articulatus* (Jointed Rush), *Equisetum palustre* (Marsh Horsetail), *Juncus conglomeratus* (Compact Rush), *Mentha aquatica* (Water Mint), and a range of sedges including *Carex nigra* (Common Sedge), *Carex pulicaris* (Flea Sedge), and *Carex panicea* (Carnation Sedge) (Conaghan et al. 2020). As a result of species richness, Molinia meadows present visually as a diverse cluster of flowering, often tall grasses. This type of plant community stems from human management, often with some mowing late in the year. As a result, threats to Molinia meadows include agricultural intensification as well as under-grazing and afforestation.

As only one of many examples, what is increasingly recognised is that changes in farm practices can shift habitats and reduce biodiversity, especially in grassland (Henle et al. 2008; McMahon et al. 2010). In recognition of this, various agri-environmental schemes (AES) use public funds to pay farmers for private farm actions meant to support grassland biodiversity, including the Rural Environment

Figure 7. Rough upland pasture in the foreground, improved fields in the background. Author photo.

Protection Scheme (REPS, 1994–2014) and the Agri-Environment Options Scheme (AEOS, 2010–2018).[1]

Farmers most likely to engage with AES are those with a high proportion of family labour, less reliance on farm activities for income, and farms with lower agricultural capacity (European Commission 2017), a description that fits most farmers I interviewed. Brennan, discussed in chapter 5, with his rushes cut in strips to encourage habitat diversity, was part of an AES, as was Darragh in chapter 3, who had fenced off a section of his field, although he intended to open it up again after the scheme was complete. Likewise, when I walked a field with the farm adviser discussed in chapter 2, we searched for plant diversity and species that would indicate rich grassland worth protecting through an AES. Similarly, when I set predator cages with the scientist and student, each pointed out different grasses and species, translating the history of the transect field into a story by reading the plants at our feet as we would read words on a page.

While the exact species composition of high biodiversity farms is frustratingly outside of human control, it appears that just enough use can create the

---

[1] The impact of such schemes is uneven (Huallacháin et al. 2016). James Moran and colleagues (2021) provide a succinct summary of the various schemes and programs implemented over the last twenty-five years that are meant to protect such high-diversity areas in Ireland.

circumstances in which the desired diversity has the potential to arise. This entanglement involves people—to a certain extent—and their entwined dependence on other, non-human species. This is the core of the concept of high nature value (HNV) farming. HNV is the recognition that the conservation of biodiversity in Europe depends on the continuation of low-intensity farming as multi-species systems. Many plants and birds rely on animal grazing, which, in turn, relies on human management.

The farmers I spoke to who pointed across their valleys to show me fields "scrubbing up" from under-use had a sense of what the farmer-field relationship should look like. While not abandonment in the traditional sense, the mutual relationship between farm activity and plants has broken down in many of these areas.

6

The Salvage Value of Rural Livelihood

Flexible Economies on the Margin

I first met Connor at his farm while I was running an errand for another community member. His house rests on the edge of a busy farmyard. While its edges were crumbling, the front of the house was tidy, with well-tended flowerpots near the door. After I had completed the errand, he invited me to drink milk poured directly from his holding tank, and we discussed the benefits of fresh milk, with reminiscences from my childhood. After hearing about my research, he invited me to come back to spend a day, and a week or so later he sent a text detailing when I should come. He told me he would be driving his Lory truck, a small semi truck he used to haul livestock, on that day. As an owner of such a truck, other farmers hired Connor to transport their cattle to the mart (market) in one of the area's larger towns. On these days, Connor picks up the animals, unloads them at the auction, and sees through the selling transaction—returning the funds to the owners afterward and charging a fee for his work. He thought it would be a good day to talk and see the countryside, and I could lend him a hand with the animals, if needed.

Connor is a late-middle-age single farmer who lives with his unmarried sister on a comparatively active, large farm in Duhallow. I met a few similarly structured households with late-middle-age siblings, male or female, sharing the home farm. The idea of unmarried siblings staying on the family farm and living with a brother who inherits it was fairly common in the past, although it is rarer with younger farming families today. After working on it for much of his childhood, Connor inherited the farm from a childless uncle. Today, he has a relatively large operation, with around thirty dairy cattle and fifty head of beef cattle. He has a thick Cork accent, rough skin on his face and hands from years of farming, and a friendly and welcoming demeanor—although he was also keen to offer criticism when needed.

On the appointed morning, I met Connor at his home. As on the first day I met him, he was wearing what I came to think of as farmers' unofficial uniform: a clean, well-worn button-up shirt tucked neatly into clean jeans, with a warm pullover wool sweater over the top. Our morning started with me hauling myself up into the vehicle's high cab and then chatting as we wound our way down the narrow roads to our first farm. Each farm we stopped at was small—often with just a few head of cattle in the yard, an old stone or concrete barn, and a small concrete house—although usually immaculate. At each house we would stop, briefly visit with the farmer, load one or two animals into the truck, and continue on our way. As we drove, I asked Connor about his life as a farmer and his history, with my recorder propped between our seats. Connor had a sizable amount of Special Protected Area (SPA) land, and we discussed the various schemes he had drawn from. He felt the Rural Environment Protection Scheme (REPS) was a good scheme, as it protected the land, and thought the Green, Low-Carbon, Agri-Environment Scheme (GLAS) was "no good." He also shared bits of advice as we drove. For instance, in speaking of an earlier scheme, he remarked: "It was too good to be true and anything too good to be true don't last. Any good never lasts. The fine weather, for instance, don't last." Building from this, I asked Connor how he felt about the various grants available, and this was his response:

> Ireland was a very poor country. I put it this right now to you. I come from the top of the country, you know what I mean [referring to the upland area]? There was no running water in houses, there was no TV, there was [sic] no toilets, there was no money, you know what I'm talking about? They see it very hardly. But once we joined the EU [European Union] in 1972, things got better and better then from that day on because there was a price for bacon, there was a price for cattle, and there was [sic] grants. Like in my grandmother's time there was starvation, famine, there was no transport, only horse and cart or a donkey cart. But like I experienced—I wouldn't consider myself old but I wouldn't consider myself young either, and I experienced it.

I learned that Connor takes in some money through his Lory work and pays other farmers to rent out their equipment when it comes time to cut rushes or seed fields. With most small farms, the need for machinery aside from a small tractor is occasional, so farmers can make extra cash by either renting out their equipment or doing the jobs themselves for other farmers. Connor sees farm advisers and scheme planners in a similar way. As most schemes require an adviser to score fields, he understands their payment as one of the many side gigs that keep the rural economy going. For example, to enter the new hen harrier scheme that was starting when I was present, he paid a woman €600 to score his fields.

When I asked Connor about the SPA, he explained that his land—over 100 acres designated—is "very poorly" and that the designation does not bother him. Some of his land is so wet that he cannot bring his tractor up to the designated SPA tracks for fear of getting stuck: "The [land] is worth less now. But I wouldn't be selling, I'm not planning on saying anything different. I wouldn't be selling. It's poor quality... I wouldn't be selling anything, but I inherited it from an uncle of mine. I've had plenty of customers for it, but hen harrier land is of poor quality. Do you know what I'm talking about?" Because Connor does not intend to sell his land or plant trees, schemes attached to the SPA are one way to draw income from land he can only use minimally for grazing.

On the subject of forestry, Connor had clear views: "I don't like trees, I'll be honest with you. They're horrible. The timbering isn't that much quality. They're not good for fence posts or they're not good for building. You know what I'm saying?" Connor has seen his neighbours' boggy land planted with trees that have stunted growth and do not yield much timber. While he does not want that for himself, he points out that forestry provides a monthly check, while beef, for the most part, is a once-a-year payment that must last for the rest of the year. He has some of both with his dairy, but others do not, and he understands the idea of planting "a bit of land."

Our day progressed as we drove through narrow winding roads, finally making our way to the auction house, where we ate cheese sandwiches in the small cafeteria and I was introduced to the other sellers. Many, like Connor, were farmers who had come with animals other than their own. After a few hours at the mart, we ran errands in town and made our way back to his farm as he spoke of other farming families in the area. I learned that for a time he had owned a piece of property near a regional park, drawing from the rental income until he sold the property to make ends meet in a rough year.

This chapter touches on some of the creative engagements Duhallow residents like Connor have with the local and global economies that produce various means of getting by. As should be clear by now, rather than development-oriented policies wiping out the small farm as predicted in the mid-twentieth century, farms and farming families have changed their shape, output, and structure while remaining fastened to the practice of inherited farms. As the past chapters have detailed, in Duhallow you are likely speaking to a farmer, even if the person is foremost the local doctor, plumber, office worker, or schoolteacher. Each is likely to live on a small family farm, or their children or siblings live on the farm and do minimal farming. If married, each is also likely to have a spouse with similar connections. Likewise, many farmers have several income-generating methods, including renting out farm equipment or fields and transporting local livestock in a creative form of capital-based reciprocity. Each is also likely to draw money from schemes and to work off-farm, and they may receive money from children or siblings abroad or in the city. This is not unique to Duhallow; flexible, adaptive economies are central to upland livelihood in Ireland and have been well documented in Irish rural research (MacClancy 2015; O'Rourke et al. 2016; Salazar 1996; Shutes 1991).

However, I see the local flexibility outlined in this chapter as an opportunity to examine Anna Tsing's (2015) unruly edges and the "riotous diversity of non-scalability." Despite being reproached for a lack of economic productivity, flexible rural livelihoods such as those I encountered in Duhallow are a commodity that can be salvaged, translated, and profited from by industry and the state. In her exploration of the global networks and flows surrounding the matsutake mushroom, Tsing emphasizes the role of salvage accumulation as a central feature of capitalist systems. She defines salvage as taking advantage of value produced without capitalist control (63), that is, existing value. Natural resources, human reproduction, cultural practices that lead to local enskillment, and, I would argue, flexible modes of subsistence all exist without being directly produced and controlled by capitalist systems. Each of these has a value that can be turned into profit through the process of salvage accumulation, "through which lead firms amass capital without controlling the conditions under which commodities are produced" (63).[1] What already exists in Duhallow that can be harnessed for profit without extensive investment? The answer is: lands primed for "rural development," a government willing to pay for investors to reach their green goals, and locals whose livelihood rests on working with a multitude of subsistence strategies and who, as a result, are often somewhat willing to participate in shifting initiatives. What already exist are also the practical knowledge, informal processes, and improvisations in the face of unpredictability that James C. Scott (1998) underscored as both central to regional functioning *and* commonly dismantled by state-led simplification and rationalization. The pages below outline some of the ways people get by and the mechanisms of translation that turn this flexibility into capital value.

MULTIFUNCTIONALITY AND RURAL LIVELIHOOD

While I discuss flexible economies in this chapter, the concept cannot be translated wholesale into agricultural multifunctionality, which is usually envisaged as

---

[1] The sites of salvage accumulation are found both in and outside capitalism's logic and are what Tsing terms *peri-capitalist*. Rather than failed projects, peri-capitalist activities are central to the functioning of the economic system, which can never entirely provide for the needs of all actors.

encompassing the discrete though overlapping domains of farm activity or output, often woven into external expectations and obligations. Instead of focusing on farm output, I want to emphasize the idea of flexibility as a *process*. This focus, I believe, is more integrated with dynamic environmental processes and farm relationships and is better captured by the concept of rural livelihood. This section details the ideas of multifunctionality and rural livelihood as they are employed in the chapter.

While the notion of multifunctional agriculture in Europe was already implicitly apparent in the 1980s (Hollander 2004), it has been a central element of the EU agricultural vision since the late twentieth century, where, as a critical feature of rural sustainability, agricultural policy increasingly began to incorporate or encourage diverse farm outputs. Within this is a core recognition of a farm's potential multiple functions, including energy production, cultural heritage, environmental services, landscape management, and agri-tourism, among others. Farm multifunctionality can include diversification, which is the creation of gainful activities on the farm using farm resources, such as making and selling value-added food products. The community member discussed in chapter 1, who declared in frustration "Lord help me if one other person suggests the ladies sell jam," was commenting on this aspect of multifunctionality as a rural fix-all. However, multifunctionality also includes broad environmental and social services that do not necessarily result in direct economic gains, such as cultural heritage conservation. Farm diversification is distinct from pluriactivity, which denotes a farm operator or manager engaging in off-farm economic endeavours, such as off-farm labour. These are terms defined by the European Union to assess program eligibility (Augère-Granier 2016), with diversification focusing on the farm and pluriactivity focusing on the farmer. However, various disciplinary differences exist in the ways such terms are employed in research.

Amalgamating multiple definitions, Martin H. Lenihan and Kathryn J. Brasier (2009, 365) define multifunctionality as "the social, economic, and environmental impact of agriculture beyond the production of food and fiber commodities." While the specifics and scales are often debated (for example, see Wilson 2009), agriculture can be understood as multifunctional when it has several functions in addition to producing a farm crop. Karlheinz Knickel and colleagues (2004) suggest that such additional activities have three main characteristics: they constitute a response to new societal needs and are an expression of new social relations; such activities represent new answers to the price squeeze; and they are part of a reconfiguration of farm resources and food chains. The Common Agricultural Policy (CAP) is supposed to exemplify the multifunctional model of agriculture, particularly with its focus on ecological outcomes—for example, through environmental schemes.

Ideally, this formalization of farm diversification is meant to recognise that farms produce many social and environmental goods while often also facing economic challenges. However, multifunctional farm rhetoric has been criticized on many fronts. Foremost, it operates within an ideology of agricultural and ecological modernization, emphasizing production and profit while disregarding local complexity. For example, Lenihan and Brasier (2009, 375), in their examination of the REPS program in Ireland, point out that in many ways, multifunctional ideology "represents a compromise between the hygienic concerns of European consumers and conservationists and the pressure for liberalization and deregulation emanating from the World Trade Organization negotiations." Such a compromise produces contradictory expectations, with little space for nuance and local context. Anthropologist Tracey Heatherington (2011), as part of a special collection that looked at case studies across Europe, is also critical of the increased expectations on farms in multifunctional discourse—in particular, the increased pressure on farms as they are expected to perform agri-tourism, eco-tourism, and heritage conservation. She notes: "These policy discourses also suggest that peasant farmers have been (or might be, with proper intervention) successfully transformed into cosmopolitan actors/consumers in their own right. This approach generates some ironies and double binds for the farmers themselves" (13). Beyond increased farm expectations, others have more direct concerns with policy outcomes. For example, high nature value (HNV) farming is often integrated into many aspects of multifunctionality regarding ecosystem services. Ideally, HNV transcends the binary of production versus environment by acknowledging the interdependence of nature and society (Folke et al. 2010). Yet as Eileen O'Rourke's (2019; O'Rourke et al. 2016) work in County Kerry has pointed out, HNV areas are far from diversity havens and instead can more often be better understood as poverty traps—characterized by social disadvantage, poor services, and population decline. Indeed, O'Rourke has argued that a focus on multifunctionality often affirms rather than counters an increasing tendency toward farm intensification and specialization.

With an eye to these criticisms, I suggest we focus instead on one of the mechanisms that often lead to diverse farm outputs: flexibility. By the term *flexibility*, I mean to emphasize the shifting decision-making and relationships required to adapt to changing policy, schemes, environmental conditions, and social and familial needs. Certainly, farm multifunctionality may be an outcome of such flexibility, but so too can the type of creative decision-making that sometimes frustrates planners or undermines scheme outcomes. Combining a recognition of this flexibility with that of rural livelihood literature helps integrate meaning making into discussions of the rural economy.

What do I mean by livelihood? Often grounded in development studies, classic views of livelihood are based on a society's techniques to meet subsistence needs according to the resources available, that is, the concrete manner in which it made a living (Kaag et al. 2004). In the discipline of geography, early ideas of livelihood were usually linked to regional studies, but anthropologists tended to tie livelihood to more material subsistence techniques, such as foraging, horticulture, pastoralism, and agriculture. However, by the 1970s, in most disciplines the concept of livelihood expanded beyond needs to include wants and desires. Looking to build sustainable livelihoods in developing nations, various development programs adopted this more inclusive idea of livelihood. As a consequence, by the 1980s the idea of livelihood was entrenched within development studies and programs.[2] Leo J. de Haan (2012), a development scholar himself, builds on the idea of livelihood by expanding it as a system that comprises the capabilities, assets (including material and social resources), and activities required for living. In this and other works, livelihood shifts away from an isolated and identifiable practice toward a collection of activities and relationships that allow people to make a living *and* make it meaningful.

An inclusive expansion of livelihood beyond mode of subsistence is central to understanding the idea of flexible rural economies today. Anthony Bebbington (2000), a geographer who has worked extensively on the idea of livelihood related to Campesinos (small farmers or peasants) in Ecuador and elsewhere in Latin America, has done extensive work on this topic. He argues that when considering livelihood or the rural poor, we need to examine the creative ways people build economically viable strategies that may be neither agricultural nor rural. In such cases, the money and resources gathered from working away, taking advantage of development programs, and creatively drawing on social resources are parts of livelihood. Like people in many marginal and underdeveloped areas of the world, the state labels Campesinos as "non-viable" and considered to be wasting resources under a neoliberal model. Bebbington argues that where rural people have not been able to improve their livelihoods, the principal reasons seem to derive from a failure or inability to defend their existing assets, identify and secure opportunities to turn assets into livelihoods, or protect existing ways of turning assets into livelihoods (e.g., by losing a place in a market). In other words, and for my own purposes, a diverse and flexible livelihood means diverse and flexible assets (material, social, and otherwise).

Ethnographic perspectives and methods lend themselves well to exploring such complexity. Rhoda H. Halperin's (1990) examination of rural livelihood in Kentucky is an excellent example of this. Halperin outlines a detailed view of what she terms the Kentucky Way—ties to land and family that confer dignity and self-esteem. Halperin explores multiple family-oriented livelihood strategies, including subsistence farming, factory work, marketplaces, and extended kin networks.

---

2 Both de Haan (2012) and Mayke Kaag and colleagues (2004) provide succinct summaries of this history.

Her work reveals the diverse and locally specific engagements between people and nature with flexibility as a point of pride and ties to land paramount. Like Bebbington's work in Latin America, Jason G. Strange's (2020) work with homesteaders in Appalachia, and countless other rural ethnographic pieces, Halperin firmly established that ways of getting by are cultural, complex, flexible, and adaptive in ways that cannot be easily folded into the farm multifunctionality rhetoric.

Building on all of this, I understand livelihood as a frame that brings attention to the various relations that collectively culminate in the material needs of life and to the meaning of that effort. As a frame, the livelihood approach pushes us to emphasize the complex relations embedded in the economic, including relations with the other-than-human, when we examine how people get by. An inclusive idea of livelihood is crucial in the ongoing effort to step away from the delineated categories that often order and measure economic productivity (income, employment, property ownership) and move toward what is actually happening on the ground, however messy or seemingly contradictory that might be. James C. Scott's (1998, 46) reminder that the simplifications necessary for statecraft "are always more static and schematic than the actual social phenomena they presume to typify" is a precursor to recent calls to question taken-for-granted categories and easily packaged questions and answers (Latour et al. 2018; Tsing 2015) and to embrace and stay with the complexity of actual life and its various messes—to stay with the trouble (Haraway 2016).

CREATIVE SOLUTIONS AND UNPREDICTABLE OUTCOMES

Like most farmers in Ireland, Connor draws income from a series of agricultural and conservation schemes. How much revenue, how often, and the expected return are variable depending on the scheme. Such monies are income, but are they "work" in the sense of productive use of land and labour? Likewise, how are other income-generating activities understood in terms of work? A livelihood frame allows for an inclusive approach to work and productivity. Inclusivity is essential because the premise of the binary productive/unproductive is central to upland development narratives and the economic and cultural evaluation of farms and farmers (whether among farmers themselves or from the outside) that I would like to question here. Many rural areas have long-standing traditions of making ends meet in various ways and keeping options deliberately open (figure 8). In such a space, land and people need to produce something, even if it is just a payment.

An example that might be useful here is my first meeting with Magda and Finn while volunteering with a rural work team. The Department of Social Protection oversees several employment schemes meant to assist skill building and work

Figure 8. Selling cows in town at the mart. Author photo.

experience among unemployed or underemployed individuals. One of these is the Tús program, in which an unemployed person who qualifies can work 19.5 hours a week on local projects. Another is the Rural Social Scheme (RSS), which is explicitly aimed at local farmers and fisher folk who receive social assistance (i.e., have low income). RSS adds to their income in exchange for services that benefit rural communities, and organizations like IRD Duhallow can be one of the organizing points for such work. Under ideal circumstances, existing skills in fencing, managing animals, building, operating equipment, and so on can be harnessed to benefit the community. Finn, Magda, and I spent the better part of three days navigating the thorny briars of tall blackberry bushes to pull Himalayan balsam and plant alder. Planting the stems of alder trees along the drainage dikes and hedges was a stipulation for pulling Himalayan balsam, as the landowner liked the look of the species on his land and deliberately let his fields fallow because, according to Magda, "he liked nature." Removing the invasive balsam was part of IRD's funding deliverables for an environmental scheme. In exchange for being granted access to his land, we worked to build up the species diversity. Unused to the terrain and the flora, my hands were cut up and filled with thorns and my feet were wet by the end of each day. However, the work gave me a good sense of what it meant to move across the landscape, engage with its various species, and talk about life in Duhallow with the other workers.

Magda had twelve acres of land and three horses. She wanted to get a herd number to be a registered farmer and be able to pull from the Common Agricultural Policy or the RSS program. I later visited her home, the original structure dating back to 1905 and heated entirely by peat. She is not Irish; she moved to the country with her husband from mainland Europe and later divorced but was keen to stay in the uplands. She had an extensive garden and drew income from numerous small sources—including selling garden goods, working odd jobs, boarding horses, and getting support from Tús—all while living as frugally as possible. She spent as much time outside as she could, and her ultimate goal was to expand her land and build up a small farm. She was smart, funny, and welcoming and was kind enough on one occasion to take me on a drive around her farm, showing me where she picked up her peat from a local harvester and taking me to a hill being developed for wind turbines, which she found disruptive and worrying.

Although he appeared much older, Finn was in his late fifties, probably only ten years older than Magda. He had seventy-three acres and grew up on the farm he still lives on. At the time of our meeting, he had "about ten cows and a few horses," though at one time the farm had had far more livestock, including sheep and chickens. He also had a wind turbine on his land that paid money each year (Finn and Magda, who were friendly with each other, disagreed on how long this would continue) and a small plot of forestry that likewise provided annual income, but for how much longer Finn was unsure (he didn't like trees but felt people should have the choice to plant if they wanted). He had worked with the RSS program for around eleven years. Finn said that RSS and the turbine and trees gave him enough money to allow him to go to the pub. By his own account and the accounts of others, this was a too-common pastime.

For Finn, Magda, and many others I met, income from a patchwork of social assistance, farm schemes, transporting animals, renting out pastures, applying silage to neighbouring fields, planting trees, having a wind turbine or two, drawing on money from children in the city, and so on is lumped together with farm income or working second jobs. Though not all these methods were equally prestigious, such diversity was the norm, and the consensus was that it was actually *good* practice to take advantage of any opportunity available. Flexible livelihoods are adaptive ways to take advantage of shifting opportunities and draw on social, cultural, and environmental knowledge, even if not always understood as "work." Finn, Magda, and Connor were doing just that.

To think more about what is valued as labour, I turned to theorist Kathi Weeks (2011), who has argued that scholars should critically examine the notions attached to work rather than focus purely on labour itself, including its reification, depoliticization, normativity, and moralization. Her broader discussion is a critique of the idea that people should live for work, reframing questions of work beyond the production of inequalities toward the political problem of freedom. All of this matters because, as she reminds us, what is produced and reproduced through labour (or its refusal) includes identities and social-political subjects.

Certainly, in Duhallow and elsewhere in rural Ireland, the productivity of farms and farmer is highly political. State and international apparatuses are structured to support and value certain forms of labour for different political purposes. Ideologically, the small-scale work of the family farm is culturally reified and even nurtured somewhat through specific funding mechanisms. Yet economically, a region's financial productivity is a key measure of development. According to state goals (and often farmers' sense of "good" farming), unproductive land should be used for something; as a package deal, this desire to have a productive environment comes with landowners who work hard and in the right way. For example, the pressure to intensify was a common theme among farmers I spoke with. This feeling was grounded in the idea that small farmers should intensify their practices, rationalize their farm operations, make better use of marginal lands, and expand their farms. Teagasc was often singled out as an organization that promoted expansion and efficiency beyond small farmers' comfort level. Beyond specific organizations, I also developed a sense that progress and success within the community had increasingly become tied to farm expansion and intensification, even in areas where such practices could be less economically viable and perhaps environmentally detrimental.

It is left to individual farmers to navigate the tensions or mistranslations between what is expected of them (the right kind of work) and what is possible or desirable on their part. While failure to be productive in the right way is often interpreted as farmers being ambivalent, unmotivated, or even lazy, in discussions with me, many farmers were openly resistant to the pressure to increase farm productivity. They questioned, for instance, whether farmers in the Vale (the common name for one of Ireland's agriculturally rich regions) were any more satisfied with all their material, labour, and capital inputs than were those with small operations. Many refused their farm adviser's suggestion to bring in more head of cattle or try to drain fields, instead remaining unruly through their steadfast commitment to schemes, a few head of cattle, and small side jobs or in-town work. Some farmers admitted to doing so because of fatigue or defeatism (they had perhaps already tried to improve fields, for example), but others, particularly younger or well-educated farmers, consciously stated a desire to raise children or work a farm on terms that best suited them. This difference in interpretation of what constitutes "good" farming or how much effort someone should put into their farm manifested as criticisms between farmers in the community and also in the less-than-favourable opinions of farm planners and Teagasc representatives who wished small farmers would modernize, educate themselves, and farm differently.

From the state's perspective, such fluidity is not ideal, for at least two reasons. First, to use Scott's (1998) terminology, local ways of knowing and getting by are illegible to state mechanisms that emphasize structured and measurable social, cultural, and natural features (22). The patchwork of incomes outlined above is unstable, does not prioritize growth, and is difficult to measure and track; it is bureaucratically indigestible. Second, flexible livelihoods can result in unpredictable or undesired outcomes from an administrative perspective.

An example of the second point is how working to scheme and moving between schemes means that farmers are both receptive to state-led plans to adjust the shape of their human-environment interactions and frustratingly fickle in their commitment to long-term landscape change. Every farmer I met in Duhallow was enrolled in at least one farming scheme, as most farmers in Ireland are. Many were also simultaneously involved in, and ridiculed the idea of, farming to scheme (undertaking the minimal effort necessary to qualify for monetary compensation). As schemes change from cycle to cycle to represent broader economic, social, and political goals, it makes sense for farmers to limit their commitment to each endeavor.

Donkeys are a good example of the creative solutions Irish farmers can use to get by. On the trip on which I was accompanied by my family, our first home was a short-term rental while we looked for something closer to Duhallow communities. To my children's delight, behind our rented home were a simple two-string electric fence and two friendly donkeys who loved to be scratched and hand-fed clumps of grass. Donkeys have a long cultural and farm history in Ireland, and the animal has become a common symbol of the Irish farm. Able to survive and work in terrain too difficult for other animals—particularly horses, which were also very expensive—donkeys were a necessary work animal until the mid-twentieth century (for an engaging overview of the Irish donkey, see Smyth 2014). Today, however, donkeys are kept as either companion animals or livestock units (LU) that allow owners to draw from the Areas of Natural and Specific Constraint (ANC) Scheme (previously known as the Disadvantaged Areas Scheme) administered by the Department of Agriculture, Food and the Marine (2021), resulting in as much as €148 per hectare in 2001. Much of upland Duhallow is considered an area of natural constraint; as such, money is available to support farmers in less favourable areas as long as they have the required number of LUs.

Because registered horses (limited eligibility after a rule change in 2012) and donkeys counted as eligible LUs, it became common practice for many upland fields and farms to host two or more donkeys. Such schemes saw a marked increase in donkey ownership in areas of natural constraint. For example, in 2008, the year the legislation was published that included donkeys in Ireland, the number of registered donkeys increased from 216 to 1,678. Although registrations fell off in the following years, they again expanded rapidly, from 426 donkeys registered in 2011 to 2,035 registered in 2012—the year changes in ANC eligibility added restrictions to horses as LUs (Collins et al. 2018). Joseph A. Collins and colleagues likewise contemplate the unintended consequences as the Department of Agriculture, Food and the Marine implements or considers new legislation including age requirements (which might produce more breeding and foals), restrictions (which might result in donkey abandonment), and concerns over donkey welfare that Ireland's very busy donkey sanctuary has taken up (including adding more farm visits, education, re-homing, and four sanctuary farms). While the ANC scheme is intended to support the upkeep of regions with difficult terrain, soil, and weather as well as to supplement farm income, its rules were creatively interpreted by Irish farmers and resulted in unanticipated outcomes such as a donkey boom in areas like upland Duhallow.

Another unpredictable component of farmer behaviour stems from local ambivalence to committed long-term change. My help with the RSS work is a case in point. Each work team member I spoke to was not optimistic that farmers would keep up the landscape changes we initiated beyond the investment of time required by the project: to mend fences, keep watch for invasive species, keep cattle out of streams, and manage hedges. That is not to say that people did not put in a strong work effort; it was just that for both project farmers and workers, the goal was their wages more than the project's deliverables. While this ambivalence might be frustrating to those trying to better the biodiversity in areas or to simplify and contain landscapes, it makes perfect sense in a place where economic, environmental, and political stability is uncertain. For instance, on Darragh's farm (the large dairy farm bordering his brother's dairy farm mentioned in chapter 3), most fields were "improved"— tidy, green, smooth. But some were wetter and closer to riparian areas. He spoke of his initial efforts at cutting hedges as required by schemes to open up these fields, then later at fencing and blocking off fields and encouraging the kind of growth he had earlier been paid to limit. As part of a current scheme, the area was fenced off to keep cattle out, although he anticipated removing the fences once the scheme was complete. The farmer in question knew the rotation of changes he was asked to implement in his one small field was nonsensical. His knowledge informed him that removing the hedges was a bad idea and that keeping out all grazing (rather than limited grazing) would encourage the growth of undesirable plants. Instead, he complied in adjusting the use of his wetter field to best profit from schemes while running the rest of his farm as he saw fit and ensuring that his entire farm was productive in some way—a field that pulls in money is productive.

The plantation decisions upland farmers make are another example of their perceived problematic choices. Recall that the lands farmers choose for plantations are often their poorest fields: areas that are steep, difficult to reach, overly wet, or small and out of the way. These fields are preferred by farmers not because they make for the best trees and therefore the most income when harvested but because they can bring in additional income without limiting the use of other lands for different purposes. As outlined in chapter 5, upland farmers who plant in less-than-ideal areas or resist planting altogether are considered illogical, irrational, or uneducated by those seeking to establish systematic and productive forests. Like abundant donkeys or less-than-enthusiastic scheme commitment, such choices make good sense for landowners whose livelihood rests on flexible and creative adaptations to getting by and who are intimately aware of their precarious relationship with the human and non-human that surround them. Likewise, farmers who break the rules—such as those I saw cutting their forested lots without permission with the hope that they will not get caught, or spraying slurry outside of the designated time frame, or maintaining older practices that the state tries to change through education programs—are problematic individuals by the measure of bureaucrats, program managers, and others whose job it is to oversee various components of landscape use in Duhallow.

Both bureaucratic illegibility and local unpredictability result in part because the materiality of nature, coupled with the complexity of the social systems that are co-constitutive of it, do not map well onto the schematic simplifications necessary to manage the unwieldy apparatus of the state. In exploring this, it is worth considering the role of the non-human environment. Building off of Weeks's ideas of work, Sarah Besky and Alex Blanchette (2019) explored labour as extended to the non-human. The authors provide a series of examples through which nature "works upon us, against us, and perhaps with us" (3), inviting speculation on the work of nature. Indeed, resources and natural systems and services have an existing value that can be salvaged (where nature turns into a resource, according to Scott), but the capacity of nature to work—or refuse to work as desired—adds another element to upland livelihood.

Farmers are acutely aware of what their fields will and will not do, and marginal areas are labeled as such precisely because they are uncooperative with broader goals of scalable production and simplification. Upland fields are filled with ruins of attempted "improvement" in the form of overgrown hedges that once clearly delineated fields, clogged drains that were too much trouble to maintain, or species composition that shows deliberate although failed attempts to turn wet areas into reliable pasture. Cultural records also hold indicators of moments when nature refused to work altogether—for instance, in stories and songs of bog slides, like the local "traveling bog" poem wherein a hillside slipped and slid through numerous farmyards. The poem was referenced in correlation with a local worry that forestry may cause such devastating moments[3] and to remind me that land can be unstable. With such stories in mind, I call Duhallow uplands uncooperative because they do not fully submit to the discipline of humans—their productivity cannot be easily scaled through the proper application of technology or behaviour. Local farmers are well aware of the land's limits, although they are still engaged in a creative relationship that tests those boundaries. Not only does land work, but it is likewise moralized—"this land is very poorly," as Connor would say. It is also politicized through its various categorizations and incorporation into planning systems, terminology, and property structures; and its normativity is undoubtedly present in attempts at scalable projects and simplification. This is all to say that nature's materiality is a social-ecological force to be reckoned with in its own right. Human labour is often an ecological relationship, and as noted by environmental historian Thomas G. Andrews (2008), the efficacy of labour is tied as much to the labouring environment as it is to human ingenuity or skill.

Flexible livelihoods make particular sense in uncooperative places, especially when we consider the role of precarity and surprise. William Boyd and colleagues (2001) explore the role of material nature in nature-centred production, and the authors posit that much political economy theory fails to grapple with the dynamics of nature itself when tackling the "problem of nature." In particular, a focus on static obstacles ignores the dynamic aspects of natural systems, rendering them variable, unpredictable, and capable of surprise (560). Surprise is an important word because it acknowledges the agency of other-than-human species and emphasizes the creative possibilities that can spontaneously emerge at any intersection of living beings and the inanimate world (bogs move, plants spread, birds roost, and so on). An approach to the non-human world that recognises the capacity for surprise is increasingly a focus for cross-disciplinary scholars grappling with the unexpected outcomes that become visible when people stay with the trouble, that is, leaning into and exploring complexity and contradiction rather than producing palatable but incomplete explanations.[4] Following Tsing (2015), I understand precarity as acknowledging that we are always vulnerable to others, including non-humans, where indeterminacy and life without the promise of stability are expected. Acknowledging precarity is also an acknowledgment of the surprise that can emerge

---

3   Indeed, with four such slides occurring in 2020, there does seem to be some potential correlation (Dykes 2022).
4   See Tsing and colleagues (2017) for an excellent example of this effort. Earlier work, such as Gregory Bateson's (1979) insistence that ecological queries (among others) remain relationship centred and therefore focus on the dynamism of the now rather than the permanency of the object, is also useful.

from nodes of intersecting relations, histories, and processes that cross species boundaries. Human lives are intermingled with and depend on the other-than-human. Farmers are well aware that strict lines between nature and culture are illusions. Part of the work they and their ancestors are involved in is producing nature. In turn, nature has produced them; they are fully aware of what precarity means.

THE SALVAGE VALUE OF FLEXIBLE LIVELIHOODS IN PERIPHERAL PLACES

Flexible livelihoods might make sense in the face of precarity (and, being cautious to avoid romanticism, I don't mean to suggest that stability and abundance would not be welcome when possible), but they are often interpreted as problematic by anyone who wants more rigid or predictable local outcomes. Poverty has very real negative consequences for upland residents, and these are concerns at the household, municipal, county, and national levels. While this is not desirable, the state and investors can utilize the underdeveloped narrative to suit existing goals because such areas are framed as in need of *something* or lacking in some way. As such, while locals may resist modernizing their practices and fully participating in new projects at times, their refusal to do so leaves open a conceptual space of possibility.[5] As long as no use-value is successfully dominant (for instance, tourism), the lack fuels potential. In such a way, marginal areas with comparable low populations primed for development can be spaces for curating particular geographic and economic narratives, a resource of untapped potential. This is especially the case because locals' inclusive and creative economies mean there is an existing receptiveness to new initiatives and projects. Even if the results are not what was hoped, many people in such areas are open to trying new schemes and land-use opportunities. Farmers like Finn, who might be thought of as old-fashioned or behind the times because of his lack of commitment to a single productive course of action, provide a potential reception point for new ideas. This space for potential is required for Robert Fletcher (2023, 160) and Mads Borup and colleagues' (2006) economy of expectation that is central to neoliberal conservation, "which attains support through the promise of concrete benefits that are perpetually deferred into the future."

The intersection of geographic conceptual emptiness and receptive, flexible economies is a particular form of fertile ground. Recent trends in the increasing commodification of nature have found success in areas like Duhallow, where the overlapping space of wind turbines, forest plantations, conservation, and upland farming is not an accident. This is particularly the case given the requirements of

---

5 Farmers at times have fully committed to waves of modernization, albeit often with upsetting outcomes. See, for example, Mark T. Shutes's work in County Kerry (1991, 2015a).

green policy and programs that need to be enacted somewhere; imaginary potential needs a place to sit.

As one quick example, I turn to forests as a climate change mitigation strategy. The 2022 Intergovernmental Panel on Climate Change (IPCC) cites afforestation/reforestation (categorized as such) as a targeted climate change mitigation strategy. New forest commitments are emerging, such as the United Nations Decade on Ecosystem Restoration in 2021 and the Glasgow Declaration on Forests, which aims to halt illegal deforestation by 2030 (UKCOP26 2021). These commitments are occurring on top of already existing commitments like the Bonn Challenge (to bring 150 million hectares of degraded and deforested landscapes globally into restoration by 2020[6] and 350 million hectares by 2030) and the United Nations Sustainable Development Goals (e.g., Goal 15: protect, restore and promote sustainable use of terrestrial ecosystems, sustainably manage forests, combat desertification, and halt and reverse land degradation and halt biodiversity loss). Forests are also often implicated in strategies to reduce carbon outputs by increasing carbon storage as well as in broad conservation goals, such as the EU Biodiversity Strategy (European Commission 2021) (with the goal of 10% of strictly protected terrestrial and marine ecosystems by 2030) and the United Nations Convention on Biological Diversity "30 × 30" target (a call for protecting 30% of the world's terrestrial and marine habitats by 2030). All of this must happen somewhere.

At the time of writing, Ireland's most recent rural development strategy (Government of Ireland 2021) is a broad look at rural development that emphasizes diverse strategic priorities, including accessible broadband, an increase in rural populations, job development, revitalized communities, and so on. Within this, a central thread is "supporting a just transition to a climate-neutral economy." Part of this thread is to deliver an ambitious plan to achieve an afforestation target of 8,000 ha/year. The report (O'Driscoll and Moore 2019) cited forestry as an important land use at the centre of Ireland's transition to a low-carbon, sustainable future and noted that 40 percent of the roundwood used in the Republic of Ireland was for energy generation.[7] The report noted that planting trees can play an important role in increasing and diversifying farm income and that by "incorporating forestry into the farming mix, agricultural production can continue alongside timber

---

6 Results for this goal are still being calculated.
7 This statistic appears to be drawn from the 2019 Timber Market Report (O'Driscoll and Moore 2019). According to this report, sawn timber, wood-based panels, and energy are the primary uses for wood in Ireland. In 2018, use of forest biomass for energy generation included using residues for fuel in the timber sector (roundwood, sawmills, and wood-based panels) such as bark, sawdust, and woodchips. It also included manufactured products such as charcoal, wood pellets, and briquettes. Use of wood for firewood is also included in this statistic.

production while delivering both economic and environmental benefits" (84). As a broad green strategy, the state suggested that wind energy, geothermal energy, forestry, water, waste management, and carbon sequestration all have the potential to support sustainable rural livelihoods in Ireland.

While conservation and a shift away from carbon-intensive economies are necessary and urgent needs, these processes and others like them also have the additional effect of commodifying nature as a scarce resource. Wim Carton and Elina Anderson (2017) provide an excellent breakdown of the processes involved in the commodification of nature by examining forestry-based offsetting as a subsumption of nature. They argue that the commodification of nature involves not just the appropriation or "grabbing" of an "already-existing" nature but also the discursive and material reworking of nature (831). This reworking makes it more amenable to particular needs, in their case, carbon market imperatives. In upland Duhallow, nature is conceptually and materially reworked to meet both development and conservation needs while playing on the natural upland aesthetic, marginal economic status, and the potential of multifunctional agriculture. In other words, "poorly land" is good for nature and therefore an economic opportunity. Locals who are receptive to ways to make a little cash or who can be framed as "in need" can ease this process. The commodification of nature through scarcity is an extraordinary economic opportunity (Smith 2006).

Let's look at plantations as an example of this dynamic. The plantation model relies on land availability, which increasingly means convincing private landowners to plant their land with trees. This model works best in areas where locals are receptive to new income streams and land-use shifts: people strapped for cash, with less–intensively used land, who have a tradition of combining different income streams and livelihood strategies. Thus, they are an existing value that can be salvaged and taken advantage of for profit. So who profits aside from some landowners or investment firms? When taken together, treed plots become a forest, a conceptual reworking that meets a specific need: the scarcity of nature. As forests, plantations meet this need and become a commodity for the state. Specifically, plantations provide something beyond wood; they are carbon storage banks needed for Ireland to meet its green goals. In this way, many things are created that, using Smith's argument, have only a momentary symbolic connection to the specific work that gave rise to them. While beef, milk, and grass production are directly tied to farmers' labour in a material way and are part of a complex relationship, forests are fairly far removed from the idea of actual production. However, they are nevertheless important exports of the region and rely on taking advantage of flexible economic strategies while packaging the entire effort as benevolent development. Forest planners might complain about farmers' uncooperativeness and somewhat erratic or contradictory planting habits, but the economic strategy that underlies this is the key to meeting tree planting targets.

Now let's turn to Special Protected Areas (SPAs). Political ecologists are well-versed in conservation as a form of resource control, which, however well-intentioned, often interferes with local livelihood while prioritizing external values in a specific place (Robbins 2019). In Duhallow, the particularly sticky issue is the EU's recognition that low-intensity farming is a desirable strategy in supporting increased biodiversity, meaning that EU strategies often recognise people as part of a co-created environment (Neumann 2014). Rather than the much-critiqued fortress protection model, the Natura 2000 network, of which the Stack's SPA is a part, was meant to contribute to a broader paradigm shift that incorporates private landowners and co-constructs management principles. Despite this effort, the protected areas that stemmed from the Natura 2000 initiative have been criticized as top-down, with science and ecology first (Bryan 2012). In examining the system's social and spatial boundaries, Sharon Bryan notes, "It is particularly ironic perhaps that the vast majority of designated sites considered of high nature value are located in these poor quality agricultural lands where livelihoods are particularly vulnerable" (85). Ireland's SPAs were established by combining existing hen harrier data with knowledge of habitat preference. As such, not only known hen harrier sites (some of which were known and not protected) but the type of land cover that is typical in marginal areas were considered prime hen harrier ground. While economically unproductive, this plan was biologically productive enough to support an endangered species of special concern.

Initially, many locals were quick to sign on to the original hen harrier scheme that would pay farmers for desired habitat type in exchange for losing potential use-value (the land could not be substantially improved). However, after it was fully realized that the SPA, like other schemes, was not an opt-in approach and the original payment scheme was discontinued, many farmers were angry about the land-use change, in part because it limited their future options. So who benefits from the SPA scheme, aside from—at least ideally—the hen harrier? Its origins at the EU level meant the Irish government was compelled to protect scarce nature (in the form of hen harrier habitat), and underdeveloped areas that met habitat requirements constituted value the state could use to meet these requirements with potential uptake (initially) by locals. Later disputes were more easily ignored because of the region's marginal status and low population density.

This is an example of the subsumption of nature (Smith 2006) in which neoliberal processes integrate nature, in increasingly complex and in-depth ways, with capital (all the way up, all the way down). Smith offers an important critique of the ways nature has become increasingly transformed into a biodiversity bank, facilitating the commodification of nature beyond the typical harvesting of raw material to excavating previously existing social-natural relations. In other words, it is not just milk, meat, or wood produced but a concept (biodiversity, carbon sequestration, habitat) that can be used as capital in strategic state and industry negotiations. However, as Smith likewise notes (20), this intensified commodification, marketization, and financialization of nature that is part of the larger project of neoliberalism is not a smooth process and is far from complete. This is not a purely theoretical problem. When researchers point out that the global and national processes that shape much of political and economic life are incomplete, the gaps that remain manifest in locally specific ways. In these local manifestations of tensions, contradictions, and decision-making embedded in local livelihoods, we can trace the ways policy and other national and international features are lived.

CONCLUSION

Neoliberalism has seen the expansion of the contract labourer, the full embracing of part-time work and piecemeal wages that results in the "gig" economy. This shift is often morally packaged together with the much-lauded characteristics of independence and entrepreneurialism (Tirapani and Willmott 2022). In Ireland, especially in less prosperous areas, this has long been the means of local independence *and* subjugation. A fine line exists between pushing against the constraints of being a productive and fully integrated member of capitalist society and becoming even more embedded within it by selling one's labour in increasingly creative ways. The willingness of marginalized people to creatively "get by" is at the heart of peri-capitalism. For farmers who are culturally entangled with the obligation and potential of land and independence, such mechanisms are interpreted in locally specific ways.

One of the core features of neoliberalism is its ability to accommodate local specificity. Noel Castree (2010), in his synthesis of works on neoliberalism and the biophysical environment, provides six broad lessons or trends he found in examining how policies born out of a neoliberal context tend to play out in actuality; all of them apply to the Duhallow case study. First, creating markets in environmental goods, services, and assets typically requires considerable state intervention, meaning this is not simply a private supply-and-demand process. We can see this in the way the state implements and subsidizes its forest and conservation goals in Duhallow. Second, careful adaptation to biophysical obstacles is necessary in this process (i.e., in this case, working with and adapting to troublesome ground and what it can provide). Third, careful adaptation to local socio-cultural and political-economic contexts is also necessary—for instance, working with and taking advantage of attachment to property and local ways of getting by. Fourth, because of this, neoliberal environmental policy tends to be impure or diverse in the sense that local contextual adaptations often produce contradictions and geographic differences in the ways neoliberal models are applied. These contradictions are part of the landscape locals navigate in their land-use decisions. Fifth, such processes tend to disadvantage the poor and powerless, for example, with loss of land control and reduced property values. Finally, creating markets in environmental goods and services produces environmental improvements as much as problems and vice versa. More specifically, in this case, Rob Kitchin and colleagues (2012) have argued that neoliberalism plays out in unique ways in Ireland, in part because, among other things, the British colonization of Ireland created a long history of conflict relating to the ownership and control of land and property. In other words, local ways of getting by that emerged historically through a colonial context and that make sense in uncooperative places can also be easily co-opted as salvage value—and to Castree's last observation, the entanglement of improvement (forest cover or hen harrier habitat, for example) and the problems such improvement creates are so common as to be expected.

Precarity is a well-known state for small farmers who are fully aware of their entangled relations with processes and beings outside of their control. I have argued in this chapter that this populace's flexible livelihoods make perfect sense when understood in this context. Furthermore, while not seen as productive by official measures, lack of conformity does provide endless spaces of intervention for state-led initiatives and, as such, is a central resource for ongoing projects. Both Ireland's SPA system and its plantation model benefit from this area's rural, marginal, underdeveloped narrative and the willingness of locals to try something new. However, they both also undo the flexibility that upland farmers use to survive. One of the most significant issues stemming from this is perhaps the fact that the SPA and afforestation limit the many forms of flexible economies in which low-intensity farming exists. The SPAs succeed in simultaneously protecting regions and undoing the mechanisms through which the desired populace might subsist, and afforestation locks in land use into the foreseeable future, even over generations. While this work has focused on a single, some might say unremarkable, region, it is almost certain that these same economic trends and development or conservation decisions extend beyond north County Cork.

7

Conclusion

During an interview, a farmer told me in frustration, "they are trying to weed us out." The statement was in reference to the policies and government officials he felt were making his life difficult to maintain, including zoning decisions, forestry expansion, conservation, and regulations on farm activity. This statement came after days of work crawling on my hands and knees through briars while pulling unwanted species from riverbanks as part of the Rural Social Scheme (RSS) work described earlier in the book. The metaphor has stayed with me since. Who—human or otherwise—was welcome in this space? Were farmers being pushed out, or were they just being difficult and contrary as a few government workers had suggested? When people weed places, they curate them, working their form into a desired shape through the joint acts of welcoming and dissuading. Both of those forces have been at play in Duhallow for a very long time.

I set out in this book to explore upland livelihood in an out-of-the-way corner of County Cork. In doing so, I hoped to braid together livelihood, environmental policy, species conservation, and rural development as a lived space occupied by those who navigate contradictions and tensions through their daily choices. This type of representation is important because it is increasingly what farming looks like in a policy-heavy environment. Our current and collective global ecological crisis is staggering in its enormity and complexity, yet the desire for increased production, propelled by massive consumption of goods, has not abated. As a result, exploration and production are moving into regions previously considered too marginal or difficult to reach and changing the social and power dynamics of places once thought to be insulated from such forces (Willow 2014). New schemes require places to occur and people to apply them after all, and I see one of these places in the small family farms of upland Duhallow.

As a so-called marginal area, the landscape is conceptually able to contain many possible futures, which—through political discourse—can draw on narratives of underdevelopment, green development, biodiversity strongholds, and family farming, depending on context and need. Such open-ended expectation results from the fundamental contradictions within and among environmental policy, economic development goals, and land-use regulations that insist that we can have it all. The changes ushered in through multifunctional farm rhetoric and associated schemes, as well as increased pressures for environmental conservation, exist in addition to farm modernization and productivity expectations, demanding increasingly more from the same spaces and people. Such contradictions, left unaddressed, threaten to undo the potential gains of any well-meaning project and add to the burden of those whose daily choices involve their navigation.

In telling the story of this area, I also endeavoured to integrate a series of parallel stories co-occurring with the lives of local farmers, in which animals and plants build landscapes in unexpected ways. The disorganized war on invasive species waged by local organizations occurs in parallel with administrative changes that make it increasingly difficult for young farmers to build new homes on their farms. Likewise, small-detail land-use policies that try to entice the presence of hen harriers or ensure clean water for the freshwater pearl mussel by cultivating certain fields occur in parallel with land-use restrictions that shape the nature of farming. Small farmers can read these efforts as an attempt to "eradicate" them from the land, yet their flexible economies can also take advantage of the income such efforts provide. When placed in a historical context, it is clear that the narrative of marginal land reflects shifting national priorities and the failure of local lands and community members to be correspondingly productive. This lack of productivity continues to be used as a framework to justify overlapping green initiatives and development goals that symbolically and materially overburden the area. Recent academic, EU, and government acknowledgments that such unproductivity cultivates biodiversity (a necessary form of productivity) have yet to manifest in any real change in the way the region and its residents are depicted. Instead, making such visions materialize is downloaded onto locals whose shoulders bear the burden of manifesting multiple, contradictory narratives.

Yet Duhallow farmers are not passive actors in this process; instead, they work to navigate this increasingly demanding political and economic environment in ways that make local sense. Understanding upland livelihood through the lens of flexible economies, including engaging in off-farm labour and securing schemes, illuminates rural longevity and local responses to various green initiatives. Such flexibility is an integral part of shifting green and development initiatives, of which afforestation is one. However, Ireland's current forest plantation model can potentially limit such flexibility more permanently than other initiatives because plantations withdraw land from private and community use, producing new forms of ownership that result in the slow-moving alienation of farmers from their farms while encouraging state and industry control over local resources. This process occurs while *discursively*, plantations supply the elements demanded by the broader forests category—including recreation, increased biodiversity, clean water, and clean air—a curated story that those who live in the area never see manifested on the landscape.

Ethnographic descriptions aim to illuminate such nuances as those described above, helping readers better understand local realities and the logic behind decision-making. Ultimately, ethnography attempts to foreground the richness of local lifeways and acts as an invitation for collective understanding, empathy, and appreciation of commonalities and differences. Through this description of what it means to live in upland Duhallow, the importance of rural places, their values, attachments, and resource calculations were central, as were the ongoing struggles of what it means to shoulder the burden of navigating systemic contradictions in the very soil one loves.

While this book represents a single case study, I believe a broader return to the rural in Irish anthropology, and perhaps anthropology more generally, is necessary to understand the implications of green neoliberalism and subsequent emerging property and livelihood dynamics in marginal regions worldwide. As noted in the book's introduction, rural areas are sites of important processes, including Europeanization and globalization, and indeed are the material focus of a green turn in capitalist production. Anthropology plays a crucial role in telling this story by concentrating on the everyday, ordinary aspects of life and using engaged methods that prioritize local voices and realities to tell the stories of environmental and social change. Specifically, it aims to express the context in which organisms live, not by idealizing or reducing these aspects into fixed notions of place and community but by embracing the tension that exists within them. As the expectations offloaded to rural places and peoples grow, ethnographic and locally grounded research can play a crucial role in documenting how, where, and why local change does or does not manifest.

Collectively, the arguments and descriptions in this book act as a material reminder that the enticing futures brought into view through the shallow rhetoric of greenwashing are not innocent. Real landscapes and residents are forced to navigate their consequences while often simultaneously labouring to produce them. However, the flexible nature of rural livelihood likewise incorporates or obfuscates the cyclical opportunities and limits that come with shifting bureaucratic landscape management. What farming, rural living, or land ownership means has historically been adaptable and continues to be so. Yet until the ideas of productivity and marginality themselves are challenged as core assumptions of what it means to have "good" land and to be a "good" farmer, efforts to reshape the human-environment relationship to cultivate human and non-human life will remain conceptual rather than material, adding yet another layer of symbolic meaning onto already overburdened areas.

References

Allan, D. H. 1973. *A History of Newmarket*. Cork Historical Guides Committee.

Allen, Kieran. 2000. *The Celtic Tiger: The Myth of Social Partnership in Ireland*. Manchester University Press.

Andrews, Thomas G. 2008. *Killing for Coal: America's Deadliest Labor War*. Harvard University Press.

Anguiano, Emeric, Catharina Bamps, Jean Terres et al. 2008. "Analysis of Farmland Abandonment and the Extent and Location of Agricultural Areas That Are Actually Abandoned or Are in Risk to Be Abandoned." *EUR 223411 EN*, Publications Office of the European Union: JRC46185.

Arensberg, Conrad M., and Solon T. Kimball. 1968. *Family and Community in Ireland*. Second ed. Harvard University Press.

Asselin, Jodie. 2022. "Plantation Politics and Discourse: Forests and Property in Upland Ireland." *Economic Anthropology* 9 (2): 336–348.

Asselin, Jodie, Gabriel Asselin, and Flavia Egli. 2022. "The Discursive Context of Forest in Land Use Documents: An Irish Case Study." *Nature and Culture* 17 (2): 170–190.

Asselin, Jodie, and Agata Konczal. 2014. "Shifting Forest Perceptions: A Comparative Exploration of Forest Perceptions in Yukon Canada and Tuchola Forest Region of Poland." *Studies and Materials of Forest Culture* 12: 9–23.

Asselin, Jodie, and Allan Mee. 2019. *Duhallow: A Living Landscape for Farming and Wildlife*. IRD Duhallow.

Augère-Granier, Marie-Laure. 2016. "Farm Diversification in the EU." *European Parliamentary Research Service.* Briefing Note PE 581.978 (April): 1–8.

Balaine, Lorraine. 2019. "Gender and the Preservation of Family Farming in Ireland." *Agricultural Economics Society and European Association of Agricultural Economists* 18 (3): 33–37.

Bateson, Gregory. 1979. *Mind and Nature: A Necessary Unity.* E. P. Dutton.

Bax, Mart. 1976. *Harpstrings and Confessions: Machine Style Politics in the Irish Republic.* Van Gorcum, Assen.

Bebbington, Anthony. 2000. "Reencountering Development: Livelihood Transitions and Place Transformations in the Andes." *Annals of the Association of American Geographers* 90 (3): 495–520.

Bellier, Irène, and Thomas M. Wilson, eds. 2000. *An Anthropology of the European Union: Building, Imagining, and Experiencing the New Europe.* Berg.

Besky, Sarah. 2019. "Exhaustion and Endurance in Sick Landscapes: Cheap Tea and the Work of Monoculture in the Dooars, India." In *How Nature Works: Rethinking Labor on a Troubled Planet*, edited by Sarah Besky and Alex Blanchette, 23–40. University of New Mexico Press.

Besky, Sarah, and Alex Blanchette, eds. 2019. *How Nature Works: Rethinking Labor on a Troubled Planet.* University of New Mexico Press.

Birdwell-Pheasant, Donna. 1992. "The Early Twentieth-Century Irish Stem Family: A Case Study from County Kerry." In *Approaching the Past: Historical Anthropology Through Irish Case Studies*, edited by Marilyn Silverman and P. H. Gulliver, 205–235. Columbia University Press.

Bogue, Pat. 2013. *Land Mobility and Succession in Ireland.* Agricultural Trust and the Department of Agriculture, Food and the Marine (Broadmore Research).

Bonsu, Nana O., Áine Ní Dhubháin, and Deirdre O'Connor. 2019. "Understanding Forest Resource Conflicts in Ireland: A Case Study Approach." *Journal of Land Use Policy* 80: 287–297.

Borneman, John, and Nick Fowler. 1997. "Europeanization." *Annual Review of Anthropology* 26 (1): 487–514.

Borras, Saturnino M., Jennifer C. Franco, Sergio Gómez et al. 2012. "Land Grabbing in Latin America and the Caribbean." *Journal of Peasant Studies* 39 (3–4): 845–872.

Borup, Mads, Nik Brown, Kornelia Konrad, and Harro Van Lente. 2006. "The Sociology of Expectations in Science and Technology." *Technology Analysis and Strategic Management* 18: 285–298.

Böttcher, Hannes, and Marcus Lindner. 2010. "Managing Forest Plantations for Carbon Sequestration Today and in the Future." In *Ecosystem Goods and Services from Plantation*

Forests, edited by Jurgen Bauhus, Peter van der Meer, and Markku Kanninen, 43–76. Earthscan.

Boyd, William, W. Scott Prudham, and Rachel A. Schurman. 2001. "Industrial Dynamics and the Problem of Nature." *Society and Natural Resources* 14 (7): 555–570.

Boyle, Mark. 2002. "Clearing up After the Celtic Tiger: Scalar 'Fixes' in the Political Ecology of Tiger Economies." *Transactions of the Institute of British Geographers* 27 (2): 172–194.

Bremer, Leah L., and Kathleen A. Farley. 2010. "Does Plantation Forestry Restore Biodiversity or Create Green Deserts? A Synthesis of the Effects of Land-Use Transitions on Plant Species Richness." *Biodiversity and Conservation* 19 (14): 3893–3915.

Brody, Hugh. 1973. *Inishkillane: Change and Decline in the West of Ireland*. Allen Lane.

Bryan, Sharon. 2012. "Contested Boundaries, Contested Places: The Natura 2000 Network in Ireland." *Journal of Rural Studies* 28 (1): 80–94.

Burton, Rob J. F., and Heike Fischer. 2015. "The Succession Crisis in European Agriculture." *Sociologia Ruralis* 55 (2): 155–166.

Buscardo, Erika, George F. Smith, Daniel L. Kelly et al. 2008. "The Early Effects of Afforestation on Biodiversity of Grasslands in Ireland." *Biodiversity and Conservation* 17: 1057–1072.

Byrne, Anne, Nata Duvvury, Áine Macken-Walsh et al. 2013. *Gender, Power, and Property: "In My Own Right."* Teagasc.

Cadogan, Stephen. 2018. "Discrimination Added to Injustice in Hen Harrier SPAs." *Irish Examiner*, February 15.

Canny, Nicholas. 2001. *Making Ireland British 1580–1650*. Oxford University Press.

Carroll, Matthew S., Áine Ní Dhubháin, and Courtney G. Flint. 2011. "Back Where They Once Belonged? Local Response to Afforestation in County Kerry, Ireland." *Sociologia Ruralis* 51 (1): 35–53.

Carroll, Matthew S., Áine Ní Dhubháin, and Ciaran Nugent. 2009. "Afforestation and Local Residents in County Kerry, Ireland." *Journal of Forestry* 107 (7): 358–363.

Carton, Wim, and Elina Andersson. 2017. "Where Forest Carbon Meets Its Maker: Forestry-Based Offsetting as the Subsumption of Nature." *Society and Natural Resources* 30 (7): 829–843.

Casey, Edward, S. 1997. "How to Get from Space to Place in a Fairly Short Stretch of Time: Phenomenological Prolegomena." In *Senses of Place*, edited by Steven Feld and Keith H. Basso, 13–52. School of American Research Press.

Cassidy, Anne. 2017. "The Agency Paradox: The Impact of Gender(ed) Frameworks on Irish Farm Youth." In *Gender and Rural Globalization: International Perspectives on Gender and Rural Development*, edited by Bettina B. Bock and Sally Shortall, 141–161. Centre for Agriculture and Bioscience International.

Cassidy, Anne, and Brian McGrath. 2014. "The Relationship Between 'Non-Successor' Farm Offspring and the Continuity of the Irish Family Farm." *Sociologia Ruralis* 54 (4): 399–416.

Castillo, Carolina Perpiña, Boyan Kavalov, Vasco Diogo et al. 2018. *Agricultural Land Abandonment in the EU Within 2015–2030*. European Commission.

Castree, Noel. 2010. "Neoliberalism and the Biophysical Environment: A Synthesis and Evaluation of the Research." *Environment and Society* 1 (1): 5–45.

Central Statistics Office. 2016. *Census Population 2016: Age Structure and Sex Ratio*. https://www.cso.ie/en/releasesandpublications/ep/p-cp3oy/cp3/assr/.

Central Statistics Office. 2018. *Farm Structure Survey 2016*. https://www.cso.ie/en/releasesandpublications/ep/p-fss/farmstructuresurvey2013/keyfindings/.

Central Statistics Office. 2020a. *Agricultural Land Prices 2020: Key National Indicators*. https://www.cso.ie/en/releasesandpublications/ep/p-alp/agriculturallandprices2020/keynationalindicators/.

Central Statistics Office. 2020b. *Census of Agriculture: Demographic Profile of Farm Holders*. https://www.cso.ie/en/releasesandpublications/ep/p-coa/censusofagriculture2020-preliminaryresults/demographicprofileoffarmholders/.

Chazdon, Robin L., Pedro H. S. Brancalion, Lars Laestadius et al. 2016. "When Is a Forest a Forest? Forest Concepts and Definitions in the Era of Forest and Landscape Restoration." *Ambio* 45 (5): 538–550.

Clancy, Clara, and Kim Ward. 2020. "Auto-Rewilding in Post-Industrial Cities: The Case of Inland Cormorants in Urban Britain." *Conservation and Society* 18 (2): 126–136.

Clegg, Stewart R. 1990. *Modern Organizations: Organizational Studies in the Postmodern World*. Sage.

Clifford, Brendan 1986. *Duhallow: Notes Towards a History*. Labour Comment.

Clinch, Peter J., Frank Convery, and Brendan Walsh. 2002. *After the Celtic Tiger: Challenges Ahead*. O'Brien Press.

Collier, Pat, Jim Dorgan, and Paul Bell. 2002. *Factors Influencing Farmer Participation in Forestry*. National Council for Forest Research and Development.

Collins, Joseph A., Patrick G. Wall, and Vivienne E. Duggan. 2018. "Use of Registered Donkeys on the Areas of Natural Constraint Scheme in Ireland." *Vet Record* 183 (9): 298.

Collinson, Paul. 2005. "Development, Democracy and the New Europe in the Irish Borderlands." In *Culture and Power at the Edges of the State: National Support and Subversion in European Border Regions*, edited by Thomas W. Wilson and Hastings Donnan, 289–320. Transaction.

Collinson, Paul. 2015. "Environmental Attitudes, Community Development, and Local Politics in Ireland." In *Alternative Countrysides: Anthropological Approaches to Rural Western Europe Today*, edited by Jeremy MacClancy, 46–60. Manchester University Press.

Conaghan, John, Jessica Hamilton, Edwina Cole et al. 2020. *Molinia Meadows (EU Habitats Directive Code 6410)*. Botanical Society of Britain and Ireland.

Connaughton, Bernadette. 2010. "The Politics of Environmental Policy." In *Europeanisation and New Patterns of Governance in Ireland*, edited by Bernadette Connaughton, Nicholas Rees, and Brid Quinn, 122–144. Manchester University Press.

Conway, Shane Francis, John McDonagh, Maura Farrell et al. 2017. "Uncovering Obstacles: The Exercise of Symbolic Power in the Complex Arena of Intergenerational Family Farm Transfer." *Journal of Rural Studies* 54: 60–75.

Council Directive 2009/147/EC of the European Parliament and of the Council. November 30, 2009. "Directive on the Conservation of Wild Birds."

Crowley, Caroline, David Meredith, and Jim Walsh. 2004. "Population and Agricultural Change in Rural Ireland, 1991 to 2002." Proceedings of the Rural Development Conference, Rural Economy Research Centre, March, Sandymount, Dublin.

Crowley, Ethel. 2006. *Land Matters: Power Struggles in Rural Ireland*. Lilliput Press.

Crowley, Tim. 1998. "The Evaluation and Location of the Economic Impact of Coillte-Owned Forests Located in the Ballyvourney Area of County Cork." MSc Agriculture, Crop Science, Horticulture, and Forestry Department, University College, Dublin.

Cullory, Anthony T. 1986. *Balydesmond: A Rural Parish in Its Historical Setting*. Second ed. IRD Duhallow.

Cunningham, John. 2010. "Oliver Cromwell and the Cromwellian Settlement of Ireland." *Historical Journal* 53 (4): 919–937.

Cush, Peter, and Áine Macken-Walsh. 2018. "Reconstituting Male Identities Through Joint Farming Ventures in Ireland." *Sociologia Ruralis* 58 (4): 726–744.

Cush, Peter, Áine Macken-Walsh, and Anne Byrne. 2018. "Joint Farming Ventures in Ireland: Gender Identities of the Self and the Social." *Journal of Rural Studies* 57: 55–64.

Davidova, Sophia, and Kenneth Thomson. 2014. *Family Farming in Europe: Challenges and Prospects*. European Parliament.

Davis, Eithne, Joseph M. Caffrey, Jaimie T. A. Dick et al. 2017. *Horizon Scanning for Invasive Alien Species on the Island of Ireland: Identification of Emerging Invasive Alien Species with the Potential to Threaten Biodiversity*. National Biodiversity Data Centre: A Heritage Council Programme. CERIS Institute of Technology.

de Haan, Leo J. 2012. "The Livelihood Approach: A Critical Exploration." *Erdkunde Journal of Human and Physical Geographies* 66 (4): 345–357.

Delestra, Denis, and Sandrine Feydel. 2014. *Banking Nature*. Icarus Films.

Demossier, Marion. 2011. "Anthropologists and the Challenges of Modernity." *Anthropological Journal of European Cultures* 20 (1): 111–131.

Department of Agriculture, Fisheries and Food Ireland. 2010. *Food Harvest 2020: A Vision for Irish Agri-Food and Fisheries*. Department of Agriculture, Fisheries and Food.

Department of Agriculture, Food and the Marine. 2014a. *Forestry Programme 2014–2020: IRELAND*. Forest Service. Department of Agriculture, Food and the Marine.

Department of Agriculture, Food and the Marine. 2014b. *Forests, Products, and People: Ireland's Forest Policy—a Renewed Vision*. Department of Agriculture, Food and the Marine.

Department of Agriculture, Food and the Marine. 2017. *National Forest Inventory Results Data*. https://wayback.archive-it.org/org-1444/20201125172921/https://www.agriculture.gov.ie/nfi/nfithirdcycle2017/nationalforestinventoryresultsdata2017/.

Department of Agriculture, Food and the Marine. 2018. *Forest Statistics—Ireland, 2017*. Johnstown Castle Estate, Co.

Department of Agriculture, Food and the Marine. 2019. *Forest Statistics—Ireland, 2019*. Johnstown Castle Estate, Co.

Department of Agriculture, Food and the Marine. 2021. "Areas of Natural Constraints and Areas of Specific Constraint (Island) Schemes." Government of Ireland. https://www.gov.ie/en/service/13d971-areas-of-natural-constraint-scheme/#how-to-qualify.

Department of Communication, Climate Action, and Environment. 2019. "National Energy and Climate Plan 2021–2030." Government of Ireland.

Dhubháin, Áine Ní, Marie-Christine Fléchard, Richard Moloney et al. 2006. *The Socio-Economic Contribution of Forestry in Ireland*. National Council for Forest Research and Development.

Dhubháin, Áine Ní, Marie-Christine Fléchard, Richard Moloney et al. 2009. "Stakeholders' Perceptions of Forestry in Rural Areas—Two Case Studies in Ireland." *Land Use Policy* 26 (3): 695–703.

Dhubháin, Áine Ní, and Sarah Wall. 1999. "The New Owners of Small Private Forests in Ireland." *Journal of Forestry* 97 (6): 28–33.

Donnelly, James S. 1975. *The Land and the People of Nineteenth-Century Cork: The Rural Economy and the Land Question*. Routledge.

Donnelly, James S. 1976. "The Irish Agricultural Depression of 1859–64." *Irish Economic and Social History* 3: 33–54.

Duesberg, Stefanie, and Áine Ní Dhubháin. 2019. "Forest Intensification in Ireland: Developing an Approximation of Social Acceptability." *Land Use Policy* 85: 368–386.

Duesberg, Stefanie, Deirdre O'Connor, and Áine Ní Dhubháin. 2013. "To Plant or Not to Plant: Irish Farmers' Goals and Values with Regards to Afforestation." *Land Use Policy* 32: 155–164.

Duesberg, Stefanie, Vincent Upton, Deirdre O'Connor et al. 2014. "Factors Influencing Irish Farmers' Afforestation Intention." *Forest Policy and Economics* 39: 13–20.

Dykes, Alan P. 2022. "Landslide Investigations During Pandemic Restrictions: Initial Assessment of Recent Peat Landslides in Ireland." *Landslides* 19: 515–525.

Egan, Keith M., and Fiona E. Murphy. 2015. "Honored Ancestors, Difficult Legacies: The Stability, Decline, and Re-Emergence of Anthropologies in and of Ireland." *American Anthropologist* 117 (1): 134–141.

Escobar, Arturo. 1999. "After Nature: Steps to an Antiessentialist Political Ecology." *Current Anthropology* 40 (1): 1–17.

European Commission. 2013. *Communication from the Commission to the European Parliament, the Council, the European Economic and Social Committee, and the Committee of the Regions on a New EU Forest Strategy for Forests and the Forest-Based Sector*. COM 659 final. European Commission.

European Commission. 2015. *Natura 2000 and Forest Guide Part I–II*. European Commission.

European Commission. 2017. "What Encourages Farmers to Participate in EU Agri-Environment Schemes?" *Science Communication Unit, Agri-Environment Schemes—Impacts on the Agricultural Environment*. Publications Office 57 (June): 37–39. https://data.europa.eu/doi/10.2779/633983.

European Commission. 2021. *EU Biodiversity Strategy for 2030: Bringing Nature Back into Our Lives*. European Commission.

European Union. 2014. Regulation (EU) No. 1143/2014 of the European Parliament and the Council of 22 October 2014 on the Prevention and Management of the Introduction and Spread of Invasive Alien Species. *Official Journal of the European Union* L 317/35.

Eurostat. 2019. *Agriculture Statistics—Family Farming in the EU*. https://ec.europa.eu/eurostat/statistics-explained/index.php?title=Agriculture_statistics_-_family_farming_in_the_EU#Structural_profile_of_farms_-_analysis_for_the_EU.

Fairhead, James, and Melissa Leach. 1995. "False Forest History, Complicit Social Analysis: Rethinking Some West African Environmental Narratives." *World Development* 23 (6): 1023–1035.

Fairhead, James, and Melissa Leach. 1996. *Misreading the African Landscape: Society and Ecology in a Forest-Savanna Mosaic*. Cambridge University Press.

Farrelly, Niall. 2006a. "The Farm Forest Resource and Its Potential Contribution to Rural Development in Ireland." Proceedings of IUFRO 3.08 Conference Small-Scale Forestry and Rural Development—the Intersection of Ecosystems, Economics, and Society. Galway-Mayo Institute of Technology, Galway, Ireland, June 18–23.

Farrelly, Niall. 2006b. "A Review of Afforestation and Potential Volume Output from Private Forests in Ireland." Internal Report, Forestry Development Unit, Teagasc, 1-28.

Feehan, John, and Deirdre O'Connor. 2009. "Agriculture and Multifunctionality in Ireland." In *A Living Countryside? The Politics of Sustainable Development in Rural Ireland*, edited by John McDonagh, Tony Varley, and Sally Shortall, 123–137. Ashgate.

"Feral Atlas." 2022. Stanford University Press. https://feralatlas.supdigital.org/.

Fitz-Henry, Erin. 2017. "Multiple Temporalities and the Nonhuman Other." *Environmental Humanities* 9 (1): 1–17.

Flechard, Marie-Christine, Matthew S. Carroll, Patricia J. Cohn et al. 2007. "The Changing Relationships Between Forestry and the Local Community in Rural Northwestern Ireland." *Canadian Journal of Forest Research* 37 (10): 1999–2009.

Fletcher, Robert. 2023. *Failing Forward: The Rise and Fall of Neoliberal Conservation*. University of California Press.

Flynn, Brendan. 2009. "Environmental Lessons for Rural Ireland from the European Union: How Great Expectations in Brussels Get Dashed in Bangor and Belmullet." In *A Living Countryside? The Politics of Sustainable Development in Rural Ireland*, edited by John McDonagh, Tony Varley, and Sally Shortall, 53–68. Ashgate.

Folds, J. S., George Petrie, and Caesar Otway. 1832. "Pobble O'Keefe." *Dublin Penny Journal* 1 (21): 166–168.

Folke, Carl, Crawford Stanley Holling, and Charles Perring. 2010. "Biological Diversity, Ecosystems, and the Human Scale." In *Foundations of Ecological Resilience*, edited by Lance H. Gunderson, Craig Reece Allen, and C. S. Holling, 118–224. Island Press.

Forde, Amy. 2018. "Forestry Threatens to Decimate Leitrim Communities." *Irish Farmers Journal*, January 8. https://www.farmersjournal.ie/news/news/forestry-threatens-to-decimate-leitrim-communities-336875.

Forestry Appeals Committee. 2021. *Chairperson's Report 2021*. Agriculture Appeals Office.

Foucault, Michel. 1991. "Governmentality." In *The Foucault Effect: Studies in Governmentality*, edited by Graham Burchell, Colin Gordon, and Peter Miller. Chicago, 87–104. University of Chicago Press.

Fox, Robin. 1962. "The Vanishing Gael." *New Society* 1: 17–19.

Fox, Robin. 1975. *Encounter with Anthropology*. Penguin Books.

Fox, Robin. 1978. *The Tory Islanders: A People of the Celtic Fringe*. Cambridge University Press.

Frawley, Jim, and Garvan Hickey. 2002. *Social Inclusion in a Rural Area of Munster*. Rural Economy Research Centre, Teagasc.

Freer-Smith, Peter, Bart Muys, Michele Bozzano et al. 2019. *Plantation Forests in Europe: Challenges and Opportunities*. European Forest Institute.

Gaffin, Dennis. 1997. "Offending and Defending US Rural Place: The Mega Dump Battle in Western New York." *Human Organization* 56 (3): 275–284.

Gasson, Ruth. 1992. "Farmers' Wives: Their Contribution to the Farm Business." *Journal of Agricultural Economics* 43 (1): 74–87.

Gibbon, Peter. 1973. "Arensberg and Kimball Revisited." *Economy and Society* 2: 479–498.

Gillmor, Desmond A. 1972. "Aspects of Agricultural Change in the Republic of Ireland During the 1960s." *Irish Geography* 6 (4): 492–498.

Gillmor, Desmond A. 1989. "The Political Factor in Agricultural History: Trends in Irish Agriculture, 1922–85." *Agricultural History Review* 37 (2): 166–179.

Girvin, Brian. 2010. "Becoming European: National Identity, Sovereignty, and Europeanisation in Irish Political Culture." In *Europeanisation and Hibernicisation: Ireland and Europe*, edited by Cathal McCall and Thomas M. Wilson, 59–93. Rodopi.

Godfray, Charles J., John R. Beddington, Jan R. Cruite et al. 2010. "Food Security: The Challenge of Feeding 9 Billion People." *Science* 327 (5967): 812–818.

Godkin, James. 1870. *The Land-War in Ireland: A History for the Times*. Macmillan.

Government of Ireland. 2021. *Our Rural Future: Rural Development Policy 2021–2025*. Government of Ireland.

Gray, John. 2000. "The Common Agricultural Policy and the Re-Invention of the Rural in the European Community." *Sociologia Ruralis* 40 (1): 30–52.

Gray, John. 2007. "Cultivating Farm Life on the Borders: Scottish Hill Sheep Farms and the European Community." *Sociologia Ruralis* 36 (1): 27–50.

Gray, John. 2009. "Rurality and Rural Space: The 'Policy Effect' of the Common Agricultural Policy in the Borders of Scotland." In *Tracking Rural Change: Community, Policy, and Technology in Australia, New Zealand, and Europe*, edited by Francesca Merlan and David Raftery, 15–40. Australian National University Press.

Graziano, Paolo, and Maarten P. Vink. 2013. "Europeanization: Concept, Theory, and Methods." In *The Member States of the European Union*, edited by Simon Bulmer and Christian Lesquesne, 31–54. Oxford University Press.

Griffith, Richard, and James Weale. 1834. *Report on the Experimental Improvements on the Crown Estate at King William's Town*. Accounts and Papers, 9 vols., session February 4–August 15. Bodleian Library, Oxford.

Halfacree, Keith H. 1993. "Locality and Social Representation: Space, Discourse, and Alternative Definitions of the Rural." *Journal of Rural Studies* 9 (1): 22–37.

Halperin, Rhoda H. 1990. *The Livelihood of Kin: Making Ends Meet the Kentucky Way*. University of Texas Press.

Haraway, Donna J. 2016. *Staying with the Trouble: Making Kin in the Chthulucene*. Duke University Press.

Harris, Rosemary. 1972. *Prejudice and Tolerance in Ulster: A Study of Neighbours and "Strangers" in a Border Community*. Manchester University Press.

Harris, Rosemary. 1988. "Theory and Evidence: The 'Irish Stem Family' and Field Data." *Man* 23 (3): 417–434.

Heatherington, Tracey. 2011. "Remaking Rural Landscapes in Twenty-First Century Europe." *Anthropological Journal of European Cultures* 20 (1): 1–9.

Hecht, Susanna B., Kathleen D. Morrison, and Christine Padoch. 2014. "From Fragmentation to Forest Resurgence: Paradigms, Representations, and Practices." In *The Social Lives of Forests: Past, Present, and Future of Woodland Resurgence*, edited by Susanna B. Hecht, Kathleen D. Morrison, and Christine Padoch, 1–8. University of Chicago Press.

Hen Harrier Project. 2021. *Hen Harrier Programme: Hen Harrier Monitoring 2021*. henharrierproject.ie.

Henle, Klaus, Didier Alard, Jeremy Clitherow et al. 2008. "Identifying and Managing the Conflicts Between Agriculture and Biodiversity in Europe—a Review." *Agricultural, Ecosystems and Environment* 124 (1–2): 60–71.

Hill, Alan. 2016. *Uplands Community Study*. Irish Uplands Forum.

Hoag, Colin. 2011. "Assembling Partial Perspectives: Thoughts on the Anthropology of Bureaucracy." *Political and Legal Anthropology Review* 34 (1): 81–94.

Hollander, Gail M. 2004. "Agricultural Trade Liberalization, Multifunctionality, and Sugar in the South Florida Landscape." *Geoforum* 35 (3): 299–312.

Huallacháin, Daire Ó., John A. Finn, Blathnaid Keogh et al. 2016. "A Comparison of Grassland Vegetation from Three Agri-Environment Conservation Measures." *Irish Journal of Agricultural and Food Research* 55 (2): 176–191.

Hubbard, Carmen, and Neil Ward. 2008. *Deliverables D8.2 Development of Socio-Economic and Agricultural Structures in Selected Rural Regions in Ireland After EU Accession*. Structural Change in Agriculture and Rural Livelihoods.

Hughes, David McDermott. 2021. *Who Owns the Wind? Climate Crisis and the Hope of Renewable Energy*. Verso.

Ilieva, Polya, and Thomas M. Wilson. 2011. "Euroscepticism and Europeanisation at a Margin of Europe." *Anthropological Journal of European Cultures* 20: 87–113.

Ingold, Tim. 2000. *The Perception of the Environment: Essays on Livelihood, Dwelling, and Skill*. Psychology Press.

Ioris, Antonio Augusto Rossotto. 2014. *The Political Ecology of the State: The Basis and the Evolution of Environmental Statehood*. Routledge.

Iremonger, Susan, John O'Halloran, Daniel Lucius et al. 2007. *Biodiversity in Irish Plantation Forests: Final Report 2000-LS-3.1-M2*. Environmental Protection Agency.

Kaag, Mayke, Rik van Berkel, Johan Brons et al. 2004. "Poverty Is Bad: Ways Forward in Livelihood Research." In *Globalization and Development: Themes and Concepts in*

Current Research, edited by Don P. Kalb, Wil G. Pansters, and Hans Siebers, 49–74. Kluwer Academic Publishers.

Kaul, Adam R. 2009. *Turning the Tune: Traditional Music, Tourism, and Social Change in an Irish Village*. Berghahn Books.

Kearney, Brendan. 2001. *A Review of Relevant Studies Concerning Farm Forestry Trends and Farmers' Attitudes to Forestry*. National Council for Forest Research Development.

Keller, Marie. 1985. *Duhallow to Oregon, 1880 to 1960*. Lakeview Duhallow Development Association.

Kelly, Roisin, and Sally Shortall. 2002. "'Farmers' Wives': Women Who Are Off-Farm Breadwinners and the Implications for On-Farm Gender Relations." *Journal of Sociology* 38 (4): 327–343.

Ketonen, Irene. 2019. "The Lens of Brexit: Examining Cultural Divisions Among Northern Ireland Farmers." *Economic Anthropology* 6: 61–72.

Ketonen-Keating, Irene. 2021. "Writing Ireland: An Anthropological Literature Review." *Irish Journal of Anthropology* 24 (1): 19–39.

Kirby, Peadar. 2013. "Transforming Capitalism: The Triple Crisis." *Irish Journal of Sociology* 21 (2): 62–75.

Kirby, Peadar, Luke Gibbons, and Michael Cronin. 2002. "Introduction: The Reinvention of Ireland, a Critical Perspective." In *Reinventing Ireland: Culture, Society, and the Global Economy*, edited by Peadar Kirby, Luke Gibbons, and Michael Cronin, 1–18. Pluto.

Kitchin, Rob, Cian O'Callaghan, Mark Boyle et al. 2012. "Placing Neoliberalism: The Rise and Fall of Ireland's Celtic Tiger." *Environment and Planning* 44 (6): 1302–1326.

Knickel, Karlheinz, Henk Renting, and Jan Douwe van der Ploeg. 2004. "Multifunctionality in European Agriculture." In *Sustaining Agriculture and the Rural Environment: Governance, Policy, and Multifunctionality*, edited by Floor Brouwer, 81–104. Edward Elgar.

Kristensen, Peter. 2003. "EEA Core Set of Indicators: Revised Version April 2003." Technical Report. European Environment Agency.

Laoire, Caitríona Ní. 2001. "A Matter of Life and Death? Men, Masculinities, and Staying 'Behind' in Rural Ireland." *Sociologia Ruralis* 41 (2): 220–236.

Latour, Bruno, Isabelle Stengers, Anna Tsing, and Nils Bubandt. 2018. "Anthropologists Are Talking—About Capitalism, Ecology, and Apocalypse." *Ethnos* 83 (3): 587–606.

Lenihan, Martin H., and Kathryn J. Brasier. 2009. "Scaling Down the European Model of Agriculture: The Case of the Rural Environmental Protection Scheme in Ireland." *Agriculture and Human Values* 26 (4): 365–378.

Leyton, Elliott. 1975. *The One Blood: Kinship and Class in an Irish Village*. St. John's Institute of Social and Economic Research, Memorial University.

Li, Tania Murray. 2007. "Practices of Assemblage and Community Forest Management." *Economy and Society* 36 (2): 263–293.

Li, Tania Murray. 2014. "What Is Land? Assembling a Resource for Global Investment." *Transactions of the Institute of British Geographers* 39 (4): 589–602.

Li, Tania Murray, and Pujo Semedi. 2021. *Plantation Life: Corporate Occupation in Indonesia's Oil Palm Zone*. Duke University Press.

Lounela, Anu, Eeva Berglund, and Timo Kallinen, eds. 2019. *Dwelling in Political Landscapes: Contemporary Anthropological Perspectives*. Finnish Literature Society.

MacClancy, Jeremy. 2015. "Alternative Countrysides: Anthropology and the Rural West Europe Today." In *Alternative Countrysides: Anthropological Approaches to Rural Western Europe Today*, edited by Jeremy MacClancy, 1–28. Manchester University Press.

Maguire, Mark, and Fiona Murphy. 2012. *Integration in Ireland: The Everyday Lives of African Migrants*. Manchester University Press.

Mahon, Marie, Maura Farrell, and John McDonagh. 2010. "Power, Positionality, and the View from Within: Agricultural Advisers' Role in Implementing Participatory Extension Programmes in the Republic of Ireland." *Sociologia Ruralis* 50 (2): 85–197.

Mahoney, Brian. 2002. *EU Complaint P2002/4259—Rockchapel*. Forest Service, Department of Communications, Marine and Natural Resources.

Matthews, Alan. 2013. "Promoting Family Farming: The European Union." *Great Insights Magazine* 3 (1). http://ecdpm.org/great-insights/family-farming-and-food-security/promoting-family-farming-european-union/.

McCabe, Connor. 2011. *Sins of the Father: Tracing the Decisions That Shaped the Irish Economy*. History Press, Ireland.

McCall, Cathal, and Thomas M. Wilson. 2010. "Europeanisation and Hibernicisation." In *Europeanisation and Hibernicisation: Ireland and Europe*, edited by Cathal McCall and Thomas M. Wilson, 11–40. Rodopi.

McCarthy, Grainne, Marina Piazza Ferrand, Timothy De Waal et al. 2016. "Geographical Distribution of Angiostrongylus Vasorum in Foxes (Vulpes vulpes) in the Republic of Ireland." *Parasitology* 143 (5): 588–593.

McCarthy, Jack, David Meredith, and Christing Bonnin. 2023. "'You Have to Keep It Going': Relational Values and Social Sustainability in Upland Agriculture." *Sociologia Ruralis* 63 (3): 588–610.

McCullagh, Ciaran. 1991. "A Tie That Binds: Family and Ideology in Ireland." *Economic and Social Review* 22 (3): 199–211.

McDonagh, John, Maura Farrell, Marie Mahon et al. 2010. "New Opportunities and Cautionary Steps? Farmers, Forestry, and Rural Development in Ireland." *European Countryside* 2 (4): 236–251.

McGrath, Brendan. 2013. *Landscape and Society in Contemporary Ireland*. Cork University Press.

McLaughlin, Eithne. 1989. "In Search of the Female Breadwinner: Gender and Unemployment in Derry City." In *Social Anthropology and Public Policy in Northern Ireland*, edited by Hastings Donnan and Graham McFarlane, 47–66. Avebury.

McMahon, Barry J., Alvin Helden, Annette Anderson et al. 2010. "Interactions Between Livestock Systems and Biodiversity in South-East Ireland." *Agriculture, Ecosystems, and Environment* 139 (1–2): 232–238.

McMillan, Robert L. 2014. "Hen Harriers on Skye, 2000–12: Nest Failures and Predation." *Scottish Birds* 34 (2): 30–39.

Moran, James, Dolores Byrne, Julien Carlier et al. 2021. "Management of High Nature Value Farmland in the Republic of Ireland: 25 Years Evolving Toward Locally Adapted Results-Orientated Solutions and Payments." *Ecology and Society* 26 (1): 20. https://www.ecologyandsociety.org/vol26/iss1/art20/.

Moser, Peter, and Tony Varley. 2012. "Corporatism, Agriculture Modernization, and War in Ireland and Switzerland, 1935–1955." In *War, Agriculture, and Food: Rural Europe from the 1930s to the 1950s*, edited by Paul Brassley, Yves Segers, and Leen Van Molle, 137–155. Routledge.

Moser, Peter, and Tony Varley. 2013. "The State and Agricultural Modernisation in the Nineteenth and Twentieth Centuries in Europe." In *Integration Through Subordination: The Politics of Agricultural Modernization in Industrial Europe*, edited by Peter Moser and Tony Varley, 13–39. Brepols.

Murphy, Thomas M., Jerome O. O'Connell, Marco Berzano et al. 2012. "The Prevalence and Distribution of Alaria Alata, a Potential Zoonotic Parasite, in Foxes in Ireland." *Parasite Research* 111: 283–290.

Nash, Roderick Frazier. 2001 [1967]. *Wilderness and the American Mind*. Yale University Press.

National Parks and Wildlife Service Ireland. 2013. "The Status of Protected EU Habitats and Species in Ireland: Overview Volume 1." Unpublished report. Department of Arts, Heritage and the Gaeltacht.

National Parks and Wildlife Service Ireland. 2015. *Natura 2000 Site Synopsis: Stack's to Mullaghareirk Mountains, West Limerick Hills, and Mount Eagle SPA*. National Parks and Wildlife Service Ireland.

Neeson, Eoin. 1991. *A History of Irish Forestry*. Department of Energy.

Neumann, Roderick. 2014. "Stories of Nature's Hybridity in Europe: Implications for Forest Conservation in the Global South." In *The Social Lives of Forests*, edited by Susanna B. Hecht, Kathleen D. Morrison, and Christine Padoch, 31–44. University of Chicago Press.

O'Carroll, Niall. 2004. *Forestry in Ireland: A Concise History*. National Council for Forest Research and Development.

O'Connell, Michael, Fergus Kelly, and James H. McAdam, eds. 2016. *Cattle in Ancient and Modern Ireland: Farming Practices, Environment, and Economy*. Cambridge Scholars Publishing.

O'Connell, Philip J., Helen Russell, and Christopher T. Whelan. 2007. "Employment Equality and the Quality of Work." In *Best of Times? The Social Impact of the Celtic Tiger*, edited by Tony Fahey, Helen Russell, and Christopher T. Whelan, 43–66. Institute of Public Administration.

O'Donnchadha, Georoid, and Niamh Ni She. 1994. "Duhallow Farm Families: Challenge and Prospect." Prepared for IRD Duhallow Ltd., James O'Keeffe Institute, Newmarket, County Cork, Ireland.

O'Donnell, Shane, and Noel Richardson. 2018. *Middle-Aged Men and Suicide in Ireland*. Report prepared by the Men's Health Forum and Health Services Executive, Dublin.

O'Driscoll, Eoin, and Fergus Moore. 2019. *UNECE Forestry and Timber Market Report for Ireland 2019*. Department of Agriculture, Food and the Marine.

O'Hara, Patricia. 1998. *Partners in Production? Women, Farm, and Family in Ireland*. Berghahn Books.

O'Hara, Patricia. 2001. "Social Enterprises and Local Development." In *The Emergence of Social Enterprise*, edited by Carlo Borzaga and Jacques Defourny, 149–165. Routledge.

O'Keeffe, Brendan. 2012. *Profile of Labour Force, Industry and Education, 1991 to 2011*. IRD Duhallow.

O'Keeffe, Brendan. 2015. "Communities, Collaborations, Cohesion, and Centralization: Contemporary Insights from Rural Ireland." In *Place Peripheral: Place-Based Development in Rural, Island, and Remote Regions*, edited by Kelly Vodden, Ryan Gibson, and Godfrey Baldacchino. Institute of Social and Economic Research.

O'Leary, Tomás N., Art G. McCormack, and J. Peter Clinch. 2000. "Afforestation in Ireland—Regional Differences in Attitude." *Land Use Policy* 17 (1): 39–48.

Ong, Aihwa, and Stephen J. Collier, eds. 2007. *Global Assemblages: Technology, Politics, and Ethics as Anthropological Problems*: Blackwell.

Organization for Economic Cooperation and Development (OECD). 2015. *New Rural Policy: Linking up for Growth*. OECD.

O'Rourke, Eileen. 2019. "Drivers of Land Abandonment in the Irish Uplands: A Case Study." *European Countryside* 11 (2): 211–228.

O'Rourke, Eileen, Marion Charbonneau, and Yves Poinsot. 2016. "High Nature Value Mountain Farming Systems in Europe: Case Studies from the Atlantic Pyrenees, France, and the Kerry Uplands." *Journal of Rural Studies* 46: 47–59.

Peace, Adrian. 1986. "A Different Place Altogether: Diversity, Unity, and Boundary in an Irish Village." In *Symbolizing Boundaries: Identity and Diversity in British Cultures*, edited by Anthony P. Cohen, 107–122. Manchester University Press.

Peace, Adrian. 1989. "From Arcadia to Anomie: Critical Notes on the Constitution of Irish Society as an Anthropological Object." *Critique of Anthropology* 9 (1): 89–111.

Peace, Adrian. 2001. *A World of Fine Difference: The Social Architecture of a Modern Irish Village*. University College Dublin Press.

Peace, Adrian. 2005. "A Sense of Place, a Place of Senses: Land and a Landscape in the West of Ireland." *Journal of Anthropological Research* 61 (4): 495–512.

Price, Linda, and Rachel Conn. 2012. "Keeping the Name on the Land: Patrilineal Succession in Northern Irish Family Farming." In *Keeping It in the Family: International Perspectives on Succession and Retirement on Family Farms*, edited by Matt Lobley, John R. Baker, and Ian Whitehead. Farnham.

Rahman, Aziz, Mary Anne Clarke, and Sean Byrne. 2017. "The Art of Breaking People Down: The British Colonial Model in Ireland and Canada." *Peace Research* 49 (2): 15–38.

Rissing, Andrea, and Bradley M. Jones. 2022. "Landscapes of Value." *Economic Anthropology* 9: 193–206.

Robbins, Paul. 2019. *Political Ecology: A Critical Introduction*. Third ed. Wiley-Blackwell.

Ruddock, Marc, Allan Mee, John Lusby et al. 2016. *The 2015 National Survey of Breeding Hen Harrier in Ireland*, vol. 93: *Irish Wildlife Manuals*. Department of Arts, Heritage and the Gaeltacht.

Rusert, Britt. 2015. "Plantation Ecologies: The Experimental Plantation in and Against James Grainger's *The Sugar-Cane*." *Early American Studies* 13 (2): 341–373.

Sacks, Paul Martin. 1976. *The Donegal Mafia: An Irish Political Machine*. Yale University Press.

Salazar, Carles. 1996. "A Sentimental Economy: The Ethnography of Farm Work in the West of Ireland." PhD dissertation, University of Cambridge, Cambridge, UK.

Save Leitrim. 2021. "Save Leitrim." https://saveleitrim.ie/.

Savill, Peter, James Bennett, Eugene Hendrick et al. 2013. *Teagasc Forestry Development Programme Peer Review*. Teagasc.

Scheper-Hughes, Nancy. 1979. *Saints, Scholars, and Schizophrenics: Mental Illness in Rural Ireland*. University of California Press.

Scheper-Hughes, Nancy. 2000. "Ire in Ireland." *Ethnography* 1 (1): 117–140.

Scott, James C. 1998. *Seeing Like a State: How Certain Schemes to Improve the Human Condition Have Failed*. Yale University Press.

Shanks, Amanda. 1994. "Cultural Divergence and Durability: The Border, Symbolic Boundaries, and the Irish Gentry." In *Border Approaches: Anthropological Perspectives on Frontiers*, edited by Hastings Donnan and Thomas M. Wilson, 89–100. University Press of America.

Shiva, Vandana. 1993. *Monocultures of the Mind: Perspectives on Biodiversity and Biotechnology*. Zed Books.

Shore, Cris. 2000. *Building Europe: The Cultural Politics of European Integration*. Routledge.

Shortall, Sally. 2001. "Women in the Field: Women, Farming, and Organizations." *Work and Organization* 8 (2): 165–181.

Shortall, Sally. 2014. "Farming, Identity, and Well-Being: Managing Changing Gender Roles Within Western European Farm Families." *Anthropological Notebooks* 20 (3): 67–81.

Shortall, Sally, Annie McKee, and Lee-Ann Sutherland. 2020. "The Performance of Occupational Closure: The Case of Agriculture and Gender." *Sociologia Ruralis* 60 (1): 40–57.

Shutes, Mark T. 1991. "Kerry Farmers and the European Community: Capital Transitions in a Rural Irish Parish." *Irish Journal of Sociology* 1 (1): 1–17.

Shutes, Mark T. 2015a. "Accidental Dairy Farmers: Social Transformations in a Rural Irish Parish." In *The Ecology of Pastoralism*, edited by P. Nick Kardulias, 211–224. University Press of Colorado.

Shutes, Mark T. 2015b. "Real Milk from Mechanical Cows: Adaptations Among Irish Dairy Cattle Farmers." In *The Ecology of Pastoralism*, edited by P. Nick Kardulias, 225–241. University Press of Colorado.

Singh, Parlo, Sue Thomas, and Jessica Harris. 2013. "Recontextualising Policy Discourses: A Bernsteinian Perspective on Policy Interpretation, Translation, Enactment." *Journal of Education Policy* 28 (4): 465–480.

Smith, Neil. 2006. "Nature as Accumulation Strategy." In *Socialist Register*, edited by Leo Panitch and Colin Leys, 16–36. Merlin Press.

Smith, Nicola Jo-Anne. 2005. *Showcasing Globalisation? The Political Economy of the Irish Republic*. Manchester University Press.

Smyth, Jim. 2014. "The Strange History of the Irish Donkey." Hydra Mule and Donkey Conference, October, Hydra, Greece.

Stacul, Jaro, Christina Moutsou, and Helen Kopnina. 2006. *Crossing European Boundaries: Beyond Conventional Geographical Categories*. Berghahn Books.

Stead, David. 2011. "Economic Change in South-West Ireland, 1960–2009." *Rural History* 22 (1): 115–146.

Stoate, Chris, András Báldi, Pedro Rui Beja et al. 2009. "Ecological Impacts of Early 21st Century Agricultural Change in Europe—a Review." *Journal of Environmental Management* 91 (1): 22–46.

Stoustrup, Sune Wiingaard. 2022. "The Re-Coding of Rural Development Rationality: Tracing EU Governmentality and Europeanisation at the Local Level." *European Planning Studies* 30 (2): 2474–2491.

Strange, Jason G. 2020. *Shelter from the Machine: Homesteaders in the Age of Capitalism*. University of Illinois Press.

Sullivan, Sian. 2014. *The Natural Capital Myth; or, Will Accounting Save the World? Preliminary Thoughts on Nature, Finance, and Values*. Education and Development School of Environment, Leverhulme Center for the Study of Value, University of Manchester.

Sutherland, Lee-Ann, Rob J. F. Burton, Julie Ingram et al. 2012. "Triggering Change: Towards a Conceptualisation of Major Change Processes in Farm Decision-Making." *Journal of Environmental Management* 104 (15): 142–151.

Taylor, Lawrence J. 1989. "The Mission: An Anthropological View of an Irish Religious Occasion." In *Ireland from Below: Social Change and Local Communities*, edited by Chris Curtin and Thomas M. Wilson, 1–22. Galway University Press.

Taylor, Lawrence J. 1995. *Occasions of Faith: An Anthropology of Irish Catholics*. University of Pennsylvania Press.

Teagasc. 2020. *A Guide to Transferring the Family Farm: November 2020*. Teagasc Agriculture and Food Development Authority.

Tetreault, Darcy. 2017. "Three Forms of Political Ecology." *Ethics and Environment* 22 (2): 1–23.

Thompson, Edgar. 1959. "The Plantation as Social System." *Revista Geografica* 25 (51): 41–56.

Tirapani, Alessandro Niccolo, and Hugh Willmott. 2022. "Revisiting Conflict: Neoliberalism at Work in the Gig Economy." *Human Relations* 76 (1): 53–86.

Touraine, Alain. 1988. "Modernity and Cultural Specificities." *International Social Science Journal* 118: 443–457.

Townsend, Horatio. 1810. *Statistical Survey of the County of Cork, with Observations on the Means of Improvement; Drawn up for the Consideration, and by Direction of the Dublin Society*. Graisberry and Campbell.

Tsing, Anna. 2015. *The Mushroom at the End of the World*. Princeton University Press.

Tsing, Anna. 2019. "The Buck, the Bull, and the Dream of the Stag: Some Unexpected Weeds of the Anthropocene." In *Dwelling in Political Landscapes: Contemporary*

Anthropological Perspectives, edited by Anu Lounela, Eeva Berglund, and Timo Kallinen, 33–52. Finnish Literature Society.

Tsing, Anna, Heather Swanson, Elain Gan et al., eds. 2017. *Arts of Living on a Damaged Planet*. University of Minnesota Press.

Turner, Michael. 1996. *After the Famine: Irish Agriculture 1850–1914*. Cambridge University Press.

UKCOP26. 2021. *Glasgow Leaders Declaration on Forests and Land Use*. https://webarchive.nationalarchives.gov.uk/ukgwa/20230418175226/https://ukcop26.org/glasgow-leaders-declaration-on-forests-and-land-use/.

Varley, Tony. 2004. "Irish Land Reform and the West Between the Wars." *Journal of the Galway Archaeological and Historical Society* 56: 213–232.

Varley, Tony, and Chris Curtin. 2002. "Communitarian Populism and the Politics of Rearguard Resistance in Rural Ireland." *Community Development Journal* 37 (1): 20–32.

Varley, Tony, and Chris Curtin. 2006. "The Politics of Empowerment: Power, Populism, and Partnership in Rural Ireland." *Economic and Social Review* 37 (3): 423–446.

Verkerk, Pieter Johannes, Philippe Delacote, Elias Hurmekoski et al. 2022. *Forest-Based Climate Change Mitigation and Adaptation in Europe*. European Forest Institute.

Vidyaratne, Herath, Akshay Vij, and Courtney M. Regan. 2020. "A Socio-Economic Exploration of Landholder Motivations to Participate in Afforestation Programs in the Republic of Ireland: The Role of Irreversibility, Inheritance, and Bequest Value." *Land Use Policy* 99: 2–8.

Vincent, Joan. 1989. *Local Knowledge and Political Violence in County Fermanagh*. Edited by Chris Curtin and Thomas M. Wilson. Galway University Press.

Walsh, Jim, and A. A. Horner. 1984. "Regional Aspects of Agricultural Production in Ireland, 1970–1980." *Irish Geography* 17 (1): 95–101.

Watts, Michael. 2000. "Political Ecology." In *A Companion to Economic Geography*, edited by Trevor J. Barnes and Eric Sheppard, 257–275. Blackwell.

Weber, Max. 1978. *Economy and Society: An Outline of Interpretive Sociology*. University of California Press.

Weeks, Kathi. 2011. *The Problem with Work: Feminism, Marxism, Antiwork Politics, and Postwork Imaginaries*. Duke University Press.

Whatmore, Sarah. 1991. *Farming Women: Gender, Work, and Family Enterprise*. MacMillan.

Willems-Braun, Bruce. 1997. "Buried Epistemologies: The Politics of Nature in (Post)Colonial British Columbia." *Annals of the Association of American Geographers* 87 (1): 3–31.

Williams, Raymond. 1975. *The Country and the City*. Oxford University Press.

Willow, Anna J. 2014. "New Politics of Environmental Degradation: Un/Expected Landscapes of Disempowerment and Vulnerability." *Journal of Political Ecology* 21 (1): 237–257.

Wilson, Geoff A. 2009. "The Spatiality of Multifunctional Agriculture: A Human Geography Perspective." *Geoforum* 40 (2): 269–280.

Wilson, Thomas M. 1984. "From Clare to the Common Market: Perspectives in Irish Ethnography." *Anthropological Quarterly* 57 (1): 1–15.

Wilson, Thomas M. 1993. "An Anthropology of the European Community." In *Cultural Change and the New Europe: Perspectives on the European Community*, edited by Thomas M. Wilson and M. Estellie Smith, 1–24. Westview.

Wilson, Thomas M. 2013. *Rural Politics in County Meath, Ireland*. Ethnographic and Historical Studies. Edwin Mellen.

Wilson, Thomas M., and Hastings Donnan. 2006. *The Anthropology of Ireland*. Oxford: Berg.

Winkel, Georg, Filip Aggestam, Metodi Sotirov et al. 2013. "Forest Policy in the European Union." In *European Forest Governance: Issues at Stake and the Way Forward*, edited by Helga Pülzl, Karl Hogl, Daniela Kleinschmit et al., 52-63. European Forest Institute.

Winkel, Georg, and Sabine Storch. 2013. "Coupling Climate Change and Forest Policy: A Multiple Streams Analysis of Two German Case Studies." *Forest Policy and Economics* 36: 14–26.

Wolfe, Alan, S. Hogan, Dave Maguire et al. 2001. "Red Foxes (*Vulpes vulpes*) in Ireland as Hosts for Parasites of Potential Zoonotic and Veterinary Significance." *Veterinary Record* 149: 759–763.

Wood, Patricia. 2017. "Travellers, Land Management, and the Political Ecology of Marginalisation in Celtic-Tiger Ireland." *Irish Geography* 50 (1): 59–80.

Woodworth, Paddy. 2019. "Rhododendron: An Ecological Disaster in Killarney National Park." *Irish Times*, May 18.

Wulff, Helena. 2017. *Rhythms of Writing: An Anthropology of Irish Literature*. Routledge.

Young, Arthur. 1780. *A Tour in Ireland: With General Observations on the Present State of That Kingdom, Made in the Years 1776, 1777, and 1778 and Brought down to the End of 1779*. Vol. 2. G. Bonham for Whitestone.

Index

afforestation, 10–11, 17, 27, 43–45, 81, 140, 163, 166; history of, 112–138; special protected area and, 113; targets, 159
agriculture, modernization of, 8, 18, 20, 39, 43, 45, 165
agriculture, multifunctional, 6, 147, 160
agricultural revolution, 35
Aldworth, Richard, 36
anthropology of Ireland, 15–19. *See also* ethnography
Arensberg, Conrad, and Solon Kimball, 15–16, 40
auto-rewilders, 55–56

Ballydesmond, 37, 40
balsam, 54, 57–58, 111, 151
Barna Bog, 40, 83–84
Bebbington, Anthony, 52, 149
Birds Directive, 23, 82, 92, 109
Blackwater River, 29, 109
bogs, 4, 5, 10, 29, 31, 35, 40, 83–84, 104, 128, 154; bog slide, 156
Bord na Móna, 40, 83, 89
Brexit, 18
Brody, Hugh, 41–42
bureaucracy, 26, 85–88, 98–100, 102, 105, 108

carbon sequestration, 4, 124, 131, 132, 133, 136, 137, 160, 162
Castree, Noel, 89, 162, 163
cattle: dairy, 9, 22, 39, 44, 47, 48, 69, 96, 144, 145; dry stock, 39, 44; prices, 39, 126, 144; suckler, 9, 48, 71, 97
céilí, 15, 62
Celtic Tiger, 11–12, 17, 50
climate change, 6, 7, 51, 92, 137; mitigation of, 6, 121, 131–132, 136, 159
Coillte, 73, 89, 99, 117, 118, 120, 123, 129
Common Agricultural Policy (CAP), 24, 33, 42, 63, 90–93, 147, 152
Council for Forest Research and Development (COFORD), 118, 123–126
creamery, 71, 40

debt, 42–43
depopulation. *See* population: changes of
Department of Agriculture (includes department of agriculture, food, and the marine), 80, 87, 89, 92, 95–96, 102–103, 123–124, 154–155
deregulation, 11, 90, 96, 148
Desmond Rebellion, 34
donkeys, 48–50, 66; as live stock units, 154–155; sanctuary, 155

189

economy, depression, 38–39, 42
economy, flexible, 8, 154, 147, 158–159, 163, 166
education, 51, 67, 69, 70, 155, 156
emigration, 12, 38, 43, 76
entrepreneurialism, 13, 162
ethnography, 6, 9, 22, 87, 149, 150, 166; in Ireland, 10, 13, 17–18, 42–43, 68; as method, 14, 16, 49, 166
European Economic Community (ECC), 17, 42, 50
europeanization, 18–22, 90, 166

farm abandonment, 44–45, 50, 139, 142
farm advisor, 46–49, 59, 87, 94–101
farm diversification, 147
Farm Improvement Program, 44
farm intensification, 35, 51, 61, 140, 148, 153
farm modernization, 18, 40, 43, 165; lack of, 8, 20, 45; scheme, 44
farm succession, 43, 53, 63, 65, 106
farming, to calendar, 96, 107
farming, low intensity, 11, 41, 45, 52, 81, 108, 122, 142, 161, 163
Fairhead, James, and Melissa Leach, 20, 123
Famine, Great, 38, 41, 66, 144
fertilizer, 38, 95, 99
fishing, 11, 16, 44, 64

Gaffin, Denis, 53
gender, 17, 26, 60, 62, 67, 69, 77
globalisation, 17, 19, 166
golden vale, 64
Gray, John, 33–34, 63
gravel, 95
green development, 7–8, 18, 28, 165
green discourse, 6, 15
green economy, 21, 25
Green Low-Carbon Agri-Environment Scheme (GLAS), 98, 100–101, 115, 144
Griffith, Richard, 37–38
gross domestic product (GDP), 11, 44, 136

Halperin, Rhoda H., 149–150
hen harrier, 32, 41, 80, 119, 137, 163; designation in Special Protected Area, 100, 163; monitoring, 3–4, 14–15, 82–85; scheme, 94, 95, 97–98, 99, 135; Threat Response Plan, 93, 113
high nature value farming (HNV), 45, 47, 52, 142, 148

horses, 22, 41, 61, 62, 66, 144, 152, 154–155

independence, Irish, 34, 39–42, 140
Ingold, Tim, 24
inheritance, patterns of, 42, 53, 60, 65–69, 71–72, 76, 136. *See also* farm succession
Intergovernmental Panel on Climate Change (IPCC), 136, 159
International Monetary Fund (IMF), 12, 90
invasive species, 15, 55–58, 79, 92, 99, 103, 151, 155, 165
Irish Farmers Association (IFA), 54, 78, 104, 118
IRD Duhallow, 13, 14, 43, 59, 61, 63, 78–80, 119, 151

joint farming venture, 64

Kanturk, 36, 38, 44, 64
Killarney National Park, 9, 58
Kimball, Solon. *See* Arensberg, Conrad, and Solon Kimball
Kinship, 15, 16–17, 78. *See also* inheritance, patterns of
Kingwilliamstown, 37
knotweed, 54, 56–58

labour, on farm, 26, 60, 66, 70, 77–78, 80, 147, 166
land abandonment. *See* farm abandonment
Land Acts, 38–39
Land Commission, 48
land, confiscations of, seizures of, 34–35, 53
land, investors, 60, 121, 146, 158
land, marginal, 24, 33–35, 44, 47, 52, 107, 114, 165
land, tenure or ownership of, 28, 39, 40, 48, 61, 78, 90, 135, 136, 163, 166, 167; leased, 62, 106
landlordism, 39–41; landlord, 36, 38, 48
Leach, Melissa. *See* Fairhead, James, and Melissa Leach
lime, 37, 38
Lounela, Anu, 24

MacClancy, Jeremy, 6, 18–19
manufacturing, 43–44
mechanisation, agricultural, 41, 43
migration, animal, 8, 82, 112
Mullaghareirk Mountains, 9, 11, 37, 82, 128
multifunctionality, 6, 18, 45, 91, 97, 113, 147–148, 160, 165; in forestry, 113, 125

National Parks and Wildlife Service, 33, 58, 83, 87, 88, 103
Natura 2000, 82, 91–92, 109, 161
neoliberalism, 21, 89–90, 162–163, 166
Newmarket, 36–37, 40
Northern Ireland, 16, 18, 40, 64, 116

Organisation for Economic Co-operation and Development (OECD), 53

Peace, Adrian, 9, 16, 17
peat. *See* turf
Plantation of Munster, 34–35
Plantation of Ulster, 34
political ecology, 9, 19–20
population: aging, 54, 65; changes of, 38, 41, 43, 148; gendered, 76; human, 11, 18, 20, 44, 61, 98, 116, 136, 161
potatoes, 43, 66, 68
precarity, 8, 52, 157–158, 163

quotas, milk, 42

rain, patterns, 8, 46, 47, 97
recreation, 6, 79, 166; in forests, 124, 129–133
rebellion, 33–36
retirement, 69, 115
rhododendron, 55, 58
Rissing, Andrea, 7
roads, development of, 34–37
Robbins, Paul, 20, 161
romanticism, 16, 19, 71, 158
rural decline, 8, 41, 52, 76
Rural Environment Protection Scheme (REPS), 118, 141, 144, 148
Rural Social Scheme (RSS), 55, 79, 111, 151, 164
rushes, 9–10, 73, 99–100, 115, 141, 144

Salazar, Carles, 10, 17, 42, 43
scalability, 41, 51–52, 143, 146
Scheper-Hughes, Nancy, 13, 16, 41–42, 74, 76
Scotland, 36

Scott, James C., 20–21, 146
Shortall, Sally, 67, 72, 78
Shutes, Mark, 16, 18, 22, 42
Single Farm Payment, 91, 95, 98, 99
Slieve Luachra, 10, 15
Special Area of Conservation (SAC), 82, 88, 92, 109
Special Protected Area (SPA), 4, 23, 82, 103, 113, 138, 163; designation of, 104, 161; farmers with SPA land, 13–14, 50, 59, 62, 97–100, 114–115, 144; Stack's to Mullaghareirk SPA, 10–11, 45, 84
spruce, sitka, 73, 118, 132
statecraft, 20–23, 150
statehood, environmental, 20–24
stem family, 66–68
suicide, 73–74

Teagasc, 51, 87, 95, 97, 100, 102, 105, 123–124, 126, 153–154
tillage, 40, 140
tourism, 11, 18, 147–148, 158
Townsend, Reverend Horatio, 36
Tsing, Anna, 25, 51, 55, 103, 138, 146, 158
Tudor Conquest, 116
turf, 4, 40; peat, 8, 83, 89, 152

unemployment, 12, 17, 43, 74

Varley, Tony, 18, 39, 40, 95

weather, 38, 46, 53
weeds, 54, 96–97, 144, 155. *See also* invasive species
Weeks, Kathi, 152, 156
Whiteboys, 36
Wilson, Thomas, 16–18, 19, 22, 25, 42, 52
wind turbine, 4, 10, 11, 27, 113, 115, 138, 152, 158; wind farm, 10, 83

Young, Arthur, 35

About the Author

JODIE ASSELIN is an associate professor of environmental anthropology at the University of Lethbridge. She coestablished the Forest Anthropology Working Group of Europe and Beyond and was a 2025 research fellow at the University of Jyväskylä, Finland. She is the recipient of an SSHRC Insight Development Grant that examines the cultural role of forests in Irish rural landscapes and contributes to a number of Canadian rural resource-oriented research projects.

www.ingramcontent.com/pod-product-compliance
Lightning Source LLC
Chambersburg PA
CBHW031151020426
42333CB00013B/606